FEDERALISM DOOMED?

European Federalism Between Integration and Separation

edited by

Andreas Heinemann-Grüder

Berghahn Books
New York • Oxford

First published in 2002 by

Berghahn Books
www.berghahnbooks.com

© 2002 Andreas Heinemann-Grüder

Library of Congress Cataloging-in-Publication Data

Federalism doomed? : European federalism between integration and separation / edited
by Andreas Heinemann-Grüder.
    p. cm.
  Includes bibliographical references and index.
   ISBN 1-57181-206-7 (cl. : alk. paper) -- ISBN 1-57181-207-5 (pbk. : alk. paper)
    1. Federal government--Europe. 2. Federal government--Europe, Eastern. 3. European
federation. 4. Pluralism (Social sciences) I. Heinemann-Grüder, Andreas.

JN15 .F386 2001
321'.3'094--dc21
                                                          2001043685

British Library Cataloguing in Publication Data

A catalogue record for this book is available from the British Library.

Printed in the United States on acid-free paper.

Federalism Doomed?

CONTENTS

LIST OF TABLES

Preface and Acknowledgments

Compared to the enthusiasm about the termination of the East-West divide at the beginning of the 1990s, the European mood at the beginning of the twenty-first century regarding prospects of integration is much more sober. Is federalism—the normative catchword for accommodation of diversity—doomed as a means for multiethnic states to survive and for supranational integration to be democratic? Ethnic, economic, and cultural legacies of the past are proving their power to constrain the imperatives of supraethnic and supra-national integration, civic constitutionalism, and democratization. Nonetheless, in the search for alternatives to the high costs of creating and preserving homogeneous nation-states, we are in dire need of appropriate political settings that provide efficiency, meaning, and stability.

Despite different legacies and trajectories, Eastern and Western Europe multiethnic states face similar challenges: how to accommodate plural ethnicities, combine efficient integration with democracy, and provide for flexibility and protected diversity? Federalism is a tool used to analyze shared and divided rule among central and noncentral actors and entities, but it is a normative concept, too. The concept itself is evolving, and its advantageousness consists precisely in its malleability. The dismissal of federal solutions in the name of national "self-determination" in the Soviet Union, Czechoslovakia, and Yugoslavia has had disastrous effects. At the same time, we see that the democratic deficit in the European Union causes nationalist backlashes among powerful constituencies in at least some of the member states. The long-term effect of dismissing federal solutions might be in both instances a strengthening of nationalist, anti-democratic, and protectionist forces.

This volume attempts to stimulate discussions about federalism in a pan-European perspective. What informs different national approaches to federalism? Does the failure of federalism in Eastern Europe teach us any lessons? And do historically formed attachments and preferences change under the influence of supranational integration? Without aiming to offer a set of unified answers to these queries, this volume for the first time connects insights from failed federations in Eastern Europe with prospects of federalizing Europe. The idea for this book originated in discussions of state constitutions at the Delaware Constitutional Seminar, organized by Daniel J. Elazar, and gained focus and momentum at "European Federalism between Integration and Separation,"a conference at the University of Pennsylvania in October 1998. The volume also grew out of many stimulating debates with Douglas Verney and with students in my graduate and undergraduate seminars on European and global federalism at the University of Pennsylvania.

I would like to express my gratitude to those people and institutions whose advice, comments, encouragement, and support made this endeavor possible: the German Academic Exchange Service, especially Barbara Motyka; the Max Kade Foundation; the Christopher Browne Center for International Relations, specifically its director, Avery Goldstein; the German Consulate General in New York, particularly its Cultural Attaché, Ludwig Linden; the School of Arts and Sciences at the University of Pennsylvania, especially undergraduate Dean Richard Beeman; and the conference commentators Jeffrey Hahn, Alan Tarr, and Ian Lustick. I would particularly like to mention my frequent discussions with Frank Trommler, whose interest and moral support were invaluable. I would also like to thank Claudia Mayer-Iswandy for her assistance during the conference. Finally, I am grateful to James Siegel, whose meticulous and reliable help was crucial in editing this volume.

Andreas Heinemann-Grüder, May 2000

INTRODUCTION

---⚬⚬⚬---

Andreas Heinemann-Grüder

The violent cycle of secessionism and "ethnic cleansing" in former Yugo-slavia, the unsettled process of nation-state building in the former Soviet Union, and Turkey's quest for inclusion in the European Union are just the most visible aspects of a larger problem. What is the positive vision of Europe beyond the mere regulation of trade, a common market, and preventing destabilizing events?[1] Ten years after the collapse of socialism in Eastern Europe, discussions about the meaning of "Europe" still concentrate on Western Europe: it may enlarge and integrate countries which are not yet members, exclude some, or put others under its tutelage, but the group claiming the power to define Europe remains the EU and the governments of its member states. Scholarly debates revolve around the EU, its institutions, decision-making procedures, and policy areas. "Europe" has been a catchword signaling spheres of inclusion and exclusion. Until the end of socialism, "Europe" had meant anti-communism, geopolitical stabilization (especially with respect to Germany), and economic integration. But the postcold war principles underlying and incentives informing the incantation of "Europe" as a political entity are rarely reflected upon. The claim that the European Union lies at Europe's heart often obscures more than it reveals: the lack of an encompassing identity, even a dialogue on Europe's postcold war ideology.[2] Nonetheless, the EU cannot escape demands to define a common political identity for its members. On what grounds, for example, should constituencies in the member states accept governance by EU law?

Notes for this section begin on page 54.

Why should soldiers be prepared to die in "Europe's name"? Why should wealthier Europeans share with poorer ones? Similarly, both prospective members as well as nonmembers have to relate their national cultures to the norms and principles governing the European integration process.

Whereas optimistic moods prevailed in the early 1990s with respect to deepening and widening integration, the beginning of the twenty-first century sees Europe in a state of indecisiveness—is there enough bonding or should one strive for more? Should national autonomy be defended or a further pooling of capacities promoted? Fears and uncertainties about expected gains determine the approaches. Meanwhile, incrementalism and functional substitutes for a European vision prevent outright exit strategies. The military incorporation of the former East is expanding but seems to be delaying political and economic integration. Furthermore, the political and economic gap between the Western European gravitational center and the area of the Commonwealth of Independent States (CIS) is widening. Finally, due to maximum expectations associated with secession, it is more than likely that the consequences of further state-seeking nationalistic trends—interethnic violence, masses of refugees, military interventions, and destroyed infrastructures—will keep Europe busy far into the twenty-first century. Following Europe's divisive experiences in the twentieth century, the meaning of "Europe" requires all the more new definitions. As Europe searches for bases of commonality, reinvented legacies of the past clash with political and economic imperatives of interdependency. Fundamental questions recur: Is Europe a type of civilization, and if so, what makes it distinctive? Where are the boundaries of Europe, and who has the power to define them? What might be appropriate political settings for preserving the structural pluralism of European cultures and meeting the requirements of governance beyond the nation-state? The following volume tries to shed some fresh light on these questions by reflecting upon the normative and institutional prerequisites of sustainable European federalism, East and West.

Observing Europe in the 1990s, we cannot fail to recognize two contrasting developments: the ongoing disintegration of three multiethnic federations in the East—contrary to most people's preferences—and a further deepening of integration around the Western European core—regardless of widespread Euro-skepticism. But the logics of disintegration and integration are highly disputed. Are actors driven by ethnic, national, or particular interests, institutional incentives, or norms and values? Employing these three concepts—interests, institutions, and norms—the disintegration of Eastern Europe's federations can be explained by the preferences of nationalist and economic elites, by institutional flaws in federal arrangements, or by the prevalence of norms such as "self-determination" instead of federal values. The same arguments can be made in order to describe the limits of integration in the EU. By contrast, integration could be advanced if it is in the self-interest of major actors, if institutions have a "spillover" effect on actors' preferences, or if basic values are shared.[3]

In the real world, academic discourses compete with a striking practical logic which holds that supraethnic or supranational integration presupposes nation-states. According to this logic of prior ethnic self-determination, multiethnic states have to dissolve and transform into nation-states before they can deliberately pool and transfer sovereignty into supraethnic or supranational settings. Integration could at some time follow the disruptive logic of "self-determination." This logic inherently provides an answer to the question of disintegration and integration: "self-determination" has to be based on an ethnically defined image of self. Wherever this self is disputed or suppressed, disintegration will ensue; wherever it is assured, integration may occur. The argument that democracy preconditions a prestatal ethnic homogeneity has been made and practically executed in Eastern Europe, but it informs the approach to political integration in the EU too. No *demos*—no European federation; no European *kratos* without a European *demos*, the argument holds. Is federation actually doomed to fail whenever a sense of belonging is missing? Theoretical and practical answers are highly divided, often they merely seem to support dogmatic beliefs rather than be based on rational calculus.

Complaints about the absence of a preexisting demos, popular sovereign, or federal culture—constantly repeated in debates about the failure of Eastern European federations as well as with respect to the prospects of federalizing Europe—mirror an obvious reality, but are to a certain extent self-serving. Most federations came into being without a preexisting federal bond. Most often the demos did not already exist. Almost all federations are "artificial," constructed, and engineered. In successful federations, the virtues of federalism have evolved as a result of the growth of shared interests, institutional development, and repeated collective gains. A federal culture—a sense of belonging to the covenant on the part of citizens and governments, partnership, and communal group norms—usually emerges from the self-interest of the constituent parts. Understanding the essential sense of federal loyalty, clearly missing among the elites of Eastern Europe's federations and critically challenged in the case of federalizing the European Union, would have to start by examining the self-interest and the pool of shared values of the constituent parts. Sustainable federations clearly require an interest in identification with the federal bond, but federal bonds are not rational in any "objective" sense; they are rather constructed by political dis-

course. Federal norms, like all social norms, are collectively designed in a
process of pooling knowledge, of gaining a sense of common interests.[4] Federal commitments may increase access to resources and distributed goods,
offer new positions, and lower the costs of action and transaction. Moreover, they may provide a sense of comfort from knowing each other, ease the
reaching of agreements, support the emergence of group consciousness, and
increase the joint success of the federated group. Federal commitments
depend upon repeated actor coordination through a shared sense of history,
a pooling of knowledge and interests, elites that coordinate constituent parts
and groups, and the institutionalized reinforcement of federal norms.
Because the virtues of federalism are not necessarily self-evident, the costs
and benefits of federalization will be constantly weighed against its alternatives. Especially in times of transition from one governmental or economic
system to another, federal norms are likely to compete with other norms—
most often with nationalism, authoritarianism, and hegemonic rule.

In most Eastern European countries, federalism has been rejected as a
device for accommodating ethnicity in a civic society and for creating a constitutionally legitimized state. The thinking of politicians and political scientists about European state forms—East and West—is still heavily informed
by the Westphalian system of sovereign states. Federalism has never been the
dominant feature among European political systems, even if attempts to federalize Western European states in the postwar period have generally been
positive.[5] In view of the breakdown of multiethnic federations in the East,
the frailty of the Russian federation, loose cooperation in the CIS, and the
questionable sustainability of the Dayton agreement concerning Bosnia, pes-
simism reigns with respect to the integrative potential of federal solutions.
Ethnofederalism—the territorialization and institutionalization of ethnicity—is widely seen as a stimulus for nationalism instead of accommodation.[6]
In Western Europe, since the early 1950s integration has been constantly
accompanied by skepticism, too, and debates about federalizing the EU are
confronted by fears of centralization and infringements on national sovereignty.[7] Compared to the beginning of the 1990s, the idea of a European
federation evokes reservations about Jacobinism, the concentration of executive power, the growth of anonymous bureaucracies, and alienation from
one's indigenous cultures. Is federalism doomed because the perceived costs
of federalizing are higher than the potential gains of lost sovereignty, because
common interests are limited, or because particular actors—ethnic groups or
nation-states—prefer particular rules instead of universal ones?[8] Paradoxically enough, integration in Western Europe faces problems structurally similar to those posed by the disintegration of multiethnic states in Eastern

Europe—how to accommodate cultural, ethnic, and economic diversity (the problem of symmetry and asymmetry); how to democratize supranational decisionmaking (the problem of democratic accountability); and how to harmonize and enforce rules and norms (the problem of deepening)?[9]

Federalism has always represented an attempt to avoid the homogenization pressure characteristic of unitary states, the imposed assimilation into one hegemonic nation; this holds especially true for multiethnic federations. Dealing with federalism thus implies studying the failures and successes of alternatives to homogeneous nation-state building. The relevance of federal solutions for multiethnic European states as well as for Europe as a whole consists precisely in their potential for avoiding the extremes of nationalism, hegemony, and anarchy. The senior scholar of federalism studies—Daniel J. Elazar—predicts the reemergence of confederal arrangements as the appropriate form to constitutionalize supranational integration.[10] Whether imperatives of integration will finally lead to more federal or confederal elements is still open. Federations react to different contexts, and so no normative type should be prescribed.

Each federation is unique in its combination of unitary, federal, and confederal elements, of symmetry and asymmetry. As a matter of fact, federations are part of a continuum including leagues, confederacies, confederations, "federacies," heterogeneous and asymmetrical federations, consociational regimes, decentralized unitary states, democratic unitary states, and authoritarian hierarchies.[11] Even if a variety of federal forms exists, federal solutions are clearly distinct from unitary ones—they include noncentralization, multilevel government, constitutionalism, powerful shared economic interests, some measure of public support, nonsubordination of people's regional, ethnic, or cultural attachments, arbitration and flexibility, and independent funds for central and noncentral authorities. In comparison to a confederation, a federal government reaches out directly to its citizenry, has enforceable laws, and strives to achieve "justice" (political, social, and economic). Some centralized federations may strengthen their confederal elements; unions such as the EU may enhance their federal arrangements.[12] Supranational forms of governance and intrastate governmental systems could converge to form new patterns of multilevel government that reflect varying degrees of policy integration. We do not yet know whether forms of supranational governance such as the EU and multilevel governance within nation-states will tend towards federation or confederation. (Con-)federalization may actually occur from both ends: the international and domestic arenas.

A number of scholars have meticulously described patterns of integration in Western Europe. Some stress the momentum of supranational integration;

others its limitations by sovereign nation-states. Nevertheless, there is a striking sense of conceptual uncertainty when dealing with processes of integration and disintegration in Europe in the last decade. Traditional conceptions
of the nation-state, sovereignty, constitutionalism, and federalism cannot
account for emerging realities in either Western or Eastern Europe.[13] Schools
of thought on disintegration and integration can be grouped roughly according to the importance they ascribe to interests (intergovernmentalism, rational choice, neorealism), institutions (functionalism, neoinstitutionalism), or
norms (culturalism, civic culture, constitutionalism).[14] This volume includes
contributions by adherents of all three approaches. The overarching question, around which the different perspectives center, addresses causes for the
failure and success of federalism. The essays in this volume deal with three
questions underrated in the workings on European integration: How can
comparative federalism instruct us about European integration? Do experiences of (dis)integration in Eastern Europe teach us any lessons? Finally, what
informs approaches to federal integration among diverse European states?
The three issues are hierarchically interrelated. The contributors explore the
complex interrelationship between federal arrangements and their effects on
integrating or disintegrating diversity in Europe. The chapters are connected
in their search for interdependencies between federalism and state-forms. The
authors have not striven for a unified approach but instead have attempted to
cross well-established disciplinary boundaries, to engage in a discourse that
connects insights on federalism from Eastern and Western Europe.

Students of federal policies, failed and successful ones, and of European
integration are usually highly specialized scholars. The disciplines mostly
reproduce their prior beliefs in a kind of self-affirmation. The academic situation strikingly resembles the picture in European politics: ten years after
the end of the cold war there is still no pan–European dialogue. One of the
prime aims of this volume is to launch a discourse between scholars of
diverse backgrounds—comparativists, sociologists, and specialists in international relations with either an Eastern or Western European specialization—on the appropriateness of federalist conceptions in analyzing processes
of integration and disintegration in Europe. The volume is not just another
account of European integration—it specifically targets the observation that
all political systems in Europe have difficulties of their own when combined
with domestic or supranational federalism. Its focus is an institutionalist perspective on difficulties faced by specific forms of government and diverse
national traditions when combined with federalism.

The first part of the volume provides conceptual and comparative frameworks that inform the discussions of future European federalism among

Europe's core states. Confederal arrangements, different representational systems, parliamentarism, and presidentalism are the main political systems in conjunction with which federal arrangements are engineered. In order to avoid abstract juxtapositions of federal with nonfederal regimes, we may be well advised to relate variants of existing federal models to the prospect of federalizing Europe. The tension between different governmental systems and federalism seems to be an old problem. The closer one looks at distinct federal systems, the more one detects warning signs: do not marry federalism with socialism, do not mix it with presidentialism, do not fuse it with a Westminster model. Federations are characterized by these tensions between unitary features of governmental systems and the quest for protected diversity. One must therefore study the effects of these interdependencies comparatively.

Are there any models for federalizing Europe? In his contribution, Douglas Verney tests American legislative federalism, German executive federalism, and Swiss assembly-based federalism as possible points of reference. Verney characterizes the emerging European Union as a type sui generis that actually incorporates elements of all three models. The main concern of his comparative study is the still unbalanced relationship between Europe's legislative and executive branches, which he identifies as the institutional reason for Europe's democratic deficit. Based on an assessment of existing EU institutions, Verney suggests the transformation of the European Commission into a genuine—meaning elected—federal government and of the Council of Ministers into the upper house of the European Parliament. Francis Campbell addresses patterns of integration in the EU from an international relations perspective. He asks whether the EU has indeed overcome state anarchy and developed into a hierarchy with centralization of powers. While stressing the incrementalist nature of, and questioning the automaticity of, functionalist spillover effects in the EU's evolution, Campbell ultimately supports the functionalist notion of "supranationalism." He envisions the emergence of a supranational state by specifically highlighting the Monetary Union as a driving force of centralization. Gretchen MacMillan, while combining in her discussion of the EU the concepts of "intergovernmentalism" and "supranationalism," and drawing on executive federalism in Canada as a point of reference, goes even further: the framework of intergovernmental relations in the EU looks more and more like the arrangement of intergovernmental relations within federal states. Her main caveats point to the lack of communal loyalty as well as deficiencies in transparency and accountability. James Caporaso observes the growth of the democratic deficit in tandem with the EU's integration, too. Yet he interprets the EU as a state, not a Westphalian state, but a regulatory one. The regulatory state is, according to Caporaso, essentially a state specializing in the control and management of international externalities. Because this state does not engage substantially in the classic functions of government—redistribution, stabilization, and provision of symbolic meaning—and because this state does not create its own security umbrella, and tax and administrative structures, it can "get by" with very little resources. The EU actually reflects a division of labor in state functions—whereas the member states focus on social and redistributional politics, the EU increasingly focuses on regulatory policy. The EU, he concludes, does not replace the identities of its member states but rather specializes in rule–making and management of a market-perfection project. Caporaso's interpretation is implicitly a functionalist one—distinct levels of government pertain to distinct functions, and states such as the EU do not require all aspects of Westphalian statehood.

The second section of the volume asks whether the collapse of Eastern European federations teaches us lessons about institutional basics necessary for the preservation of multiethnic federations. The attempt to rebuild federal or confederal arrangements in Russia, the CIS, and Bosnia should be seen in this light. Jim Seroka provides three major explanations for the failure of federations in the East: the lack of a cultural commitment to federalism, institutional flaws, and economic inefficiency. System change exacerbated these common defects as federal institutions actually became, according to Seroka, an impediment to change and were thus dismissed by both nationalists and reform-oriented elites. Sustainable multiethnic federations thus have to provide for a supranational identity, enforceable norms, and incentives for economic growth. In other words, they require meaning, obedience to norms, and functionality.

Rhetorics of national self-determination, rather than searches for federal solutions have largely accompanied system change in Eastern Europe. The activation of nationalist myths by self-interested elites and the ensuing interethnic wars in former Yugoslavia and on the territory of the former Soviet Union were the price for the dismissal of federal solutions. Nonetheless, the international community is cautious in outrightly promoting secessionism, especially if it is combined with the violation of minority rights. After mass-scale "ethnic cleansing" in Bosnia, the Dayton accord attempted to impose a multiethnic federation under a strong international protectorate. Lenard Cohen critically assesses the results of Dayton's endeavor to engineer a multiethnic federation. He concludes by stating that a purely territorial federalism is unlikely to find support among Bosnia's divided ethnic groups once the Stabilization Forces (SFor) leave the country. Self-sustaining federalism in Bosnia requires elements of ethnofederalism, yet avoidance of the well-known pitfalls of territorialization of ethnicity at the same time. Instead of integrating ethnic groups, territorially assigned rights may become a resource for secessionism and independent nation-state building.

Russia, too, inherited ethnofederalism, from the Soviet Union, but it did not fall apart, even if Chechnya's secessionism challenges its integrity. Comparing Russia's federalization with the failed federations in Eastern Europe, I argue that Russia's failed nation-state building, transformation "from above," and federal institution-building—including asymmetrical arrangements—contributed to the preservation of Russia's federal unity in the 1990s. Russia combines unitary, federal, and confederal elements in its unique "contractual federalism in action." It has been argued that the Commonwealth of Independent States could develop into a union comparable to the EU. Mark Webber applies the confederal test to the CIS, and his answer is more than skeptical. The CIS will not mature into any confederal form of governance, instead it will follow a logic of disintegration. Bilateral ties will prove more important than the loosely coupled structures of the CIS. Webber explains this disintegrative prospect by highlighting the fear of Russian dominance, the lack of a community of values, and the absence of congruent political regimes among CIS member states. Positively formulated, one could thus argue that prerequisites of (con)federal integration are absence of hegemony, shared values, and a congruence of political regimes.

The third section of the book is concerned with possible directions of European federalism: the interdependencies between regional, national, and supranational attachments, and European actor strategies. Is there a community of shared pan-European values at all, something like a European civilization? Starting with the observation that Europe means "structural pluralism," not homogeneity, Willfried Spohn classifies the approaches to European integration of various European nation-states. He highlights the historical path-dependency of European integration. Following the tradition of Stein Rokkan, Spohn discerns three factors that determine diverse national approaches to European integration: distinct trajectories of state formation and nation-building; different economic policies (liberal-anti-statist, state-interventionist, and peripheral); and belonging to special religious-cultural zones (Anglican protestantism, Lutheran protestantism, Catholicism, interconfessionalism, and Orthodoxy). The salience of these legacies limits prospects for centralization of the EU. Henry Teune's contribution supports this finding. Based on interviews concerning democratic cultures among several thousand local political leaders in Western, Eastern, and central European countries, Teune argues that the simplest single piece of information that predicts the most about the responses is where local leaders are from. The salience of historically formed regional attachments, primarily molded by state-building, and local affinities, forged by urbanization, constrains the diffusion of political cultures by increased interaction with neighbors. Instead of a consolidation of supranational unions such as NATO and the EU, Teune expects that all kinds of subnational regions will emerge as prime units of global economic interaction. Globalization as well as democratization will actually free local economies from the tutelage of large nation-states. Teune implicitly questions the nineteenth century rationale for nation-building and supranational integration as important to enhancing industrial growth in the twenty-first century.

Michael Kreile completes this volume with an assessment of the institutional implications of EU enlargement. Federalism, as Kreile observes, has been rejected by most EU member states as a synonym for centralist state institutions, and Eastern enlargement is likely to strengthen the anti-federalist forces further, including those in the prospective member states. In contrast, academic debates treat federalism much more flexibly—the union may not be a state, but a community with federal and confederal elements, such as two independent and coexisting levels of government, a common market, supranational law, and common citizenship. Even if federalism is not the favored arrangement of most national constituencies for European integration, federal elements may, as Kreile concludes, be used as a source for proposals to increase the efficiency and legitimacy of the EU system. Enlargement would clearly require more flexibility and differential treatment. He remains cautious in predicting a "creeping federalism" as a result of added flexibility.

Future academic and political debates about federalism in Europe will have to address three issues. First, what are the jurisdictional and economic demarcation lines for asymmetry—or opt-out clauses—the crossing of which undermines the governability, cohesion, and efficiency of central authority?[15] Ethnic, regional, and supranational integration evidently requires protected diversity and flexibility. States confronted with regionalist or secessionist movements will have to allow for asymmetry in order to accommodate otherwise radicalizing quests for independence. The EU faces similar challenges, especially with its enlargement. With respect to common foreign and security policy as well as social policy, the EU already allows for opt-out clauses. The more countries entering the EU, the more diversity will be added, resulting in multiple speeds and levels of policy integration. The study of asymmetry thus refers not only to ethnic and cultural diversity but to economic discrepancies and diverging policy preferences as well. The

Soviet Union, Russia, Yugoslavia, Spain, and Belgium have gathered valuable experiences with diverse forms of asymmetrical federalism that deserve further comparative study.

Second, given the general discouraging experiences with ethnofederalism in Eastern Europe, we are in dire need of comparative studies on the impact of ethnofederal institutions on ethnic mobilization. Students of federalism—including those, whose work is brought together in this volume—are deeply divided over the benefits and disadvantages of ethnofederal institutions. Does the territorialization of ethnicity induce nationalism, thus preventing multiple identities to coexist and emerge? Are ethnofederal institutions actually fostering ethnic divisions at the expense of civic identities?

Finally, what are the prerequisites for the emergence of civic, supraethnic, and supranational communities bound by shared democratic norms and federal virtues? Can a common political demos, a supranational popular sovereign, emerge from a shared constitutional patriotism, or will and should political loyalties rest with nation-states? Some authors stress the importance of constitutional founding acts, while others defend an ethnically and culturally defined community as the only legitimate basis of sovereignty. Debates about European constitutionalism evidently bear high normative charges, with opposing camps defending or attacking an exclusive national sovereignty in the name of democracy.[16] Whereas a United States of Europe, substituting older affiliations, is an unlikely prospect, multiple, inclusive, competing, and coexisting identifications may nevertheless emerge, similar to the multilevel attachments inside federations. At least three basics seem to be crucial for the development of supranational, civic loyalties: a consensus on shared values, effective participation in decision–making, and dense political communication.

Evidently, Europe is not a preexisting given; instead it displays a wide-ranging pluralism in culture, politics, and economics. In trying to find adequate forms of articulating this pluralism, Europe is defining its new insider and outsider relationships, but without yet expressing a clear vision of its meaning and constitutional character. It is, therefore, still easier to characterize what Europe is not than what it is: it is not a nation-state, a demos, a federation, or a mere treaty community or alliance for limited purposes. With the prospect of further widening and deepening of the EU, the quest for a pan–European delineation of the EU's constitutional guiding principles and its governmental structure will become more urgent. The past incrementalism, accompanied by often merely descriptive accounts among scholars, must be replaced by a more pro–active approach. It will have to include Eastern Europeans as equal partners of this dialogue, not primarily as a means to make good for past exclusion but as a prerequisite for successful inclusion and future affiliation.

Notes

1. F. Scharpf, *Regieren in Europa. Effektiv und demokratisch?* (Frankfurt/Main, New York, 1998).
2. See B. Laffan, "The Politics of Identity and Political Order in Europe," Journal of Common Market Studies, 34, no. 1, (1996): 81–102; W. Weidenfeld, "Die Bedrohung Europas. Wie die Identitätsschwäche des Kontinents zur Gefahr wird," *Frankfurter Allgemeine Zeitung*, 12 May 1999.
3. P.H. Gordon, "The Limits of Europe's Common Foreign and Security Policy," in *Centralization or Fragmentation? Europe Facing the Challenges of Deepening, Diversity, and Democracy*, ed. A. Moravcsik (New York, 1998), 164f.
4. On the construction of group norms, especially ethnic ones, see R. Hardin, *One for All. The Logic of Group Conflict* (Princeton, 1995). A specific pledge for "social constructivism" in the analysis of the EU is made by T. Risse-Kappen, "Exploring the Nature of the Beast: International Relations Theory and Comparative Policy Analysis Meet the European Union," *Journal of Common Market Studies* 34, no. 1, (1996): 54–80.
5. F. Knipping, ed., *Federal Conceptions in EU Member States: Traditions and Perspectives* (Baden-Baden, 1993). On federalist discussions covering the postwar period see A. Döpfner, "Keine Angst vor Europa. Umbrüche, alte Ideen und neue Formen des Föderalismus," in *Keine Angst vor Europa. Föderalismus als Chance*, ed. A. Döpfner (Zürich, 1992), 12–41; J.J. Hesse, V. Wright, "Federalizing Europe: The Path to Adjustment," in *Federalizing Europe? The Costs, Benefits, and Preconditions of Federal Political Systems*, ed. J.J. Hesse, V. Wright (Oxford, 1996), 389.
6. R. Brubaker, *Nationalism Reframed* (Cambridge, 1996), 13–178.
7. On federalist discussions surrounding the Maastricht Treaty see H. Laufer, Th. Fischer, *Föderalismus als Strukturprinzip für die Europäische Union* (Gütersloh, 1996).
8. The argument has been made that federation requires some external or internal enemy or object of aggression in order to aggregate resources, and that only political idealists would assume that protection of liberty is enough to federalize. See W.H. Riker, "European Federalism. The Lessons of Past Experience," in Hesse, Wright, *Federalizing Europe?*, 20.
9. A. Moravcsik, "Europe's Integration at Century's End," in Moravcsik, *Centralization or Fragmentation?* 1–58.
10. D.J. Elazar, *Constitutionalizing Globalization. The Postmodern Revival of Confederal Arrangements* (Lanham, 1998).
11. D.J. Elazar, *Exploring Federalism* (Tuscaloosa, 1987).
12. This view is supported by M. Burgess, "Introduction: Federalism and Building the European Union," *Publius: The Journal of Federalism* 26, no. 4 (1996): 1–15.
13. For an astute critique of narrow constitutional definitions of federalism, proposing instead the hypothesis of "fused" joined forces and instruments of regulatory and distributive

action in the EU, see W. Wessels, *Die europäischen Staaten und ihre Union – Staatsbilder in der Diskussion* (Munich, 1994): 51–69.

14. Forsyth describes the functionalist and normative approaches as two souls or spirits that dwell within the European integration process, with the "technical-functional" dominating over the "federal-constitutional" spirit. See M. Forsyth, "The Political Theory of Federalism: The Relevance of Classical Approaches," in Hesse, Wright, *Federalizing Europe?* 40. An overview of different international relations theories applied to the EU is preserved by R.G. Whitman, "The International Identity of the European Union: Instruments of Identity," in *Rethinking the European Union: Institutions, Interests and Identities*, ed. A. Landau, R.G. Whitman (London, 1997): 54–71.

15. For an overview of literature on asymmetry, see R.L. Watts, *Comparing Federal Systems in the 1990s* (Kingston, 1996).

16. For an early discussion of linkages between national and European democracy, see M.R. Lepsius, *Interessen, Ideen und Institutionen* (Opladen, 1990), 264–68, and M.R. Lepsius, "Nationalstaat oder Nationalitätenstaat als Modell für die Weiterentwicklung der Europäischen Gemeinschaft," in *Staatswerdung Europas? Optionen für eine Europäische Union*, ed. R. Wildenmann (Baden-Baden, 1991), 19–40; Peter Graf Kielmansegg, "Integration und Demokratie," in *Europäische Integration*, ed. Markus Jachtenfuchs, Beate Kohler-Koch (Opladen, 1996); Joseph H.H. Weiler, *The Constitution of Europe: Do the New Clothes Have An Emperor?* (Cambridge, 1999).

FEDERALISM AND STATE FORMS

Chapter 1

CHOOSING A FEDERAL FORM OF GOVERNANCE FOR EUROPE

———— ⊸⊶⊷ ————

Douglas V. Verney

For many observers until very recently, any consideration of "a federal form of governance for Europe" seemed premature. The European Union (EU) remained in many ways a collection of independent and sovereign states. However, with the die cast in favor of a European currency, which took effect on 1 January, 1999, it would seem shortsighted to assume that European federation will not one day be a much-debated issue. It is by no means premature to consider the options facing the Europeans.

Understanding the European Union: A Unique Set of Political Institutions

The European Union (EU) is unlike any other political institution in the world.[1] It is often called "supranational," but this does not mean that it is a superstate. It means simply that the EU is an association of nation-states. It is not a sovereign state comparable to Russia, which is also a collection of different nations, and it may never become one. Certainly the European Union is not yet a federation. Some observers liken it to a confederacy, that

---

Notes for this section begin on page 36.

is to say a combination of states that collaborate for certain purposes but that retain their powers as sovereign states. Confederacies delegate limited powers to the confederate authorities. For example, the member-states of confederacies do not allow the confederate government to deal directly with their citizens. However, the European Union is more than a confederacy. It enjoys some of the powers that normally pertain only to states. For example, in a number of areas the European Union is allowed to deal directly with the citizens of member-states. It is therefore tempting to classify the EU as something more than a confederacy, but something less than a federation. This is, however, to assume a simple classification of states from unitary to confederate, with federations in the middle of the spectrum. For a number of reasons it is doubtful whether the European Union can be classified in this way.

The first reason is that the EU is not only more than a confederacy and less than a federation, but is also a work in progress and changing all the time. It is a political institution unlike any other, whether federation or confederacy.

Secondly, its members are sovereign states very different from the provinces and states in traditional federations such as Canada and the United States. Member-states like the United Kingdom and France have a long history of independence as sovereign states. By contrast, no modern federation, or confederacy, has been based on the coming together of a group of large, long established independent nation-states willing to submit to higher authority in certain matters.

In the third place, there are various types of government in Europe. In most federations there is considerable political uniformity. The provinces, states, or *Länder* that together with the national government compose the federation, share a similar form of government. In Canada, India, and Germany, this takes the parliamentary form. In contrast, the fifty states of the United States, like the federal government, have adopted the separation of the executive from the legislative branch of government. In other words, while these federations differ from one another in their form of government, within each federation the form adopted is uniform throughout. In their political institutions the member-states of the European Union are more heterogeneous than these federations.

However, Europe is not unique in its asymmetry. The 1993 Russian constitution allows the eighty-nine regional governments of the federation to select their own system of government. Some have governors, others have presidents.

The European Union does share one important characteristic with modern federations. The member governments are all assumed to be committed to liberal democracy. Indeed no state can join the European Union until it becomes a liberal democracy with free elections and a free press.[2] If we turn from the member-states to the European Union itself, we find that it is difficult to classify its institutions of governance. Vivien Schmidt has suggested that it displays a dynamic "confusion" of powers "insofar as the directly elected legislature is primarily consultative, the indirectly elected executive, which is made up of member-state representatives, plays mainly a legislative role, the bureaucracy takes on most executive functions, and the judiciary overlaps with the executive and legislature in its highly activist role."[3] There is no "government" in the normal sense of the term. There is simply a Council of Ministers of the European Union (CEU) and a European Council (EC) consisting of heads of government.[4] Without a prime minister or president in charge of the CEU or EC, both these councils are governed by a collegium of the fifteen member-states, with the chair revolving every six months. The unicameral European Parliament (EP) is a legislative body that is separate from the three executive bodies. As a primarily consultative body it does not have anything like the powers of legislatures in federations. Although its powers are gradually increasing, especially with regard to membership of the Commission (the administration of the EU executive) it cannot hold the ministers or commissioners responsible to it in parliamentary fashion. Nor do its committees have the clout of committees of the U.S. Congress, with their control over finance. There is neither the responsible government associated with parliamentarism nor the presidentialism's checks and balances.

Moreover, there is no second chamber representing the member-states, though the Council of the European Union already appears to play the role of a second chamber. In addition to the peculiar separation of the legislature from the executive bodies there is an extraordinary physical separation of the various institutions of governance. They are located in Brussels (the Commission), in Strasbourg (the European Parliament), and in Luxembourg (the European Court of Justice). As for the European Council, not only does the chair rotate every six months but meetings take place in the member-state of the current chair, and not necessarily in the capital. Hence at meetings in the Netherlands, treaties were signed at Maastricht and Amsterdam, neither of which is the country's capital. So far, then, there appears to have been a desire to prevent any city from becoming the political capital of Europe, though this in itself is not surprising.[5] Another feature that makes the EU unique is the absence of anything like a constitutional convention such as the one held in Philadelphia in 1787. Modern federalism was invented there by the framers of the American constitution. Because of its success, federalism supplanted confederacy, the older form of federation. American federalism provided the model for other federations, notably the Swiss Federation in 1848 and the Dominion of Canada (misleadingly called

"Confederation") in 1867. Although neither of these countries adopted the American system of government, both were influenced by the American experience. For example, their federations were established as a result of the equivalent of the American constitutional convention, a meeting of framers that resulted in a carefully crafted constitutional document.

The European Union has not followed this path. There has been no constitutional convention, and consequently, no constitution. Instead, the sovereign member governments have signed a number of important treaties, each of which has taken the development of the institutions of European governance a stage further. The process has been slow, one of gradual evolution. The wording of the treaties has often been ambiguous. The political style of the leaders of the various member-states has been characterized by pragmatism, a willingness to try things out before embodying the decisions in a treaty. Two features of this pragmatism distinguish the operation of the EU from most nation-states and federations. The first is that wherever possible, decisions have been left to lower bodies. Among these are member parliaments and local governments. In trying to ensure that policies are formulated as far as possible not in Brussels but at the national (and even local) level, the EU is following the principle known as "subsidiarity." Subsidiarity merely means the decentralization of decision-making as far as possible, in order to bring government nearer to the people. In addition, so far as possible the whole process has been governed by a preference for consensus. Only gradually has the system of voting known as qualified majority voting (QVM) been adopted when consensus proves impossible.

How could such a unique—and almost apolitical—set of institutions have developed? To understand the peculiar nature of the European Union, one has to go back to its origins in the European Coal and Steel Community (the ECSC) of 1951. The brainchild of the leaders of France, Germany, and Italy, the ECSC was primarily an economic organization. The goal of those who created it was to integrate the coal and steel industries, then the sinews of countries at war, in such a way that a third great European war would be inhibited. In other words, the primary aim was economic integration on a limited scale, not political union.

Over the years, a great deal of progress has been made towards some form of union. Indeed the term "European Community" has been discarded in favor of "European Union." Yet the fact remains that after nearly fifty years, the EU remains primarily an economic union. The member states remain sovereign in very important ways, notably defense, foreign policy and taxation.

In sum, the European Union is unique in a number of respects. It is neither a confederacy nor a federation, and yet in some ways is treated as a state. Its member-states remain in many ways sovereign. There is no symmetry among these states' institutions: Their systems of government vary. The institutions of the European Union are different from those of any of the members. The Union has evolved gradually without a constitutional convention or a constitution. It tries to operate according to the principles of subsidiarity and consensus. Above all it is a work in progress, and has been ever since the European Coal and Steel Community was established in 1951. Clearly the European Union has an intriguing set of governmental institutions. If it ever becomes a federation it will be different from the two main forms: systems based on the principles of federalism, such as the United States and Switzerland, and the parliamentary systems of such countries as Canada, Australia, and India where federation was added on. In trying to discern a road map for the future of Europe, we need to note the different ways in which federations generally have developed.

What Form Might the Federation Take?

In addition to confederacies, however, there are two types of federation. First, there are federations like Canada, India, and Germany, which were established primarily as *parliamentary*. Only secondarily were they federations. Second, there are states such as the United States and Switzerland. These two states were primarily *federal*. This means that they were based on federal principles. Their form of government (presidential and assembly) was determined by their federal character. In considering what form a European Federation might take, it is necessary to distinguish between the three types of federation:

1. Parliamentary federations (e.g., Germany and Canada)
2. Confederacies (notably the American Articles of Confederation in the 1770s, and the Southern Confederacy in the 1860s)
3. Federal states (the United States and Switzerland).

Parliamentary Federations

Not surprisingly, when there emerged new states like Canada, India, and Nigeria, in which one nation was not paramount (as England was in the United Kingdom), the nation-state did not provide the model. Instead there were efforts to establish forms of governance in which there was a federative element. One such type was called the parliamentary federation. Here one of the principles of federalism, the distribution of powers, was added to the parliamentary form of government, creating a new type of state. A number of European countries, including Belgium, Spain, and Austria, have since 1945 adopted elements of federation. The most important European federation, and one with a much longer history, is Germany. In view of Europe's familiarity with parliamentary government, and the establishment of a number of parliamentary federations, one might expect this to be the form that a European federation would take. For under the federal principle of the constitutional distribution of powers, there are autonomous regional governments. However, the European Union itself, as distinct from its member-states, has not been based on parliamentarism.

Confederacies

An alternative might seem to be confederacy. After all, in trying to classify the European Community, many observers concluded that it was more like a confederacy than a federation. But traditionally confederacies were intergovernmental arrangements and had no place for direct links between the confederate government and the citizens of the various member-states. This was why the leaders of the American states came together in Philadelphia and invented a new form of government called federalism. Until recently, scholars were much more interested in federations than in confederacies. However, in the past few years, in part because of the success of the European Union in preserving its character as a form of "confederacy," confederations have begun to attract more attention.[6]

Federal States

If the EU is not a parliamentary federation, and if its confederate status turns out to be a stage on the way to federation, not many models are left. Among them are the United States and Switzerland. Unlike Canada, Germany, and India, they did not adopt parliamentary government and then add on the distribution of powers. Instead, their starting point was federalism itself. This involved not only a constitutional distribution of powers but also three other principles:

1. The separation of the executive and legislative branches of government
2. A division of the legislature into two roughly equal chambers
3. A special role for the legislature, including the upper house, in protecting the interests of the people.

The Separation of the Executive and Legislative Branches

In deciding to make federalism the basic principle of governance, the Americans and the Swiss retained the old doctrine of the separation of powers, that is, separation of the executive from the legislative branch of government. Whereas in parliamentary systems the executive and the legislature were fused to create a parliament, a body in which members of the government usually sat both as ministers and as members of parliament in the United States and Switzerland, the two institutions were kept separate. To be a member of one meant that one could not be a member of the other.[7] This principle has not been implemented in the European Union. Today, in both the European Council and the Council of Ministers of the European Union, ministers tend to be members of their own national parliaments. On the other hand, so far there has been a separation within the organs of the EU itself. Members of the European Parliament are not members of either the European Council or the Council of the Union.

Two Equal Chambers

In all federations there is a bicameral legislature in which the upper house is elected from the regions. There is no upper chamber in the European Union. So far the European Parliament has been unicameral. However, any further development towards a federation would probably raise the question of bicameralism, and the form this might take. In the United States and Switzerland the legislative branch has been divided into two roughly equal chambers. By contrast in parliamentary government the chambers are not equal. The emphasis has always been on the lower house, the chamber elected according to population. It is to this chamber that the government is responsible, in part because it has been presumed to be more democratic than the upper house.[8] Government is based in principle on majority rule in the lower house. While there might be an upper house representing the regions, such as the Senate in Canada and Australia or the Rajya Sabha in India, it has played a lesser role. A much more significant role is played by the German upper house (the Bundesrat), though even in Germany the Bundestag alone is sometimes called "parliament."

The federal principle of the division of the legislative power, especially as adopted in the United States, rejected the emphasis on the popular house. In the United States the Senate has always played a very important role as the representative of the states, as the states are very unequal in population.

This means that the Americans are not governed according to the parliamentary principle of majority rule. Today, eight of the American states have such small populations that the total of all eight is only about five million people. These eight states elect sixteen senators. By contrast, California has a population of thirty-one million. Yet although California returns fifty-two members of Congress (to a House with 435 members), it has only two senators, the same number as each of the small states. Such equality of representation is rare in parliamentary federations, the most important example being Australia, where the six states have six seats each. In Canada the two largest of the ten provinces share nearly half the seats in the Senate. In India in 2000, the five largest states out of a total of twenty-five have 111 seats out of a total of 245 members of the Rajya Sabha. In Germany the larger of the sixteen Länder return more members to the Bundesrat.

The Role of the Upper House of the Legislature in Representing the People

It is unthinkable in genuine federations for the legislative branch of government to play a consultative role. Yet in the European Union only that has long been the role of the European Parliament. Hence the assertion that the system has a "democratic deficit." In all liberal democracies the legislature plays an important role in holding the government accountable. In parliamentary federations the government depends on the goodwill of the lower house of parliament for its continuation in office. In other federations there are other checks and balances to prevent the executive from exercising too much power. Unlike parliamentary federations, which give prominence to the lower house, the American and Swiss federations give equal weight to the upper house. This means that smaller states and cantons have a disproportionate role in governance. This is defended, on one hand, on the grounds that territorial minorities must be protected. In both federations there was some concern from the beginning that such minorities, for example French–speaking and Italian–speaking Catholics in Switzerland or farmers in the American heartland, could be overwhelmed by a Protestant or urban majority. It is opposed, on the other hand, on the grounds that it tends to give rural, and usually conservative, minorities the opportunity of vetoing progressive legislation.

What Form Might a European Federation Take?

In theory, the European Union could settle on being a parliamentary federation, a confederacy, or a novel form of federal state, like the United States
and Switzerland. Clearly, the European Union is not about to become a
super nation-state. It has too many nations to bring together. Like many
other large countries, such as Russia or India, a United States of Europe
would have to be multinational. The choice is between some form of federation or confederacy. Could Europe become a parliamentary federation? It
is true that most of Europe's member-states have a parliamentary form of
government, but it is unlikely that a *European* parliamentary federation will
evolve. Europe has long moved in a different direction. It is therefore too late
to think of the European Union adopting a parliamentary form of government, with a federation added on. Since 1951 the Europeans have been
developing a form of governance that is not parliamentary at all. There is a
European Parliament, but that body has not been a parliament in the true
sense. Far from fusing the executive and legislative branches, the European
Parliament has met separately in Strasbourg, not in Brussels where the European Commission has its headquarters. The European Union, then, will be
neither a super nation-state nor a parliamentary federation.

How relevant is the second form, confederacy? In some ways, the European Union already is a form of confederacy. It is based on a number of
treaties and other intergovernmental arrangements between its member-
states. There is general agreement that all the members have to give up a
degree of their sovereignty, a fact that has made Europe more like a confederacy than, say, an alliance. There is also a widespread belief (especially in
countries like the United Kingdom) that this intergovernmental union is as
far as the European Union ought to go in the direction of federalism. However, Europe is already more than a confederacy. It is probably too late to
prevent a movement towards a more intimate union. We noticed earlier that
one distinguishing feature of a traditional confederacy was simply that it
was an intergovernmental arrangement. The confederate government, such
as it was, had no authority to deal directly with the citizens of the member
states. Yet the European Union does deal directly with the individual citizen.
While it is not a "state" in the ordinary sense of the term, it is treated as a
state in a number of ways.

If, then, the European Union is not a nation-state; if it is most unlikely
to become a parliamentary federation; and if it has progressed beyond a traditional confederacy, what then? Now it becomes necessary to think about
what for many is unthinkable: the extent to which the European Union is, or

could evolve into, a novel federal system. It is hard to visualize the EU going that far. This is partly because it differs from other federal systems in two important respects. First, it does not conform to the federal principles discussed above. There is no European constitution in which the powers are distributed between the Commission and the member states. Instead there has been a succession of treaties. There *is* a separation of powers, but it is very lopsided, with three institutions making up the executive branch, and one institution representing the legislative branch. As for the federal principle of a bicameral legislature, there is no second chamber, no upper house representing the member states. Nor does the legislature have the powers that it has in countries like the United States and Switzerland that are based on federal principles. The Council of the Union is an executive body meeting in private, and can hardly be compared to a legislative body engaged in public debate. The European Union has had very little to do with federal principles.

There is another respect in which the EU is hardly a federal system. It is not a form of governance that can be explored and analyzed in the normal fashion of political analysis. It remains "a work in progress," so much so that whatever is said about it today is unlikely to apply ten years from now. As we noted at the beginning, the EU is sui generis. The European Union could perhaps be moving from an "intergovernmental arrangement," which is how many governmental observers officially view it today, toward some form of federation that is unique. Just as the United States and Switzerland established unique federal systems—very different from the parliamentary federations that followed—so the EU, if it does become more integrated, will be unique and will require a novel form of classification. It is already a unique form of "state." Whatever it becomes is also likely to be difficult to classify, if only because—unlike other states—the EU may always be in the process of becoming something else!

What Other Systems of Governance Should Be Explored?

A "system of governance" refers to the main institutions of government, notably the executive and legislature. There are only two "classical" systems of governance, parliamentarism and presidential-congressionalism. Both date from the eighteenth century, and both have been widely copied. Without some understanding of how the European Union developed, one might reasonably have expected a federal Europe to be either parliamentary (like Germany or India) or presidential (like the United States). Parliamentarism has proved to be very adaptable. In the twentieth century it was adopted by states throughout the world. It has run into difficulties in large heterogeneous societies such as Canada and India. As for the other classical form, presidential-congressionalism has succeeded in the United States because (thanks in large measure to the important role of the Senate) it is associated with federalism. Elsewhere, notably in Latin America, it has frequently resulted in a struggle between the executive and legislature. Outside the United States, presidential government has not worked very well.

If both parliamentarism and presidential-congressionalism are nonstarters, is there an alternative? The end of the eighteenth century saw experimentation with a third classical form of governance. This was a convention-type government in which all power was given to the people's representatives. The term "convention" is used because it is associated with the convention government adopted in France in 1792. That "government" is remembered today largely because during its heyday the Convention freely used the guillotine. It is remembered in history as "the Reign of Terror." For this reason convention theory is generally regarded as disastrous. However, it may be worth taking another look at a modification of convention theory known as "assembly government." This was adopted in the year 1848, sometimes called "the year of revolutions." It was in that year when the Swiss formed their modern federation, influenced by convention theory. However, their National Assembly did not attempt to govern as a convention. It remained an assembly and elected as government a federal council of persons outside the legislature. In rejecting the two classical forms, presidential and parliamentary government, the Swiss adopted something else: collegial government. The Swiss federation had several novel features. It attached considerable importance to what is now called "subsidiarity" by allowing the cantons, and local government in general, as many powers as possible. It established a federal executive council, a body elected by the Assembly. It then ensured that the executive council took its decisions as a collegial body. Instead of a prime minister or president, there was a rotating chair. Proposed constitutional amendments were submitted to the people. This "assembly-based" system does not appear to have been tried elsewhere, though it has been suggested as an alternative for India. Might Swiss federalism offer some insights into what has been developing in Europe?

Finally, there is a fourth form of governance, the French presidential-parliamentary hybrid introduced in 1958. This novel and flexible system has worked in France, just as presidential government has worked in the United States. It is novel because it combines presidential government with an element of parliamentary government under a prime minister and cabinet. It is flexible because it can handle situations where presidents find themselves dealing with prime ministers from an opposing party. In France the president is elected for seven years, the National Assembly for four. On several occasions the president's party has subsequently been defeated in the National Assembly elections. Then the system reverts to one of parliamentary government, with the prime minister, not the president, formulating policy in what the French call "cohabitation." When the system is working as De Gaulle intended, with the president in charge, it can hardly be called parliamentary. A more precise term for such a system is "presidential-quasiparliamentary."[9] France, of course, is not Europe. It is a nation-state. However, a modified form of presidential-quasiparliamentary government has been introduced in the Russian federation following the adoption of the 1993 constitution. It is too early to say whether it offers yet another model.

What Political Systems are Most Suitable for Federations?

Parliamentary Federations

When parliamentary, presidential, and assembly-based government are assessed with regard to their suitability for federations, a different picture emerges. Parliamentary government, especially British parliamentary government with its emphasis on the supremacy of parliament, appears to conflict with the distribution of powers characteristic of federations. Because of the failure in Canada of what we may call the "legislative federalism" practiced by the Senate in the United States, there has developed an "executive federalism." The most serious constitutional issues have been debated not by the Senate but by meetings of the prime minister and the ten provincial premiers. With the passage of the 1982 Constitution Act, the formerly ad hoc First Ministers' Conferences have been constitutionalized. An interesting feature of executive federalism is that each of the provinces is represented by its premier, thus placing tiny Prince Edward Island on a par with Ontario. Germany has never tried an American-style legislative federalism. Instead, it has adopted an interesting variant of executive federalism. The upper house, or Bundesrat, is not elected to represent the people of the various *Länder*. Instead it represents the *Länder* governments.

Presidential Federalism

The only good example of presidential federalism is the American. It may be more precisely classified as "presidential-legislative federalism." This system has been in existence since the constitution was framed in 1787 and appears to work reasonably well. Whether the American "presidential-legislative federalism" can be recommended for other states is more doubtful, because the political system of the United States was not originally based solely on presidentialism. Nor was it based on a supposed balance between President and Congress. The secret of its success was that it was firmly based on the principles of federalism. How else would the American people have accepted a system in which such power was given to a body like the Senate?

Assembly-Based Federalism

We noted in the previous section that convention government has not worked in nation-states. However, assembly-based federalism has worked well in Switzerland. The revolutionary year 1848 had a profound effect on the Swiss framers, who based much of their new constitution on the principles associated with convention government. That the Swiss system survived was due in part to the fact that the Swiss established a new type of government, "assembly-based federalism." They modified convention government in two very significant ways. Although the victorious cantons were Protestant, they did not impose their will on the Catholic minority, who were given equal representation in the upper chamber. Secondly, the Swiss decided to enable the executive to have a separate existence.

Nevertheless the Swiss preserved several important features associated with convention government. In the first place they arranged for the executive to be elected by the assembly. Secondly, they substituted a collegial federal council for government by either a prime minister or a president. Thirdly, the seven members of the Council were expected to work collegially. It is therefore more accurate to classify the Swiss system as one of "assembly-based collegial federalism." Naturally, there had to be someone to chair this body. Rather than appoint a president, the Swiss decided that the members of the council should take the presidential chair in turn for a year apiece. Nor was this all. The Swiss did not adopt the American principle of judicial review of the constitution by the courts. Instead of instituting judicial review of the constitution, the Swiss decided that the proper way of amending this document was for the people to decide by referendum. Switzerland is one of the few states to have opted for popular referendum and to have limited judicial review largely to cantonal legislation.

In sum, when we turn from the nation-state to federations, the form of government that would be most suitable changes. Parliamentary government, which has proven very adaptable to all sorts of unitary states, appears less adaptable in federations. The Westminster form of parliamentary government, with its stress on the supremacy of parliament and majority rule through the lower house, conflicts with all three federal principles: the separation, division, and distribution of powers. By contrast, presidential and assembly government have both worked well in federations. Both the presidential–legislative federalism practiced in the United States and the assembly-based collegial federalism of Switzerland have been successful.

Presidential-Quasiparliamentary Federalism

Yet another type of federation appears to be emerging in Russia, where there is both a president and a prime minister and cabinet on the French model. But Russia is not France. It is a large heterogeneous federation with eighty nine regions recognized in the constitution. The French presidential-quasiparliamentary system has had to be adapted to Russian needs through what we may call "presidential–quasiparliamentary federalism." This awkward terminology is necessary if we are to classify both the new (French-style) presidential-quasiparliamentary Russian constitution of 1993 and the federation adopted in 1992. The Russians, therefore, offer yet another model for Europeans to consider.

A Suitable System for a Federative United States of Europe

It has already been argued that, although most member-states are parliamentary in form, the Europeans are unlikely to adopt a parliamentary federation because this would require the dismantling of the collegial decision-making structure that is already in place. Nor are the Europeans likely to adopt the American system of government. Might the Russian presidential-quasiparliamentary form of government be a possibility? That seems doubtful. It is unlikely that the Europeans would want to venture into something as novel, and relatively untested, as this form of government.

This leaves assembly-based federalism, a system that appears to work in Switzerland but has not been adopted by any large heterogeneous society. However, it is not a system to be dismissed out of hand, if only because some of its institutions are comparable to those of the European Union. There is little doubt that the system chosen would have to fit into Europe's own fifty-year old tradition of governance. That tradition has had nothing to do with the two main classical forms of government, the parliamentary and the presidential. Nor, it must be conceded, is the EU assembly-based like the Swiss. So far, unlike the Swiss National Assembly, the unicameral European Parliament has played a minor role. As we saw earlier, the European Union is top-heavy with executive bodies, and weak on the legislative side. It has what many observers have called "a democratic deficit." Something needs to be done about the executive-legislature relationship to bring the two into balance.

One option is to transfer one of the three executive bodies to the legislative side of the equation. In the American tradition of governance, which we have called "legislative federalism," there is an upper house to represent the people of the various regions, either directly or indirectly. Even where the upper chamber is indirectly elected, as in the United States before 1913, it has been the legislatures of the regions that have elected the members of the chamber. In Germany, however, where the Bundesrat and its predecessor the Reichsrat have traditionally elected *governments*, there is a form of "executive federalism." Since Germany is the leading state in the European Union, and the one with the longest experience of federation, it may well be the German form that is selected.[10] It makes sense, therefore, to consider the possibility that there will one day be a European Bundesrat representing the fifteen governments. How can this be achieved?

When we turn to the existing institutions of the European Union we find that there already is an institution representing the governments of the fifteen member-states. It is the Council [of Ministers] of the European Union. Like the existing German Bundesrat it has fluid membership, depending on the issues being discussed. Could the Council of the European Union, at present an executive body, be suitably modified to become part of the European Parliament? Certainly there would be no need to change its name: "the Council of the European Union" sounds fine. Were the Council of the Union to become a legislative body, it would operate differently from the way it currently conducts its affairs. First, as a legislative body it would have to debate in public, not behind closed doors. This would remove one objection to the present set of institutions: that they are not democratic. Secondly, as a legislative body, the bicameral European Parliament would elect, rather than appoint, members of the European Commission. (The present unicameral European Parliament has already been granted the right to approve members of the Commission.) In electing the Commission, the new Parliament would overcome the main objection to the Commission: that, because member-governments appoint it, the Commission contributes to the democratic deficit.

The European Commission would now become the government of the European Union. It may be argued that to have the Commission elected by both chambers of a bicameral Parliament would be something that no member-state has experienced. That is true. For while German chancellors are elected by parliament, "parliament" is the Bundestag. There is, however, something of a precedent in Switzerland. The two chambers of the Swiss legislature, acting as a national assembly, elect a separate Federal Council. However the Swiss body, like the Council of the European Union, has no permanent chair. By contrast, the European Commission does have a permanent chair in the chief commissioner, elected for a five-year term.

So far, we have proposed arrangements for two of the three executive bodies. We have suggested a new use for the European Council of Ministers, transforming it from being one of three executive bodies into a legislative body, into the upper house of the European Parliament. We have also proposed transforming the European Commission from a government-appointed body into an elected executive. Neither reform would involve the creation of a new institution—though the transformation of the European Commission into a genuine federal government would be even more revolutionary in its implications than the creation of a common (federal) currency. The European Council [of heads of government] is a different matter altogether. There is no way that the biannual meetings of the heads of the member-governments can be converted into a legislative body. If the experience of other federations is any guide, however, politicians from the member-states will quickly gravitate to the new federal government. Failing such a transfer, the European Council will have to remain as it is, at least for the time being. If the new arrangements proved to be successful, there will be less need for meetings of heads of government. However, these "First Ministers" could continue to meet so long as member-states remained hesitant about the transfer of sovereignty to the European Union. In due course, assuming the new system proved to be effective, the number of meetings would decline.

How Unique Is the New Europe?

We began by assuming that the institutions of the European Union were sui generis. We will end by suggesting that an attempt to transform the Union into a federal system will not require much that is new in the institutions of governance. To understand the European Union it is necessary to examine it in the context of the various strands in modern federalism. We have suggested that the American model of federalism has been one of "legislative federalism." This is best represented by the American Senate, a body very different from Germany's Bundesrat. The Bundesrat serves as a representative of "executive federalism." Both types of federalism are different from the assembly-based collegial federalism of Switzerland. It is the Swiss and German models that appear to have most relevance for a federal European Union.

In addition to taking into account the experience of the American, German, and Swiss federations, it is necessary to recall Western Europe's earlier attempts at some form of unification. It is useful to recall that the European

Union originated with the European Coal and Steel Community. That Community owed much to statesmen influenced by the example of Europe's ancient Middle Kingdom, a kingdom close to Switzerland. It could be difficult for the citizens of centralized nation-states like the United Kingdom and France to come to terms with something like the German and Swiss federations. All the countries are liberal democracies. But there have been different interpretations of "liberal democracy" in Europe, some being more democratic than others. As federations, both Germany and Switzerland have become used to "pressures from below" on their systems of government, pressures unfamiliar to nation-states like France and England. For the English in particular, who are still coming to terms with the aspirations of Ireland, Scotland, and Wales, it will require a reappraisal of the nature of federalism and federations. In sum, the uniqueness of Europe consists in its evolution into a novel form of federation. This requires a reappraisal of existing federal practice and of Europe's own history.

Redefining the American Model: Legislative Federalism

Traditionally, students of federalism have started from the assumption that the model for modern federations is the United States.[11] With regard to the three principles of federalism, this is correct. As the United States discovered, there has to be a constitutional distribution of powers. In the European Union this will be between the Commission and the member-states. There also has to be a separation of the executive and legislative powers (something that is missing in parliamentary federations, including Germany). And there has to be a division of the legislative power into two powerful chambers, one of which (like the Bundesrat) represents the governments of the member-states.

However, it is not necessary to assume that all departures from the American model are deviations from federalism. It may be possible for the European Union to adopt a system of government different from the American, and yet be federal. As far as the distribution of powers is concerned, it may not be necessary to convene a constitutional convention where everything is finalized. Europe could continue to be a work in progress with powers gradually being shifted to the European Commission in Brussels. For a long time to come, the European Commission could remain more of an administrative rather than a political body. Nor is it necessary to have a single president as head of the executive. Europe's collegial form of government could continue. It is true that the president of the European Commission is more than first among equals, and it is conceivable that future presidents might be allowed to exercise more powers than they have been permitted to do so far. However, to judge by the debate preceding the appointment of the president appointed in 1998 there is still some concern lest the office be transformed into something more presidential than was originally intended.

A Form of Executive Federalism: The German Bundesrat

The European Union has to be examined in the context of German as well as American federalism. The German variant of "executive federalism," a Bundesrat representing the *Länder* governments, is very different from the Canadian. In Canada the term "executive federalism" refers to meetings of First Ministers, yet another indication that there are alternatives to American legislative federalism with its powerful Senate. Admittedly, the European Union is at present top-heavy with institutions that represent the executives of the member-states. However, it does not follow that institutional reform would lead to legislative federalism on the American model. The Europeans will probably adopt some form of executive federalism.

Assembly-Based Federalism: The Swiss National Assembly

In Switzerland, as in the European Community and the European Union, there has long been a preference for a collegial executive. The two chambers of the legislature, acting as the National Assembly, elect the executive, the Federal Council. Assuming that the European Commission gradually develops into the European executive, the nature of its election becomes crucial. Traditionally, responsibility for the appointment of the members of the Commission has lain with the Council of the European Union. More recently this responsibility has been shared with the European Parliament. Under the new dispensation, the Council of the European Union would form the upper house of the European Parliament, performing a function similar to that of the Bundesrat in the German Parliament. The appointment of the European Commission could easily be transformed into an election—on the Swiss model—by the bicameral European parliament. From an American perspective, the democratic deficit would persist in the absence of a powerful and directly elected upper house. However, executive federalism has established itself elsewhere, and in the medium term at least, may be the only form of federation acceptable to the member-governments.

Europe's History: The Middle Kingdom

When the ECSC was created, it was noted that all three of the leaders of Germany, France, and Italy (Konrad Adenauer, Robert Schuman, and Alcide De Gasperi) were Roman Catholics. In addition, they all came from a part of their respective countries that was close to Charlemagne's Middle Kingdom and that later became part of the Holy Roman Empire. It has often been suggested that they must have been inspired by these earlier attempts to bring the peoples of Europe together.[12] Certainly it is hard to imagine a Prussian, a Breton, or a Neapolitan having the same feel for the new Europe as imbued these three founders. Incidentally, it needs to be remembered that Germany has traditionally been a federation. The centralized state established by Adolf Hitler lasted only twelve years. Even Bismarck's German Empire, a state in which Prussia played such a dominant role, was in some respects a federation. It has also been suggested that Switzerland was able to develop its unique form of federalism because it was located close to the Middle Kingdom and the Holy Roman Empire. One writer has suggested that the European Union is following in Switzerland's footsteps.[13] Its institutions may be novel, but not the concept of Europe as an entity.

European Democracy: A Variety of Styles

While all members of the EU claim to be liberal democracies, they have different styles. All have political parties, but some have more than others. (At the last count there were forty-seven parties in Italy.) Federal states like Germany and Switzerland are accustomed to pressures on the federal government from below. Nation-states like France and the United Kingdom take the dominance of Paris and London for granted. It is likely that member-states of the European Union will preserve not only their diverse political cultures but also their different forms of government.

European Federalism: A New Form?

In 1787 the United States burst out of the confines of the nation-state and established the first modern federal system. Eighty years later its neighbor Canada became the first parliamentary federation. Meanwhile, in 1848, a third Assembly-based federal system emerged in Switzerland. Today a fourth type of federal system may be in process of being created. The European

Union has incorporated elements of the American, Swiss, and German federations. It will be interesting to see whether a novel federation will emerge over time, or whether at some point the Europeans will actually "choose" a new federal form of governance through a constitutional convention and a referendum. Europe's form of governance will continue to display many of the features with which students of federalism have long been familiar. But it will also be unique, because the European Union is unique.

Notes

1. Having suggested that to the casual observer the European Union's "basic institutional structure seems to resemble a typical federal system," Vivien Schmidt goes on to say "On a closer look, however, it becomes clear that the European Union (EU) fits no traditional model of governance." See "European 'Federalism' and its Encroachments on National Institutions," *Publius: The Journal of Federalism,* 29, 1 (1999): 19.
2. In early 2000, when a right-wing party joined the government, Austria discovered just how deep this commitment was.
3. Schmidt, 20.
4. For anyone not intimately connected with the European Union, the use of the official terms "Council of the European Union" and "European Council" may be somewhat confusing.
5. The capitals of both the United States and the Province of Canada rotated until Washington and Ottawa were selected as permanent.
6. See, for example, Daniel Elazar, *Constitutionalizing Globalization: The Postmodern Revival of Confederal Arrangements* (Lanham: Rowman and Littlefield, 1998.)
7. In some parliamentary systems, for example the Netherlands and Norway, the older doctrine of the separation of powers remains. Members of parliament are required to give up their seats on being appointed to the cabinet.
8. The terms "upper" and "lower" house have nothing to do with superiority. They date from the time when the House of Representatives met on the lower floor and the Senate on the upper floor of Congress Hall in Philadelphia.
9. In *The Analysis of Political Systems* (London: Routledge, 1959), I analyzed parliamentary, presidential, and convention government. The French hybrid of presidential-parliamentary government had only just been adopted. I made no attempt to incorporate federalism or federations in my analysis.
10. Alternatively, the Europeans might conceivably want to consider the Russian equivalent of the Bundesrat. Half of the members of Russia's Council of the Federation represent the governments of the eighty nine regions. The other 50 percent of the members represent the regions' legislatures.
11. For example, K.C. Wheare, in his classic work on federalism began his second paragraph with the sentence "The modern idea of what federal government is has been determined

by the United States of America," K.C. Wheare, *Federal Government* (London: OUP, 1946), 1.

12. Some scholars have taken the idea of Europe back thousands of years. See for example James O'Connell, "The Making of Europe: Strengths, Constraints and Resolutions," *A Constitution for Europe*, ed. Preston King, (London, 1991), 23–61.

13. "The European Union, which now surrounds it, has begun to develop into a loose, multi-national confederation not unlike what Switzerland was at an earlier stage. ... [T]he long struggle from 1291 to free the Swiss Confederation from the Holy Roman Empire may end with Switzerland joining that Empire's unlikely successor, the European Union." Jonathan Steinberg, *Why Switzerland?* 2d ed., (Cambridge, 1996), 232.

Chapter 2

FEDERAL ARRANGEMENTS, NEGARCHY AND INTERNATIONAL SECURITY

The Philadelphia System and the European Union

———⊸⊰⊱⊷———

Francis Campbell

European integration was first conceived by its founding ethos, to prevent the outbreak of hostilities between its member states by engaging them in an integrative process.[1] This process would simultaneously replace the old anarchical relationship between the different European States and yet guard against the formation of an overall hierarchical central power.[2] The argument put forward here holds that some contemporary EU initiatives threaten the original architecture of concurrently preventing anarchy and hierarchy by moving towards a hierarchical structure in some key policy areas. Anarchy is taken to mean a series of independent states that live in order, but engage in little formal integration. Hierarchy, on the other hand, has a centralization of powers. The European Union is not easily located along the anarchy—hierarchy continuum. But clearly, it is neither a collection of states living an ordered, yet anarchical existence, nor does it possess one centralized hierarchical power structure.[3] Thus, one of the core tasks will be to locate the EU along the anarchy-hierarchy axis and then determine a threshold beyond which the Union falls into the ambit of hierarchy, albeit novel. The three

---

areas examined in the following are some of the most sensitive for contemporary governance: the economy; foreign and security policy; and citizenship.

Integration in sensitive areas is occurring at a European level. In fact, political discourse among European leaders centers on what the appropriate level for governance actually is.[4] Over the past forty years, the same question has occupied many generations of European leaders. Some saw a challenge to the primacy and permanency of the nation-state.[5] For example, Walter Hallstein, the first President of the European Commission (1958-67), wrote "it does not follow that this type of nation-state, highly centralized, non-federal, and neglectful of regional interests, is the highest and only form of political organization known to man".[6] Reinforcing the point, he sought solace from that other great observer of new phenomena, Alexis de Tocqueville. He said of America, "a form of government has been found out which is neither exactly national nor federal; but no further progress has been made and the new word which will one day designate this novel invention does not yet exist."[7] De Tocqueville's observations could easily be ascribed to the contemporary European Union.

A good starting point for defining the Union is "Governance without Statehood. "[8] This mirrors what de Tocqueville first observed in the "Philadelphia system," laying ground to the emerging federalism in the United States.[9] Governance without Statehood exposes the complexity of the problem in hand. Too often observers wear nation-state lenses when defining the Union and thus our ability to think outside of this framework is severely impeded. But the structure of the Union is not without historical precedent. Similarities can be found in the Swiss Confederation (1815–1848), the United Provinces of The Netherlands (1579–1795), and the United States (1789–1865). In the following, some of the similarities between the American states union 1789–1861 and the EU will be explored. In its present form, the Union falls short of a complete fusion of states. While a European identity is advancing, its has not yet reached the stage where all of the members have lost their identity as states. It is doubtful whether this will occur in the near future. But the Treaty of Maastricht, signed in 1992, introduced the concept of European citizenship. The Treaty of Amsterdam, agreed in 1997, amended article 8 (1) of the Maastricht Treaty to make explicit that European Union citizenship was complementary to and not a replacement of national citizenship. But Maastricht's introduction of citizenship could be seen as signifying a shift from what the preamble to the 1957 Treaty of Rome called "laying the foundations of an ever closer union among the peoples of Europe" to a European demos. Such a change though gradual, could over time see the emergence of European consciousness. Often developments in European integration outpace theory—thus it is necessary to take stock of what impact the developments have on International Relations theory.

Hierarchy and Anarchy

One of the foremost neorealist thinkers, Kenneth Waltz, envisages order as being either hierarchical or anarchical. The neorealist tradition does not make provision for anything in between the anarchy-hierarchy relationship.[10] Classically the concept of hierarchy is associated with the contemporary nation-state in its postwestphalian mode. The structure of order within the unit is along hierarchical lines. Conversely, outside the realm of this hierarchically constructed unit there is anarchy. This hierarchical model has a working definition of being "a hierarchically organized protection-providing entity monopolizing violence in a particular territory and possessing sovereignty and autonomy."[11] "Westphalia's" location of sovereignty in the state ensured that no higher or supranational sovereignty was recognized to exist outside of the state. Thus, states could be characterized as states in anarchy concerned primarily with their own survival and/or the maximization of power.

Realist thought holds that international relations takes place within an anarchical framework with sharp divides between domestic and foreign frontiers. Domestically, states living in the anarchical system possess a monopoly on legitimate violence within their territory. Beyond domestic borders no such monopoly exists.[12] Historically the international system, that is all the states, has been considered "anarchic," because it was based on unequally distributed power and was deficient in higher, that is supranational authority. Its units, the independent, sovereign nation-states, were constantly threatened by stronger powers and managed to survive by engaging in the balance of power system.[13] Anarchy could be characterized as "a relationship between states that involves economic rivalry, security dilemmas, arms races, hypernationalism, balancing alliances, and ultimately the threat of war."[14] Simply put anarchy is characterized by the absence of hierarchy, but harboring rights and responsibilities. The first of those responsibilities is the mutual recognition of each other's right to exist as a state.[15] States within the anarchical structure are in constant search of security and this is manifested by balancing—balancing with other states to achieve security.

One of the first real efforts at replacing the European anarchical system of balancing came with the creation of the League of Nations in the aftermath of World War I. The League was the first U.S. inspired attempt to engender more cooperation between European nation states. Woodrow Wilson attempted introducing a cobinding institution to Europe. This effort failed because of continuing U.S. isolationism, and it was not until World War II that more solid cobinding institutions emerged in the shape of NATO and the WEU and on this occasion with the direct participation of the United States. As seen by their continuing popularity, these cobinding institutions were not simply the byproduct of a Cold War world riddled with fear and insecurity. The multilateral institutions founded in Europe after the Second World War have either accepted or are preparing to accept applicants from the former Warsaw Pact. If applicants of membership and further strides towards cooperation are indicative of anything, then such institutions are not on the wane.[16]

Negarchy

The concept of "negarchy" is borrowed in its entirety from Daniel Deudney. He calls it the arrangement of institutions necessary to prevent both the emergence of hierarchy and anarchy.[17] While he coined the concept of negarchy from his analysis of the system existing in the American states-union from around 1787–1861, it can also be applied with considerable success to the European Union.[18] Negarchy is achieved by a system that at once negates against the formation of anarchy and a hierarchy. Deudney says, "the overall system architecture negates, so it is appropriate to call the structural principle of such orders 'negarchical' and the overall order a negarchy."[19] The European Union has managed to achieve a system that while mitigating against anarchy does not create a hierarchy. It mirrors the American system from 1787–1861 as described by Deudney. He described the American state-union as a spectrum in the middle whereby states are circumscribed and embedded in a constitution of the negative—a cross cutting architecture of binding and bound authorities. Deudney's American union combined separation of powers, popular arms control, and sectional balance of power to simultaneously solve insecurity threats.[20] Likewise, the EU has a series of cross checking architectures ranging from the role of the European Court of Justice to the function of the Commission in pursuing the Community interest. The separation of powers and the balancing that Deudney describes in the Philadelphia system are similar to the compromises that underpin the EU.

Negarchy is an order peculiar to more liberally minded states. While such states face the security threats from the anarchical system, they engage in a form of security cobinding as a means of responding to anarchy and thus they avoid the "realist" response, balancing. Cobinding commits each state to mutually constraining institutions and thus reduces the uncertainties associated with anarchical systems.[21] According to Deudney, this cobinding is mutual and reciprocal, and while overcoming the effects of anarchy it does not produce hierarchy. Such a framework fits the EU as one can point to the different, and sometimes conflicting mechanisms that simultaneously promote a community interest, but ensure that the member states powers are not eroded.

The concept of negarchy in the American states-union (Philadelphia system) would not label the government's powers national, because its jurisdiction only extended to certain enumerated objects. The different states had a residuary and inviolable sovereignty over all other objects.[22] When Madison described the American Constitution of 1789, he said it was neither national nor federal, but a composition of both—a mixed constitution.[23] For Madison the member states in the Philadelphia system retained a residuary and inviolable sovereignty over those areas not specifically delegated to the central government. Hamilton also believed that sovereignty was divided, like coequal sovereigns. He supported a stronger central power and yet insisted on the equality of the center and the parts. It was a mixed federal and national system. In the Philadelphia system the numerous factions, that is, different member states, served as a powerful bulwark against the formation of a central power. Similarly, the European Union has developed a guard against the formation of a central power by developing the concept of subsidiarity.[24] In many respects, this concept reflects Madison's and Hamilton's divided, but complementary views of sovereignty under the Philadelphia system.

The EU, in its present form, has many of the features of a negarchy, that is, its structure prevents anarchy between its member states while at the same time guarding against the creation of a new coercive central and over-arching authority. How long the EU will remain a negarchy is unclear. Three developments threaten the EU's negarchical existence: the reinvigorated Common Foreign and Security Policy; Economic and Monetary Union; and Justice and Home Affairs. It has been quite some time, if at all, since one could describe the EU as the interaction of sovereign states in an anarchical society.[25] Although the contemporary EU has not become a state, the level of integration that has developed in the EU has widened considerably in scope and depth over the past forty years. Thus, it occupies ground somewhere between anarchy and hierarchy. Negarchy is a label that fits well with the contemporary EU. But, with developments in the field of Common Foreign and Security Policy (CFSP), Justice and Home Affairs (JHA), and Economic and Monetary Union (EMU), negarchy may indicate the bounded threshold, beyond which EU developments will pass and thus the EU will no longer be a negarchy, but will be closer to a hierarchy, albeit novel. The EU possesses strong elements of hierarchy in the shape of the European Commission and the European Court of Justice. However, the present EU is a structure that simultaneously negates against the formation of anarchy and hierarchy. It is constantly in a state of flux. When the full integrative impact of EMU is felt this will strengthen the hierarchical element in the Union. Therefore, presently the structure of the EU is negarchical.

What is the EU?

Discovering the EU's contemporary nature is not easy. The EU has moved far from its first premise of making war among its member states unthinkable. So what is the contemporary EU? Is it a community of values? Some indications from the EU's enlargement policy provide us with some useful insights. The prospective EU applicant states (thirteen in all) must subscribe to criteria laid down at the 1993 Copenhagen European Council.[26] These criteria envisage a community of common values based on democracy, capitalism and respect for human rights.[27] But while enlargement conjures up certain norms to which willing applicants must subscribe, it also serves to concentrate existing member states minds on what the EU is and what they want it to become.

Many times throughout the history of European integration, pundits have predicted its demise yet it has survived. Political leaders have challenged it in a variety of forms from de Gaulle[28] to Thatcher, but it has grown in scope and depth over the past forty years. There is no greater testament to its success than its growth from six member states in 1957 to the possibility of twenty-seven in the near future. Similarly, the American states-union also managed to absorb states into its union: Utah and Vermont and the two independently recognized states of California and Texas. Agreeing that the applications indicate a measure of success is one thing, achieving a definition is an entirely different matter. The member states of the EU are embedded in a series of treaties. The EU is a cross-checking architecture of binding and bound authorities. The bound authorities do not eradicate conflict altogether, but they do channel it. It is a balance between the center and the periphery, the small and the large. There is no hegemon with a concentration of power. Increasingly the EU emancipates regional identity long since suppressed by the nation-state.

The cooperation in the early years of integration was facilitated by the destruction of Europe's old international order. Thus, there was a tremendous opportunity to experiment with new structures of governance. Similarly the Philadelphia system followed close on the heels of war and rebellion and thus an opportunity was available to develop new structures of governance. During World War II, some thinkers were developing an order that would replace the one that had delivered two devastating wars in Europe within one generation. The Second World War made it very clear to the European leadership that the old order had failed and integration was the only possible response to prevent war and yet maintain the integrity of the state. The state had failed to supply that basic requirement, security. Integration promised to deliver this, but maintain the state as a viable entity. Therefore, it is argued that this process, far from stripping sovereignty away from the EU's member states, actually restored it.[29] This is also a feature of the Philadelphia system, which argues that the American states-union actually preserved the states in a viable form.[30]

However, arguments about peace and security some forty years after the Treaty of Rome ring hollow. The war generation has passed from political power and with them the strong desire and conviction for securing peace. Thus contemporary dynamics must be unearthed that answer the EU's continuing appeal and growing mood towards integration. War could have been prevented by a degree of integration considerably narrower in scope than what we have in today's EU. The collapse of Soviet influence in Central and Eastern Europe in 1989 raised another possible explanation for the EU's existence: the Soviet threat. With the demise of such a threat, many seriously questioned the EU's ability to survive.[31] However, the EU's main impetus did not emanate from external threats.[32] Primarily the EU served the purpose of providing order within its borders; it had delivered predictability on the European political arena thereby making war unimaginable. A form of cobinding that created institutions of mutual constraint such as the European Commission or the European Court of Justice achieved this. This cobinding pacified otherwise anarchical states into predictable patterns of behavior that gradually removed armed conflict from the repertory of member states. European integration provided a comprehensive framework for governing relations within Western Europe, which may have initially arisen out of fear, but had matured greatly by 1989. From the very moment communism began collapsing in Central and Eastern Europe there was a unanimous European resolve to tackle and manage the problem on a European level. This had two fronts: what to do with Central and Eastern Europe; and how to strengthen the EU itself? The response to the former was to start the countries of Central and Eastern Europe on a path towards membership of the EU. The response to the latter was the Treaty on European Union signed in 1991 and the

Treaty of Amsterdam signed in 1997. By 1989, the European Union was more than an entity designed to prevent war or Soviet aggression. In other words, it had matured from its postwar and Cold War roots into being a sophisticated comprehensive system of government on an entirely new and novel level.

Locating the Contemporary EU

Descriptions of the European Union are somewhat à la carte in that one can choose from a menu what aspects they want to highlight to argue for either the intergovernmental or the supranational theories. Soul searching by EU analysts throws out labels such as supranational, intergovernmental, federal state, union of states, system of states, community, perpetual league, multi-tiered, multilevel governance, confederation, a loose federation, supranational polity or merely an international forum. These are matched by an earlier myriad of labels from the 60s and 70s such as federalist, functionalist, neo-functionalist and transactionalists. However, while some proponents of these schools claim to offer the definitive decoding sheet for the EU, no one perspective fully encapsulates its dynamic.

Supranational

"Intergovernmentalism" would gravitate more towards the anarchical end of the continuum, while "supranationalism" would rest closer to the hierarchical. The realist tradition within international relations has great difficulty in theorizing about the EU. The contemporary EU no longer possesses a sharp divide between the domestic and the interstate arenas. European integration touches so many facets of domestic policy that it is unfair to continue putting European affairs under the foreign policy banner. Blurring the domestic and foreign policy lines vis-à-vis Europe can be best depicted by the Europeanization of the member states civil services.

As more progress is made in the process of European integration, it is harder to argue that states are the primary units in this system. Those who believe that state power is being eroded only have to point to the existence of the European Commission, with its exclusive right of policy initiation in the Community pillar; the supremacy of European Community law; the European Court of Justice, whose rulings are applied in national courts via the preliminary reference; and the increased powers for the European Parliament. Furthermore, the increased use of Qualified Majority Voting (QMV) moves the EU closer to supranationalism and away from intergovernmentalism. While majority voting was rarely used because of the Luxembourg compromise, which in effect gave each member state the power to veto Council decisions, it has made a significant comeback in recent years. The Single European Act, which came into force on 1 July 1987, introduced a new legal basis for majority voting in internal market, economic and social cohesion, research and development, and environment.[33] The development of qualified majority voting, coupled with the supremacy of European Community Law, meant it was no longer tenable to argue that the member states in the EU enjoyed a monopoly of sovereignty.

Presently the use of national veto powers via intergovernmentalism is confined to certain matters, for example, fiscal harmonization. But with the implementation of the Treaty of Amsterdam on 1 May 1999, qualified majority voting was extended to a further fifteen areas (four existing and eleven new) and codecision.[34] with the European Parliament was extended to a further 23 areas. Some areas to benefit from the extension of qualified majority voting are employment, social policy, public health, research and development, and the coordination of national provisions on foreign nationals' rights of establishment.[35] The extension of qualified majority voting also takes place against a backdrop of enlargement when the nature of voting alliances will be overhauled. Presently, the system has 87 votes and a qualified majority-voting threshold of 71 percent, that is, 62 votes and a blocking minority of 26. Enlargement, will take in a further twelve member states and this will see the blocking minority increase to 39 votes and the qualified majority voting threshold increase to 94 votes out of a total of 132.[36] Thus, it appears that the Amsterdam Treaty does much more to strengthen the supranational element of the Union at the expense of the intergovernmental. Further extensions of the qualified majority-voting base would indicate a shift from negarchy to hierarchy.

Intergovernmental

The intergovernmental school stressed the primacy of the nation-state in the European integration project and indeed one can point to a variety of mechanisms that would support such a case. Some view the EU as a form of close cooperation between nation states, arguing that national governments are the primary actors in the integrative process. It is national governments that agree to coordinate their policies and these are implemented by national institutions. Even the "Community pillar" is more consensual, with the European Commission acting like a broker between the different vested positions in Europe. Furthermore, the Commission is made up of a vast number of national civil servants, called "detached national experts. " Finally, the ultimate indication of intergovernmentalism is the use of unanimity as a voting base. But the use of the veto is done sparingly, because of the normative constraints involved in using it. In most member states of the EU, European integration harbors a great degree of legitimacy. States can adhere to policies for the sake of Europe that would otherwise be unachievable. Examples include the economic policies adopted by the Italian and Spanish governments in order to meet the economic and monetary union convergence criteria.[37] But such a school gives exaggerated importance to the role of the state and marginalizes the sub- and suprastate actors. Intergovernmentalists also fail to realize how much the state has been influenced by the process of European integration. Too often one is led to assume that European integration has not affected the contours of the West European state. But as contact has increased throughout Europe, old suspicions have slipped away and thus the nature of the state's interest has altered dramatically.[38]

Why the EU Is Not a State

The concept underlying the Community holds that states surrender part of their sovereignty or, rather, pool their sovereignty. Writing in 1972, Hallstein could say categorically that the Community was not a state because, he believed, "A state is competent in all matters touching public policy, but unlike a state, our community is competent only in certain limited spheres which are already laid down in the treaty."[39] Today, if one were to use Hallstein's litmus test of statehood, in an era when the Community has greatly extended its scope of competence, one would be hard-pressed to deny the Community the label state. Finding appropriate labels to fit the Community in 1972 was difficult, but locating the contemporary European Union is even more difficult. So much competence of the member states originates from the Community. Over 70 percent of the legislation governing U.K. business emanates from the Brussels-based institutions. It is difficult to find areas of national policy that do not have an EU angle. The European Union is much more than yet another multilateral entity. Member states must share a stage with the European Commission and subordinate their relevant national law to rulings of the European Court of Justice. Those states that are part of the Euro zone are subordinate in matter of monetary policy to the

European Central Bank. Thus, with time it is harder to argue that member states are the dominant units in this entity. Even in domestic matters, member state sovereignty is curtailed by European norms in that citizens can appeal to a variety of overarching European institutions. There is certainly no monopoly of sovereignty within the European Union.

Analysis of the EU demands new concepts. It is not sufficient to benchmark the EU with dated notions. Now the depth of integration is so great that we are forced to examine its structures and processes and thereby generate a new concept of order. What is clear is that the numbers of multilateral entities are growing. Those that exist attract more and more applications for membership. It would be very wrong to approach the study of the EU preoccupied with the question whether or not it is a state. However, it is excusable to apply this label in order to advance analysis of this novel form of government. It is doubtful that the EU will ever become a state in the traditional sense. To begin, it does not have a shared collective experience, and, with enlargement on the horizon, this will seem even more remote. However, neither is it merely just another multilateral entity, the restriction of national sovereignty is too great for it.

The Dynamics of Integration: Spillover or Political Will?

The functional analysis of the EU tells us about the development of linkages between separate communities. These in turn generate transaction flows and if these transactions increase, then the assimilation of peoples and thus their integration into larger communities will be encouraged.[40] One of the first proponents of linkage creation was David Mitrany; he suggested integrating in technical areas first with the expectation that the success of this strategy would spill over into other areas. This dynamic would embed states into a series of crosscutting relationships and as contact increased, so would the possibility of assimilation into a new set of complementary loyalties.[41] Integration resembles state formation in the sense that the state absorbed regional entities under its hegemony.[42] However, it differs from state formation in that coercion plays an entirely different role. The increasing presence of liberal democracies, international social ties, and international institutions result in the development of a form of coercion that does not base itself on power relations.[43] The dynamic moves from communities to community and then from community to state. Integration precedes amalgamation; sentimental change precedes institutional change; social change precedes political change.[44]

Nevertheless, some felt that communication was not having the desired results within Western Europe. The theoretical linkage between transaction and assimilation was coming under strain because of reemerging provincialism and nationalism. But with hindsight, one can see that although the process of European integration did unleash a newfound separatism and provincialism, these were not directed against European integration. The integration dynamic assumed a life all of its own and in so doing not only altered the state's interest by adding a new European layer, but also and more fundamentally, altered the underlying distribution of power.[45] Suddenly hitherto small entities became viable again under the new European umbrella. European integration emancipated a substate identity while complementing state identity with a European seal.

Further efforts at integration require political will to push the reforms through; they do not just happen. While some could validly argue that economic and monetary union is a mere spillover from the integration of markets and the eradication of obstacles to trade, it would be harder to sustain this claim when examining integration over the past forty years. Integration should be seen over a longer period and then a different continuum can be recognized. Moving to a single market does not happen automatically as the spillover hypothesis would have us believe. Instead, its impetus was an ambitious political project aimed at moving the stagnating integration process forward. Equally, one could argue that the Maastricht Treaty was not the product of spillover, but a political response to the unification of Germany. We are told that Maastricht was designed to give the EU the instruments it needed to meet contemporary challenges.[46] The question is therefore whether it was strictly the product of political will or rather the product of environmental conditionality which gave rise to the possibility of spillover.

The Treaty on European Union: Maastricht

Maastricht was innovative in two senses: monetary union and further integration of social policy. The Treaty on European Union also put the Council in charge of the common foreign and security policy and cooperation in the field of justice and home affairs. The European Commission was to be "fully associated" with the work carried out under these pillars. Where spillover works it produces a dynamic that few can control and often member states meet merely to sanction inevitable measures. But the desire to move to a common foreign and security policy was a political initiative; it was not the product of a spillover from European political cooperation. The political process can also thwart spillover and this was witnessed in the early years when the French National Assembly rejected the formation of a European Defense Community.[47] Some argue quite persuasively that while intergovernmentalism is an important dynamic it is not the sole or indeed primary one.[48] Member states have often been confronted with a scenario where further integration was inevitable. The integrative process took on a life of its own. Often the integrative process was fueled by actions taken by the Commission or the European Court of Justice. It is noteworthy that the blueprint for the Treaty on the European Union came to life as a report of the European Parliament. Thus, it appears equally implausible to rely on nation-states as the sole actors in this dynamic.

EU Policy Developments

While one could focus on many policies to indicate developments in the process of European integration, few are as sensitive as the areas of foreign and security policy, justice, and the economy. The Maastricht Treaty dealt with economic and monetary union and laid out the three-stage timetable for creating the single currency. Developing a single unit of currency throughout the EU may yet serve as a catalyst for the centralization of powers in the realm of fiscal policy. Furthermore, the Treaty of Amsterdam deals comprehensively with two of those areas; justice and home affairs (JHA) and the common foreign and security policy (CFSP).[49] Developments in these important sectors will show that the trend is increasingly shifting towards hierarchy and away from the initial structural design, negarchy.

Economic and Monetary Union: A Catalyst for Change

Economic and Monetary Union (EMU) has a long history within the process of European integration. The idea first appeared from a gathering of the Community's heads of state at a meeting in The Hague. The result was the Werner Plan of 1970, which envisaged the creation of a monetary union over a period of ten years. However, the oil crises of the early 1970s and the subsequent global economic downturn greatly undermined the political will to bring this project about. Some twenty-one years later the concept was embodied in the Treaty of European Union.[50] It built upon the existing success of the European monetary system (EMS), which began life in 1979. In 1988, the then president of the European Commission, Jacques Delors was commissioned to produce a report that would propose concrete stages leading to economic and monetary union. The report proposed a three-stage process. Stage one began on 1 July 1990 and was aimed at increasing monetary coordination by bringing all member states into the EMS and completing the Single Market. The second stage, which began on 1 January 1994, witnessed the establishment of a European system of central banks. Finally, the third phase, which began with eleven of the fifteen EU member states, started on 1 January 1999. This last stage irrevocably fixes the exchange rates and moves to a single currency.

Why should this development act as a catalyst for further change? Already in stage one the member states were expected to move towards greater coordination of their monetary policy. By stage two they had begun to meet within the confines of the European system of a central bank; and the forerunner of the European Central Bank, the European Monetary Institute, had come into being. By the third and final stage, eleven member states of the EU had irrevocably fixed their national currencies and formed one currency region. It is interesting that in moving to this third stage the prospective members had to embrace rather strict convergence criteria.[51] These criteria severely curtailed the economic policies, both monetary and fiscal, of the member states. Many of the southern European member states pursued economic policies that were harmful to them in the short term. Interestingly enough the prospect of economic and monetary union seemed sufficiently attractive in Italy and Spain to fight off pressure for a shift from anti-inflationary policies and towards one aimed at reducing excessive unemployment.

But currency is more than just a medium of exchange or a unit of account. Currency has a major role in a country's constitutional and political fabric. Like recognition by the UN, it is one of the key indicators of sovereignty. Thus it is quite wrong to see EMU as a mere technical measure, it possesses rich symbolism. There is no doubt that governments will lose influence as more and more multinationals think outside the national frame of reference. This is not to say that national identity will be eroded entirely. The impact that EMU will have both internally and externally for the EU is without precedent. Internally the political consequences will be momentous. Economic and monetary union has already added another supranational entity, the European Central Bank, to the EU's architecture without creating any corresponding political union. This will only fuel the calls for more legitimacy by reducing the democratic deficit. The eleven members that form part of the Euro zone are examining ways of intensifying their cooperation under the new "Euro X Forum. " This body consisting of European finance ministers is envisaged as an embryonic political counterweight to the ECB. Economic and monetary union is already requiring greater coordination of macroeconomic policies so that member states economic cycles are more in tune.

It is said that the success or failure of EMU depends on either greater labor mobility or some form of extensive transfers from the center to the periphery.[52] The 1986 Single European Act called for the creation of a single market by 1 January 1993. In many respects, this process was a Trojan horse for EMU in that a single market for goods and services led to calls for a single medium of exchange aimed at entrenching confidence across borders. A single monetary policy could see the EU evolve from its current position as a structure concurrently guarding against anarchy and centralization, into a federal state. If a single monetary policy results in a single fiscal policy within the EU, then the process of integration will have reached and encapsulated some of the core sovereign areas traditionally reserved for the state. Economic and monetary union involved a three-pronged process where the EU witnessed convergence of monetary policies within the EU. The restrictive nature of the convergence criteria, assessed independently by the Commission, has had a huge impact upon the member states' ability to formulate their own fiscal policies. One could be forgiven for concluding that EMU will act as a catalyst for a common fiscal policy within the EU, in other words, for uniform taxation and social security. In December 1997, EU governments agreed to a voluntary code of conduct restricting unfair tax competition and the Commission is working on draft legislation. Already there is fiscal coordination within the EU in the shape of the European Finance Minister's Committee. There is little doubt that EMU will require some form of fiscal federalism in order to help the economies of the Euro zone should they face different shocks.

The external impact of EMU also deserves attention. EMU will bring immense global responsibilities for the EU and these responsibilities could well hasten further efforts at fiscal harmonization to induce greater integration in the political sphere. Responsibility brings power and at present, there is little semblance of an effective political structure within the EU to manage such a powerful global economic weight. EMU will certainly put pressure on the Euro zone for greater coordination with the United States on economic policy so that the international financial institutions will become less lopsided and thus reduce their dependency on the dollar. Rectifying the problems associated with EMU means labor mobility or monetary transfers. The EU, unlike the United States, has many more natural and cultural barriers that prohibit movement of excess labor from one region to another. Thus, it is suggested that in an area with a single monetary policy there should be a single fiscal policy. A uniform redistributive policy within the EU would compensate for the lack of labor mobility and therefore rectify one of the central problems for economic and monetary union. In matters of trade, the EU is represented by the European Commission and it successfully concluded the GATT Uruguay round. The Commission attends all G7 meetings on an informal basis, but is examining ways to bring it status onto a more formal footing. What is more important on the external front will be the role of the Euro as a new reserve currency. This could ensure a dramatic shift from a unipolar world financial system to a bipolar one. Since 1 January 1999 the EMU bloc is the world's largest exporter and importer, it accounts for 20.9 percent of the world's trade.

If monetary union is indeed to result in fiscal union then can one safely declare that the EU is no longer a negarchy, but a rather novel form of hierarchy? It may still be called "governance without statehood" if there is not a significant and complementary alteration in the political design. If fiscal harmonization emanates from economic and monetary union in the way that economic and monetary union emanated from the creation of the single market, then yet another core area of statehood will be embraced at the European level.

Common Foreign and Security Policy

When European integration reaches core areas of sovereignty, integration seems to take a marginal role. Despite a highly developed mechanism for gaining a common position on matters of international importance, something falls short in the area of the common foreign and security policy.[53] Clearly, Maastricht failed in the common foreign and security policy area and this was reinforced by the reports submitted by the European Commission, Parliament, and Council to the Reflection Group, which were preparing for the 1996 Intergovernmental Conference (IGC).[54] For many, the failure rests with the system and it shows the limits of integration. After all European Political Cooperation, the forerunner of the common foreign and security policy had been around since 1969 and it had little success apart from the odd solemn declaration. However, the breakup of Yugoslavia was seen as the ultimate failure of the common foreign and security policy. While recent developments in the Treaty of Amsterdam go far in attempting to rectify these shortcomings they may ignore the idea that the integrative process was not designed from the outset to evolve a common foreign policy and the subsequent centralization of power that this would create.[55]

Before identifying a common foreign and security policy as a step too far for integration, it is important to examine clearly, how the Treaty of Amsterdam envisages enhancing its effectiveness. The changes put forward are the fruit of the Intergovernmental Conference that met from 29 March 1996 to the 17 June 1997. "Amsterdam" attempts to move away from stalemate in the Council by moving towards consensus and away from unanimity. More and more the Union tends to speak with one voice in international forums. Already the U.K. and France, as permanent members of the UN Security Council, are obliged under the Treaty of European Union (Maastricht) "to ensure the defense of the positions and the interests of the Union, without prejudice to their responsibilities under the provisions of the United Nations Charter."[56] To avoid the stalemate that plagued the Union during the Bosnian conflict, the Council of Ministers intends to implement common strategies, which will usually be decisions based on qualified majority voting. Member states retain the right to hold up the process by referring the matter to the heads of government for discussion. A further measure aimed at moving the process forward is the concept of "constructive abstention" whereby Member states can remain apart from a project in which they do not want to participate, but which they do not oppose in principle. Finally, the newly packaged common foreign and security policy will have a public face with the secretary-general of the council having the responsibility of being the common foreign and security policy high representative.[57] The High Representative will have a central cadre of specialists of foreign policy staff called the Policy Planning and Early Warning Unit (PPU).

Will all these changes be enough to make foreign policy integration as effective as its economic partner? There is no doubt that there is much coordination within the EU on matters of foreign policy, but much division remains. Nowhere can this be seen more clearly than in the United Nations. The European Community was granted Observer status at the 1971 General Assembly (it can make its views known, but does not have the right to vote).[58] The Community is represented by the permanent representative of the member state holding the presidency of the Council of Ministers and by the head of the delegation of the European Commission. The Community has been granted full participation at many UN conferences; because of its competence in the relevant field.[59] Increasingly the profile of the EU is more visible at the UN, especially in the Security Council where it is now common practice for the presidency to make a statement on behalf of the EU. In circumstances where an individual EU member state wants to make an individual contribution to the debate, it is customary that they prefix their contribution with a statement aligning themselves with the EU presidency statement. The practice of having one EU voice at the UN resulted in the opening of an "EU Council Secretariat liaison office at the UN. " This inter- action among EU diplomats outside the EU and the impression of solidarity given in such a forum as the UN does much to add to the standing and pro- file of the EU.

However, when it comes to deciding on critical areas of interest the capacity of the Union is very weak. The UN crisis with Iraq showed how difficult it is to achieve a definitive EU position in the Security Council. Such divisions are deeply embarrassing for the EU, and it is doubtful that the Treaty of Amsterdam will rectify these difficulties in the short term. Surely, divergences of national positions indicate more the limits of inte- gration than mere failures of the structure. However, what was integration designed to achieve? It was designed to prevent centralization of power, while at the same time preventing conflict. The common foreign and secu- rity policy is beyond the boundary of integration; it is a step too far and if achieved will alter the uniqueness of the EU. There can be a gradual con- vergence of positions in foreign policy, but to develop a common—or do we mean a singular?—foreign policy could bring the EU into a federal state. The Commission's director general for external relations, speaking in 1995 said: "The pursuit of any foreign policy is based on a clear awareness of one's interests and objectives and the preparedness to defend and pro- mote them through appropriate means of action. ... This is already the case in the field of external economic relations. However, diplomacy and defense continue to be dominated by the perception of larger member states in particular that the pursuit of national interests should be given pri- ority over common action. There will be no genuine common foreign pol- icy if member states are not convinced that national and common interest coincide on given matters."[60]

Common foreign and security policy occupies one of the three pillars of the EU, thereby acknowledging the primacy of intergovernmentalism; it is nonetheless central to the integrative process. But while acknowledging that the key decisions will continue to be taken on a unanimity voting base (in EU jargon "common strategies"), implementing decisions, with the excep- tion of those which have military or defense implications, may be adopted by qualified majority voting. While this is a major shift towards more inte- gration in the field of common foreign and security policy, intergovernmen- talism is given an emergency brake provision to veto actions in case of "important and stated reasons of national policy."[61] Unanimity voting in common foreign and security policy results until now in decisions based on the lowest common denominator and were thus weak and ineffective—which clearly restricts central power and results in the continuation of a negarchical structure.

Justice and Home Affairs

In the justice and home affairs field (JHA), the EU is also moving towards presenting a common face towards the rest of the world. Political scientists often believe that it is impossible to present a common face externally if relations between the states concerned remain "external." Despite the common foreign and security policy each EU member state continues to exhibit traditional diplomatic norms, such as the exchange of ambassadors and large embassies vis-à-vis one another. This raises questions about the real impact of the common foreign policy and the inability to conceive of new and enhanced forms of intra-EU representation. A common external face necessitates a new internal order between the constituent parts or member states. "These relations must therefore become 'internal' at the same time as a common exterior is constructed. ... States become a part of something which has its own 'inner' and 'outer', its own state-like interests. ... This new body is not a state, it is not a union of individuals in a body politic, but a union of states in a body politic."[62]

That the process of integration is a process designed to create a change of attitudes among the populace is hardly revolutionary. Integration if it is to be long lasting needs to create a shared identity and to manufacture common experiences. In tangible form, this can be seen most clearly from the use of EU passports, and a common and recognizable flag. Shared identity could be seen as symbolizing the existence of shared values.[63] The Maastricht Treaty introduced a new layer of identity, European citizenship for citizens of EU member states. While the citizens enjoyed rights of establishment and movement under the single market legislation, it was only in 1991 that the concept of European citizenship emerged. European citizenship complements national citizenship. Concrete civil rights are accorded to the European citizen, such as the right to vote, to stand in municipal or European elections, and to petition the European Parliament. Furthermore, where a citizen's own nation does not have diplomatic or consular relations, they enjoy the protection of the other member states.

EU citizenship, though complementary and reliant on national citizenship, raises the possibility of a shift from the "peoples of Europe" as mentioned in the 1957 preamble to the Treaty of Rome, to a European demos.

European integration has significantly altered what has classically been meant by citizenship. Indeed, the very acts of integration are themselves inducing a European citizenry. The emergence of a European Union citizenship, albeit novel, may be a key point in determining the locus of the EU along the negarchy-hierarchy pathway. Many of the driving forces of European integration initially emerged as mere gestures only to mature later into key components of integration. Thus, EU citizenship could well move beyond its formal inception in the Treaty of Maastricht and develop a shared consciousness among the citizenry of Europe. Such a development would unquestionably move the EU into the realm of a hierarchy.

The integration of justice and home affairs (JHA), the so called "third pillar," is also engaged in harmonizing rules concerning third-country nationals. The aim is to have EU-wide immigration rules for third-country nationals and to harmonize asylum policy. The cooperation in matters of justice and home affairs has been brought to an even deeper degree of integration through the Schengen Group. The agreement aims to accompany the abolition of border controls with a comprehensive program of security measures covering the harmonization of the rules governing checks at external borders, visa policy, the right of asylum, and the rights of aliens. By a special protocol on the Schengen *acquis* this will be incorporated into the institutional and legal framework of the EU in respect of thirteen member states.[64] While Ireland and the U.K. have opted out of this degree of integration, it is noteworthy that those states applying for membership of the European Union must subscribe to this *acquis*. In the field of JHA, the shift from negarchy to hierarchy is quite noticeable if one compares the Maastricht Treaty in 1991 to the Amsterdam Treaty in 1997. Major areas of the JHA portfolio have shifted from the intergovernmental realm to the supranational.[65] The Treaty of Amsterdam ensures open frontiers for the people of Europe and the abolition of all identity checks within a five-year period.[66] Over a five-year period, member states will harmonize their rules on issuing visas and granting asylum to non-EU citizens.[67] While under the Maastricht Treaty JHA was firmly in the intergovernmental realm it has now moved into the community pillar and thus has come under the jurisdiction of the European Court of Justice. If one believes that the EU is moving from a negarchical structure towards a form of a European hierarchical framework then one can look at the remaining elements of the JHA pillar as some possible elements for future integration. Amsterdam focuses the JHA pillar principally on combating crime, with an expanded role for Europol. There is a mechanism whereby member states can empower the ECJ to give preliminary rulings on criminal matters.[68] This could well prove an embryo for a future harmonization of criminal law across the EU and thus move the EU away from a negarchy and closer to a hierarchy.

Conclusion

The European Union in its current form occupies a middle ground between anarchy and hierarchy. Anarchy in this sense means a series of independent states that live in order, but engage in little formal integration. Hierarchy possesses a centralization of powers in a number of essential areas, namely foreign and defense policy, economic policy, and justice. The EU is much more than anarchy, but is not yet a hierarchy. However, many policies are currently underway that could well transform the EU into a hierarchy. The transformation of the EU into a hierarchy could be brought about by economic and monetary union, common foreign and security policy, or cooperation in justice and home affairs. What is certain is that a gravitational shift will occur as a result of economic and monetary union where the EU will be located much more towards the hierarchical trend than the position it currently occupies.

The Union itself is under no illusion that the structural work is complete. The building of Europe is happening incrementally, but maybe the threshold has been passed and the issues raised do warrant a more comprehensive settlement to determine the future trajectory of the EU. The centralization of monetary policy will lead to greater centralization of fiscal policy. Such moves would subsequently deliver a more hierarchical structure. EMU and its impact on the EU's role in the global economic order will induce swifter developments in the realm of common foreign and security policy. The tension caused to the integrative process by trying to achieve consensus in the common foreign and security policy is significant. If a genuine common foreign and security policy is to emerge and if the EU becomes a unitary actor in the realm of foreign policy in a manner similar to the economic forum, then a threshold has been crossed and the EU will no doubt own some of the fundamental vestiges of statehood. It will possess a single currency, and a single citizenry living under similar economic policies, and will speak to the outside world as a unitary actor. Should this happen, then the EU, as a unique model of integration, will be no more.

Notes

1. The author is a member of the Foreign and Commonwealth Office, London and was Thouron Fellow at the University of Pennsylvania from 1996–98. The views expressed are the author's own and do not represent the views of the British government or the Foreign and Commonwealth Office. The author would like to thank Paolo Camoletto, Colin Budd, Ambassador Boselli, Andreas Heinemann-Grüder and Daniel Pruce for their helpful comments on earlier versions of the text.

2. See D.A. Lake, "Anarchy, Hierarchy, and the Variety of International Relations," *International Organizations* 50, no. 1 (Winter 1996): 1–33.

3. The concept of a hierarchy-anarchy continuum relates to the idea of federalism as a process or spectrum. This idea would bound the continuum with unity/centralized and differentiation/peripheralized.

4. Romano Prodi, President of the European Commission, *2000–2005: Shaping the New Europe*. Address to the European Parliament, Strasbourg 15 February 2000.

5. See H. Spruyt, *The Sovereign State and its Competitors* (Princeton, 1994). Spruyt traces the evolution of the sovereign state and the demise of other competing forms of governance such as the Hanseatic League and the Italian city-states.

6. W. Hallstein, *Europe in the Making*, translated by Charles Roetter (London, 1972), 15.

7. Ibid., 38.

8. W. Wallace and H. Wallace, *Policy Making in the European Union* (Oxford 1996).

9. D.H. Deudney, "The Philadelphia System: Sovereignty, Arms Control, and the Balance of Power in the American States-Union, 1787–1861," *International Organization* 49, no. 2 (1995): 191–228.

10. For a full overview of the concept of anarchy see K. Waltz, *Theory of International Politics* (Reading, 1979); John Gerard Ruggie, "Continuity and Transformation in the World Polity: Toward a Neorealist Synthesis," in *World Politics, Neorealism, and its Critics*, ed. R.O. Keohane (New York, 1986), 131–157; and B. Buzan, C. Jones and R. Little, *The Logic of Anarchy: Neorealism to Structural Realism* (New York, 1993).

11. D. H. Deudney, "The Philadelphia System," 192.

12. Wight Martin, *Power Politics* (London, 1978), 168–186.

13. J.H. Herz, "Rise and Demise of the Territorial State," *World Politics* 9, no. 4 (July 1957): 473–493.

14. D.H. Deudney and G.J. Ikenberry, "Structural Liberalism: The Nature and Sources of Postwar Western Political Order," Paper presented at a conference on "Realism and International Relations Theory after the Cold War," Harvard University, December 1995.

15. M.R. Fowler, and J.M. Bunck, *Law, Power and the Sovereign State: The Evolution and Application of the Concept of Sovereignty* (University Park, 1995).

16. C.C. O'Brien, "The Future of the West," *The National Interest* 30 (Winter 1992/93): 3–10; O. Harries, "The Collapse of the West," *Foreign Affairs* 72, no. 4 (September/October 1993): 41–53.

17. D.H. Deudney, "The Philadelphia System," 208.

18. Ibid; D.H. Deudney, "Nuclear Weapons and the Waning of the Real-State," *Daedalus* 124, no. 2, (Spring 1995): 209–231.

19. D.H. Deudney, "The Philadelphia System," 208.

20. Ibid., 194.

21. Ibid.

22. M. Forsyth, *Unions of States: The Theory and Practice of Confederation* (New York, 1981), 107.

23. J. Madison, A. Hamilton, and J. Jay, *The Federalist Papers*, no. 40 (London, 1987).

24. Treaty of the European Union (TEU), Article 3 b: "The Community may take action in areas which do not fall within its exclusive competence 'only if and in so far as the objectives of the proposed action cannot be sufficiently achieved by the Member states and can therefore, by reason of the scale or effects of the proposed action, be better achieved by the Community."

25. H. Bull, *The Logic of Anarchy* (Oxford, 1977).

26. These include, stable institutions guaranteeing democracy, the rule of law, human rights and respect for and protection of minorities, a functioning market economy, the capacity to cope with competition within the EU, and the capacity to adhere to the aims of the EU.

27. Except for Greece, these shared values have always been the criteria for previous applications for membership, but this was the first time they were explicitly stated.

28. From 1 July 1965 to January 22 1966, France, under the leadership of de Gaulle, operated an empty chair policy. French ministers stayed away from Council meetings. At this time the French were fearful of the supranational influences associated with integration, and with a move to majority voting imminent, de Gaulle perceived that the nation state was being eroded. De Gaulle successfully ousted the President of Euratom and established a precedent whereby ambassadors would be accredited to the Council and not the Commission. Majority voting would be dealt a severe blow.

29. A. Millward, *The European Rescue of the Nation State* (Berkeley, 1992).

30. D.H. Deudney, "The Philadelphia System".

31. J.J. Mearsheimer, "Back to the Future: Instability of Europe after the Cold War," *International Security* 15 (Summer 1990): 5–57; C.C. O'Brien, "The Future of the West," 3–10; K. Waltz, "The Emerging Structure of International Politics," *International Security* 18 (Fall 1993): 44–79.

32. J.G. Ikenberry, "Creating Yesterday's New World Order: Keynesian 'New Thinking' and the Anglo-American Postwar Settlement," in *Ideas and Foreign Policy: Beliefs, Institutions, and Political Change*, ed. J. Goldstein and R.O. Keohane (Ithaca: 1993).

33. Single European Act, signed 17 and 28 February 1986, came into force 1 July 1987.

34. TEU Article 189b: legislation is adopted in a multi stage procedure involving both the European Parliament and the Council. If disagreement persists after the Parliament's second reading, Parliament can convene a conciliation committee made of equal numbers from either side. If disagreement persists, an act cannot be adopted.

35. Articles 46 (2), 125, 129, 135, 137, 152 (4), 166, 172, 285, 280 EC and Declaration 23.

36. This calculation assumes no reweighting of the current votes, but assumes that the following applicants have these votes: Poland 8, Romania 6, Czech Republic 5, Hungary 5, Bulgaria 4, Slovakia 3, Lithuania 3, Latvia 3, Slovenia 2, Estonia 2, Cyprus 2 and Malta 2.

37. Donald J. Puchala, and Raymond F. Hopkins, "International Regimes: Lessons from Deductive Analysis," in *International Regimes*, ed. S. Krasner (New York, 1983), 61–92.

38. J.S. Duffield, "International Regimes and Alliance Behavior: Explaining NATO Conventional Force Levels," International Organization 46 (1992): 819-55.

39. W. Hallstein, *Europe in the Making*, 39.

40. Donald J. Puchala, "International Transactions and Regional Integration," *International Organization* 24, no. 4 (1970): 732–63.

41. D.A. Mitrany, *A Working Peace System* (Chicago, 1966).

42. C. Tilly, "Reflections on the History of European State Making," in *The Formation of National States in Western Europe*, ed. C. Tilly (Princeton, 1975), 3–84.

43. A. Moravcsik, "Liberalism and International Relations Theory," Working Paper, Center of International Affairs, Harvard University, 1992.

44. Donald J. Puchala, "Integration Theory and the Study of International Relations," in *From National Development to Global Community: Essays in Honor of Karl W. Deutsch*, ed. R.L. Merritt and Bruce M. Russett (London, 1981).

45. Contact between states can alter state preferences over time and thus socialization into a more consensual or community way of thinking develops. This is seen each time the EU enlarges with the existing member states fearful that the new arrivals may not adhere to the traditional philosophy. See T. Risse-Kappen, ed., *Bringing Transnational Relations Back In: Non-State Actors, Domestic Structures, and International Institutions* (New York, 1995).

46. Dr. Günter Burghardt, Director General, DG 1A, External Relations, European Commission, in a speech to the Twenty-fifth Session of the Asser Institute Colloquium on European Law "The Treaty on European Union—Suggestions for Revision," The Hague, 16 September 1995.

47. This was rejected by the French National Assembly in 1954.

48. A. Moravcsik, "Preferences and Power in the European Community: A Liberal Inter-governmentalist Approach," *Journal of Common Market Studies* 31, no. 4 (1993): 473–524.

49. The process of ratifying the different EU treaties by the EU Member states mirrors the earlier process of ratifying the American Constitution by the independent sovereign states in America.

50. Articles 102a–109m of the EC treaty.

51. In the second stage member states must allow their central banks to become independent of the political authorities, discontinue their overdraft facilities with their central banks and their privileged access to financial institutions and endeavor to fulfill the following five convergence criteria: an average rate of inflation that does not exceed by more than +/- 1 percent that of the three best performing member states during the year preceding the third stage; a budgetary deficit not exceeding 3 percent of GDP, or at the very least close to that level, provided that it has declined continuously; government debt not exceeding 60 percent of GDP, or at the very least approximating to that level owing to a sharply diminishing trend; a long term interest rate that does not exceed by more than 2 percent the average of the three best performing member states in terms of price stability; maintenance of the national currency within the normal fluctuation margins of the EMS for at least two years, without devaluation. See Article 104, 104c, and 109j of the TEU (Treaty on European Union, Office for Official Publications of the European Communities, Luxembourg, 1992).

52. Barry Eichengreen, "European Monetary Unification," *Journal of Economic Literature* 31 (September 1993): 1321–1357.

53. Established in Title V of the TEU.

54. European Commissioner for External Relations, Hans van den Broek, High-level Group of Experts on the CFSP, *First Report: European Security Policy Towards 2000: Ways and Means to Establish Genuine Credibility* (Brussels, 19 December 1994).

55. Treaty of Amsterdam agreed June 1997, signed October 1997, came into force on 1 May 1999. *The TEU-The Meaning of Amsterdam, Representation of the European Commission* (London, July 1997).

56. Article J5, Paragraph 4, TEU.

57. Article 18 and 26, TEU.

58. Observer status was not extended to the European Union because it does not possess legal personality.

59. 1992 Earth Summit at Rio, The 1994 Cairo Conference on Population and Development, the 1995 Social Summit in Copenhagen, and the World Conference on Women in Beijing.

60. Dr. Günter Burghardt, Speech to the Twenty-fifth Session of the Asser Institute Colloquium.
61. Article 23, TEU.
62. M. Forsyth, *Unions of States*, 7.
63. L. Lindberg and S. A. Scheingold, *Regional Integration: Theory and Research* (Cambridge, 1971).
64. TEU/TEC, Protocol 2.
65. Asylum and immigration policy transfers from the third pillar to the Community Pillar and this includes an expanded visa policy. The decision base will remain unanimity for at least the first five years.
66. Article 62 (EC), (ex Article 73j), Treaty Establishing the European Community (consolidated version; the amendments and renumbering made by the Treaty of Amsterdam will only be effective on its entry into force, as provided for in Article 14 (2) of that treaty.
67. Article 63, *EC Treaty Establishing The European Community* (consolidated version), Office for Official Publications of the European Communities (Luxembourg, 1997).
68. Article 35, TEU.

Chapter 3

THE EUROPEAN UNION

Is It a Supranational State in the Making?

⌒⌒⌒

Gretchen M. MacMillan

The European Union (EU) is an unique political and economic experiment. The pooling and sharing of sovereignty by fifteen western European states, primarily for economic, but also for political reasons, remains sui generis. Is the EU a potential supranational state? The answer to that question, the subject of this chapter, is a qualified yes. In order to understand both the question and the answer it is important to understand the nature of the decision-making process in the EU, including the role played by the member-states in the EU's institutions and the degree to which this process can be made accountable to the people of the EU.[1] The position that the EU has the potential to be a supranational state is supported by the following argument: the decision-making process within the EU institutions is quite similar to domestic federalist decision-making. To be more specific, this chapter uses the term intergovernmentalism and links it to the concept of executive federalism. This approach to decision-making assumes the dominance of executive decision makers even while it acknowledges the presence of supra-national, intranational, and subnational actors (institutional and noninstitutional) in the decision-making process. Moreover, it acknowledges that

executive federalism does not resolve the problems of democratic accountability and transparency. It concludes however, that the problems of
accountability and executive federalism are not peculiar to the EU, but occur
in other parliamentary federalist systems as well.

The word "state" comes loaded with emotive and ideological baggage.[2]
Any definition of the word must include a conceptual framework of institutional relationships, including that between institutions and the underlying society that it governs. The organization of the chapter takes this into
account. Initially the concept of the state will be discussed in connection
with what is meant here by the term supranational state. Second, there will
be an examination of federalist decision making, with an emphasis on executive federalism and federalist intergovernmentalism. In particular the discussion will center on some aspects of the differences in decision making in
the EU under the Treaty on European Union (TEU), known popularly as the
Maastricht Agreement. Third, there will be a discussion of some of the issues
of accountability and legitimacy created by the institutional process and
decision-making structures of the EU.

The Building of a Supranational State

The institutions created to carry out the policies agreed upon by the founding states of the EU, first in the Treaty of Paris, 1951 and then reinforced in
the Treaty of Rome, 1957 and the Merger Treaty, 1965, are usually referred
to as supranational institutions. They were different from institutions created in international organizations, like the United Nations. The political
actors in these new institutions could make decisions legally binding on the
member-states. However, the institutions differed from those in a federal
state since control over coercive force remained with the member-states. The
new arrangement was an integrated set of institutions that operated above
and separate from the member-states even while composed of political
actors from the member-states. The institutions had an separate existence
from the member-states. They could and do influence and change the member-states. This is often referred to as pooling sovereignty, which is unlike an
international organization where sovereignty remains with members and
also unlike a federal state where coercive force accompanies the sovereignty
of the central body.

The founders of the EU were interested in more than just a customs
union. Some perhaps did envisage a new European state, that would be in
many ways analogous to the traditional state within which they lived, but

would replace local national loyalties with a broader European loyalty. It became apparent however that this degree of integration was unlikely. Opposition came from the political leadership of the existing states, as well as from the members of their societies.

In the first decade of the European Communities (EC), the completion of a customs union and removal of internal financial tariffs went a long way to consolidate its foundation. However, further major developments did not occur until the 1980s. Since then, there has been a remarkable series of treaties negotiated and ratified by the member-states. These treaties have resulted in an increased role for the supranational institutions in many areas of political life. They have included not only the completion of the internal market and the final steps to the creation of an economic and monetary union with a common currency, but have also provided a new role for the supranational institutions in both internal and external issues of security and foreign policy, through the Common Foreign and Security Policy and Cooperation on Justice and Home Affairs.

These developments have been the subject of much debate, both at the level of practical politics, as well as by scholars who have attempted to understand and explain the EU. The debate centers on three broad frameworks: functionalism and neofunctionalism; intergovernmental institutionalism, liberal institutionalism, and regime theory; and federalism, neofederalism, and cooperative federalism.[3] These three might be briefly defined as supporting respectively: a single state; an international organization; a confused federal arrangement. None of these classifications sufficiently explain the development of the EU. The longer the historical experiment endures the less it looks like an international organization, but it is also not a single state. It has taken on many of the characteristics of federal states. The classification of the EU as a "potential supranational state" allows us to examine these arrangements. At the same time as a "potential supranational state," it reminds observers that the processes observed in the EU reflect state building rather than state maintenance.[4] The concept of supranationalism is usually linked to the theoretical approach associated with neofunctionalism, rather than to that of federalism. The idea of neofunctionalism is quite useful but limited by the expectation that integration would lead inexorably towards a new statehood that would resemble a traditional state. Neofunctionalism's underlying principles of incrementalism and spillover are valuable because the process of development in the EU has been incremental, but it has not been uniformly progressive and there have been periods of stagnation and retrenchment.

Institutions, once established, usually take on a "life of their own." The political actors who control them at any given time both act upon the institutions and are shaped by them in turn. In this way the institutions of the EU: the European Commission, the Council of the European Union (Council of Ministers), the European Parliament (EP), and the European Court of Justice (ECJ) are quite typical. It has not been an arena in which they have been bystanders.[5] These institutions have affected both the states and the societies which they have acted upon. At the same time this experience in the EU is not unique. In all states the institutions are established for certain specific reasons and overtime take on new aspects as new issues develop. In that way it could be argued that the experience of federal states such as the United States and Canada fit into the model of neofunctionalism and spillover. It would also be true of unitary states as well. Two countries that might be examined in a similar manner would be France and Ireland. What all four of these states have in common with the EU is that the institutions and structure of the states were consciously set down in a document. This is true of many, if not of most, states. To further develop this argument it is important to look at some common characteristics of the modern state.[6] The state is often defined as a separated set of specific institutions from society that leads to identifiable public and private spheres. According to this definition, the European Union could be defined as a state, since it does have a set of institutions separate and differentiated from European society. The fact that the members of the institutions of the EU are chosen by and from the leadership of the member-states does not invalidate this separation. Such arrangements exist in varying degrees in all federal states. The evolution of the rules of the game in federal units may over time increase or decrease the autonomy of federal and subfederal units, but in all cases the rules allow for some intervention by the one level in the powers and memberships of the other level.

A major characteristic of all states is sovereignty. Public law, the creation of the state's institutions, are backed by coercive force, over which the state has a formal monopoly. Moreover, the state's formal monopoly of force extends its control over all individuals and political actors in the territory. This is clearly a gray area of statehood in any discussion of the EU. It certainly lacks the ability to enforce its rules by coercive sanctions and it laws are not backed by any formal monopoly of force. The EU is dependent on the good will and law abiding nature of the member-states to enforce the legislation of the EU and to recognize its laws as sovereign and supreme. Yet again this is not entirely unusual in federal states. Certainly the individual states of the United States in its formative period prior to the American Civil War were able to insist on their sovereignty and act in defiance of the federal unit. Undivided sovereignty is a characteristic primarily of unitary not federal states. In federal states the legal monopoly over force is usually divided between the federal and subfederal units. In some federal units, such as the United States, the ability to enforce law is divided between federal and state law enforcement and courts, while in others, such as Canada the court system is united and the subfederal units may or may not use federal law enforcement officers.

The degree of ability of federal and subfederal units to operate separately in areas of law making is always an issue in the evolution and development of the federal states. In some, the divisions of powers between federal and sub-federal units are better defined than they are in others. In all federal states, in any conflict between federal and subfederal laws in areas in which the federal state is paramount, the laws of the subunits must give way to the federal laws. It is in this area perhaps more than most that the EU looks and acts like a federal state. The ECJ through its decisions and the compliance of the member-states in these rulings has reinforced the federal nature of the EU.

Two other characteristics of the modern state that are significant here are the administrative nature of the state and its ability to extract resources, especially financial resources from the state. The EU is certainly administratively sophisticated. Its bureaucracy is similar to those of the member-states, even if in size it is much smaller. One way in which the bureaucratic nature of the EU is apparent is that many of the laws (regulations and directives) of the EU are regulatory in nature.[7] Its ability to extract resources from the society is limited. The EU does not possess the capacity to directly extract revenues from the population of the Union. It does have its own tax base (which makes it unlike an international organization), but taxes are collected by the member-states. The EU cannot itself run a deficit. Its budget is determined by the Council of Ministers the supranational body controlled by the member-states. Yet, since the Council of Ministers must come to an agreement, pressures for consensus within the body can counteract the forces provided by the national government. Moreover, the budget must be approved by the EP, which, while it cannot change broad areas of the budget, can through their threat of a veto influence decisions made by the Council of Ministers.

The extraction of monetary revenues is often divided between federal and subnational units. However, the making of fiscal and monetary policy, along with the establishment and control of currency is associated with the state, and in federal states, with the central institutions. The establishment of economic and monetary union (EMU) and the common currency (Euro) will place control in new supranational institutions. While political, economic, and social union is often seen as characteristic of the state, the degree of union varies among and within federal states. The United States is clearly an economic and monetary union with no internal barriers to trade, but Canada is a monetary union with internal barriers to trade. In the United States there is no social union, but Canada has been proactive in the establishment of a social union.[8]

In summary then, the EU lacks certain characteristics that we associate with the traditional state whether it is unitary or federal. The most significant of these, is that the monopoly on coercive force remains with the member-states who are responsible for both internal and external security. The other major difference is the limitations placed on its ability to extract resources directly from the people of the EU. However, do these restrictions mean that the EU cannot be described as a state? To answer that question it is important to examine the differences between an unitary state and federal state. In an unitary state the powers and authorities associated with the state are concentrated at one level, but in a federal state they are divided or shared. The division within a federal state leads to a question about why would the state divide its powers. Certainly those who support the idea of the EU as a "federal state" or even a "supranational state" have often emphasized the importance of increasing and consolidating the powers of a highly centralized and "logical" set of institutions in the EU, which would weaken the member-states. This varies from the historical factors that influenced the establishment of federal states. In all federal states, the presence of preexisting societies and communities led to the creation of nonunitary systems because of the fears of one or more or all of these communities of being swallowed by a larger political community.[9] Over time the boundaries of the federal state as well as those of the internal units have become fixed. Loyalty to subnational units at the expense of national units is not uncommon in some federal states.

It is important to remember that the societies of the member-states are sometimes older than the states themselves. Some of them as "states" are younger than the Anglo-American federal upstarts of Canada, the United States, and Australia. Moreover, the subnational units of the member states often reflect even older and more substantive divisions, which have grown in significance in the past three decades. Change at the subnational level in the EU has occurred for some of the same reasons that decentralization has occurred in federal states such as Canada and the United States: cultural and linguistic, as well as economic and social. A major difference then between unitary and federal states relates to the homogeneous nature of the underlying societies. The greater the differences, whether based on historical, cultural, linguistic, religious and/or geographical differences, the more likely some form of devolution will occur. This is certainly reflected in the member-states themselves. It could be argued then that the supranational state will reflect even greater differences on these grounds in the underlying units. It has been argued that federal states (and this certainly would be true of Canada and the United States) were created out of previous entities that joined together because of external threats.[10] Because of this it was in the interests of the former colonies or states to give to the central government control over foreign and security policies. In federal systems the process leads to the legitimization of a process that will result in a foreign and security policy that, while it affects the constituent parts, is meant to advance and protect the national interests of the central government and all of the state. A supranational state might well be defined as one formed to ensure the peace and stability between and among the members by pooling and sharing sovereignty to prevent the constituent parts from harming each other militarily. However, pooling and/or ceding control over coercive force to the supranational institutions would be counterproductive. In short in a supranational state the protection and preservation of common values might well mean that the tools of force remain under the control of the constituent parts. This does not mean that the central institutions cannot acquire an external identity and even a legal personality. It will probably mean that the decision-making process will take on different characteristics. Federal states are constructed to take into account the interests of both citizens and subunits. Supranational states must also take into account the interests of the national units.

Executive Federalism and Intergovernmentalism: The Cornerstones of the Supranational State

State-building is not usually an orderly evolutionary process. It does not move from a pristine set of architect's drawings to a final house built to prior specifications. The process needs to be understood as a series of developments often punctuated by crises that can both promote and retard development. If the supranational state of the EU is to be understood in institutional terms, then a comparison to an evolving federal state or a federal state in crisis is of more value than to a mature federal state, not in crisis. Any comparison between the contemporary United States and the EU would have to take into account the increased decentralization that has occurred in the United States over the past two decades. A better comparison would be to the evolution of the American currency or the building of the national administrative framework in the nineteenth century.[11] The contemporary Canadian federal system supplies us with an even better model because the cooperation in this decentralized and increasingly fragmented state has resulted in some of the same institutional problems and political discourse one finds in the EU. One particular way in which the problems within the Canadian federal system have been addressed is through the process known as executive federalism.

Donald Smiley defined the decision-making process used in Canadian federalism, as executive federalism. This was, he argued "a system of government which is executive dominated and within which a large number of important public issues are debated and resolved through the ongoing interactions among governments."[12] Executive federalism was combined with the executive dominance associated with the Westminster parliamentary model. The emphasis on the prime minister, the premiers, and their cabinets as the principal decision makers further encouraged centralization of policy making in the executive and administration.[13] The growth of the role of governments in all modern societies meant that the areas of conflict between the two levels of governments increased. In order to resolve these issues there was an increased emphasis on intergovernmental relationships, including meetings between the premiers without the prime minister and also between cabinet ministers responsible for specific areas of public policy meeting with their counterparts, with and without the presence of their federal counterpart. These intergovernmental meetings of cabinet ministers have been recently referred to as Councils of Ministers.[14]

Intergovernmentalism refers to relationships between two or more governments. Intergovernmental contacts can occur between political actors from two or more sovereign states, the way the term is used in international relations, but it can also be used to describe the relationship between a central government of a state and its subnational units or between political actors from the subnational units of a federal state. The actors are usually members of the executive and their respective civil servants. The combinations among actors can be many: heads of government, members of cabinets, and members of civil services in any number of combinations. What does this mean when applied to the EU? First, intergovernmentalism can be used to discuss how the units of a federal state play a significant role in the decision-making and policy processes of the central institutions.[15] Second, it can also be used to describe how units in an organization maintain control over decision making by excluding or limiting the role of the central institutions. This sense of the word is similar to that associated with international relations. This is a type of decision making in which control remains in the hands of the subunits, in this case the nation-states in the Union.[16] Third, the term can be used to describe the process by which the rules of the game can be changed in a federal system. It certainly would apply to the changes associated with the Single European Act (SEA), the Treaty on European Union (TEU), and the Treaty of Amsterdam.[17] Changing the rules of the game in a federal state is always intergovernmental.

The emphasis in this discussion will be on the first two uses of the term intergovernmentalism: the processes associated with federal domestic decision making and international relations decision making.[18] Since Maastricht the policy-making process in the EU has been divided into three major areas, usually referred to as the three pillars. Under the first or the Community pillar issues of social and economic policy in which the Union and member states have shared competency are addressed, while the second and third pillars address issues that are primarily the responsibility of the member-states: external security, under the rubric of Common Foreign and Security Policy (CFSP), and internal security, under the rubric of Cooperation of Justice and Home Affairs (JHA). The policy-making process under the first pillar as it now exists can be described as federalist.[19] The Commission is responsible for initiating legislation and both the Council of Ministers and the EP must approve the legislation.[20] Moreover, all decisions are justiciable before the ECJ. This is not true of the decision-making process under the second and third pillars of the TEU. While the supranational executive (the Commission) has a consultative role and can initiate policy, neither the ECJ or the EP have a role to play. To that degree, the complexity of the decision-making process under the first pillar (along with roles for interest groups and policy advocates), which is matched, as Wallace points out, to the complexity of the American federal level of governance, is limited under the second and third pillar.[21] Attempts to resolve conflicts between the member states in areas of foreign and security policy and judicial issues use the institutions of the supranational level of government but do so at the expense of the supranational institutions of governance. Yet if the supranational institutions are used for these purposes a pattern is developed in which CFSP and JHA might come to be perceived as supranational, more than intranational or subnational, issues.

The institution in which all three pillars meet for decision-making purposes is the Council of Ministers.[22] It provides for representation of the member-states in the Union and is central to the intergovernmental nature of European Union decision making. It brings together the appropriate ministers of the member-states, on a regular basis, to make decisions affecting the entire Union. Their control over the agenda of the EU has ensured the dominant role of the member states. The growth of their role is further linked to two bureaucratic functions: the need to have a chair at each meeting and the need to have civil service support. The first was provided by the six-month rotating presidency of the Council, while the second was filled by the Committee of Permanent Representatives (COREPER).

The role of the presidency has grown tremendously since the 1970s. This is due in part to the creation of the European Council which has increased the profile of the member-states and their leaders.[23] The highest profile goes to the head of government of the country holding the presidency, but all Council of Ministers affairs under all three pillars are all chaired by politicians and civil servants of the member-state. The presidency brings the different types of intergovernmentalism and decision making both within and outside the treaties and both within and outside the supranational institutions together. The makeup of the Council ensures that national interests are protected. However, the complexity of the decision-making process means that much of the day-to-day activities in Brussels are carried out by their permanent representatives in Brussels through COREPER. The tasks of COREPER are to act for and to keep the home government informed. At first, this might seem to be an international task (the heads of each of the permanent representatives has ambassadorial status in Brussels), but most of the activity is concerned with domestic policies that are similar to the concerns of subnational units in a federal state. It is therefore an important link in the preservation and development of the intergovernmental "federal" model of decision making in the EU. While they are representatives of the member-states and defend their interests at Brussels, they are also an important link in increasing the integration of the national units into the supranational institutions. Members work with representatives of the other member-states. They both explain their state's position to other member-states' representatives and have other states' positions explained in return.

The process of integration within the Union cannot be separated from the evolution and development of the intergovernmental role of the Council of Ministers and its bureaucracy. This is particularly obvious in the evolution and development of the European Council, which brings the heads of government and state into the process. Its twice yearly meetings linked to the presidency of the Union provides a framework for the institutional year in the Union's calendar. The political clout of its members makes it the most important institution in setting the Union's agenda. It has been this Council that has furthered the movement towards integration and been the major force behind the Single European Act, the Treaty on European Union, and the Amsterdam Treaty. The institutionalization of the meetings of the heads of government and state and the intergovernmental bodies created under their auspices, present the interesting paradox of the member-states' executives providing the framework for closer integration through the intergovernmental structures of cooperation acting through the supranational institutions. The institutions that they have been responsible for include the European Monetary System (EMS) and the Exchange Rate Mechanism, the European Political Cooperation, the "Trevi Group" (which became Common Foreign and Security Policy/CFSP, and, finally, Cooperation on Justice and Home Affairs JHA). Moreover, by using the Council of Ministers to implement these extralegal functions, the member-states confused and blurred the lines between the supranational institutions and their own institutions. At the same time, the degree to which these increased common mechanisms for shared decision making actually work is subject to much debate. Theoretically, increased common decision making in these two areas associated with the sovereignty of the nation state might be seen as leading to increased federalist decision making. Many of the issues under CFSP are central to the nation-state's role in defending the citizens against outside enemies. The JHA is primarily concerned with issues that might be seen as affecting the nation-state's internal security role, including issues involving police, immigration, refugees, drugs, and crime. In reality as many examples demonstrate, including of course the EC/EU's response to the crises in the former Yugoslavia, in practice the decision-making process is more often flawed to the point of nonexistence. Similarly the JHA's actual coordination of activities has been directed to the lowest common denominator. At the same time, the presence of JHA in the supranational institutions is significant. The two areas under Article J and Article K of the Maastricht Treaty go to the very core of the state's existence: protection of the citizen and society against internal and external enemies and preservation of boundaries. While analysis of both CFSP and JHA often invokes criticism of what they are not, less emphasis is placed on what their presence within the supranational institutions does entail: an attempt to make decisions on national issues within the supranational framework.

Criticism of the ineffectualness of the CFSP in particular is premised on the role that foreign policy plays in an unitary or federal state. Yet, in an examination of a supranational state, it becomes apparent that a major obstacle to further integration of this component of state policy is the lack of identity between citizen and the EU. There is no sense of national territory that needs to be protected, nor is there any sense of any national political, economic, social, or cultural interests to protect at the European level. It is also unlikely that the major states that have played key roles in European and world politics will give up control over foreign and security policy to the

Commission. Foreign policy differences become even more complicated when defense issues are added to the mix. Defense, even more than foreign policy, is linked to state sovereignty. Furthermore some states have a greater defense capability than others (and in the case of the United Kingdom and France this includes a nuclear capability) and some are more willing than others to use it. Finally the differences between states with external defense agreements and states that are neutral has to be taken into account.

Issues under the third pillar, while not having the high profile of second pillar issues, are perhaps more complex in terms of decision making and state structures. They cover a mixture of policies that are meant to maintain internal security, while also allowing for free movement of individuals across the internal borders within the Union. This possesses a logical relationship to the economic agenda of a free internal market. The cornerstone of the internal market is the free movement of goods, services, labor, and capital among the member states. In order to achieve this, it would mean an end to all internal border controls within what is now the European Union. Not surprisingly it has been more difficult to achieve this in practice than it was to agree to it in theory. The 1992 internal market did remove most of the barriers to the movement of goods within the European Union. They also removed most barriers on capital movement and many of the barriers on services and labor. The establishment of the internal market raised other questions that went to the heart of the role and authority of the nation state: protection of citizens and national borders. Since most border controls and markings have been removed the question of how these states are to control movements not only of refugees but also of criminals, terrorists, and drug traffickers has become more significant. There are at least two different sets of problems associated with free movements of persons and services that go beyond simple economics and enter into the political realm: the maintenance of law and order within the state and the admission and treatment of third country nationals. How do you maintain open economic borders but also ensure order and stability and protection of the community against disorder, crime, and economic disruption?

The issues under the third pillar are perhaps more significant for purposes of governance than those under the second pillar. Foreign policy issues often have less direct effect on the lives of citizens, especially if the state is in no danger of attack. Issues involving refugees, immigrants, both legal and illegal, along with questions of criminal jurisdiction, police, and border controls are issues that citizens are likely to encounter on a more regular basis. It is therefore not surprising that some of these areas, including free movement of persons, checks at external borders, asylum, immigration and protection for the rights of nationals of nonmember countries as well as judicial cooperation in criminal matters, will move from Pillar III to Pillar I when the Treaty of Amsterdam is fully ratified. In this development, Community rules governing the operation of supranational institutions under Pillar I will apply to these areas of policy. Over time, the Treaty makes provisions for the Commission to have the right to initiate legislation, for the Parliament to have a say in the final legislation, and for the Court of Justice to have jurisdiction in certain cases.

The Council of Ministers within the supranational institutions wears at least three hats. Under the first pillar the process is federalist, under the second and third pillar it is cooperative and sometimes follows rules similar to international organizations, and when changing the rules through intergovernmental conferences it is constitutionalist. It is not even clear if they always manage to change their hats when they move from role to role. Thus, the Council and its activities do not fit into any preordained category, but the Council could be described as supranationalist. Its behavior makes it difficult for scholars who want to find nice clear-cut explanations for its behavior and of who controls the agenda at any given time: supranational actors, national actors, regional actors, interest groups, or citizens. The major actors are probably going to remain representatives from the member states.

Intergovernmentalism is not, of course, the most transparent form of governance.[24] The lack of transparency is not peculiar to the supranational system and often occurs in federal and unitary systems, as well. Obviously, the problem is greater than just at the top of the multilevel tier of governance in the Union.

Multilevel Governance and Questions of Accountability and Transparency

There are now several tiers of political institutions that act on the people of Europe. This leads to questions about accountability of the institutions and the transparency of decision making. The development of supranational institutions in the EU has occurred alongside an increased decentralization within the member-states. Governance is in many ways an updated term that takes into account effective and efficient government through political institutions that are both responsible and representative of and to the people over which they govern. The EU is multilevel, but the EU is in many cases not just a third level but is a fourth level of governance. The increasing number of states in the Union which possess federal or quasi-federal governments or at least some degree of devolution indicates that the levels of government in relation to the citizens of Europe is increasing not decreasing. The problems of multilevel governance and democratic deficit found in the EU, as opposed to the issues of institutions, are not entirely different from those to be found in several other states. Issues of accountability from local government boards and regional authorities to the decisions of intergovernmental meetings in federal states arise as they do in the EU. In federal states such as Canada, these continue to be addressed through intergovernmental meetings including first ministers' conferences, all of which exist outside the legal and constitutional mechanisms of governance.

Governance then is a problem not just for the EU but for the member-states as well. However, the very size of the EU and the complexity of decision making required to allow for consultation and cooperation among and between the several levels of government that make up both the European Union and its member states only add to the difficulty. The growth of the EU, both in terms of its membership and the scope of its activities and responsibilities, has meant that the Byzantine nature of European Union decision making has increased. Given the number of states, regions, and societies, languages, and administrative and political cultures involved as well as the incremental nature of the process, this is not surprising. It is also not surprising that executive federalism along with intergovernmental decision-making has been the main form of governance. Yet if the Union is to become legitimate, both on grounds of efficiency and efficacy, it will need to be—and be seen to be—more accountable. This need for accountability and transparency by institutions governing liberal democratic states and societies is not peculiar to the EU. However, the supranational, national, and subnational structures and networks that have grown and developed over the past thirty years makes this often quite difficult. In fact is it possible?[25] At present, the possibilities are limited. The degree to which the accountability and transparency of the supranational institutions could be rectified by removing the imbalance between the legal and political powers of the supranational institutions and the member-states' institutions is limited. This is not only because of the unwillingness of the states to transfer any more powers to institutions they cannot control (such as the European Parliament), but also because there is little support for such a transfer among the citizens of the member-states of the Union.

The Union is not a unitary or federal state. It is probably safe to argue that it will not become one in the future. This is not only because coercive force remains with the member-states. The supranational institutions and the role they play in the lives of Europeans is not the only change that has occurred over the past three decades. In many states, power and authority has shifted downward even while at the same time it has moved upward to the supranational Union. This along with the increased linkages that exist at all levels of governments within the Union has meant that a multilevel form of governance has emerged. The multitiers of governance along with the complexities created by federal and quasi-federal states within the supranational framework means that the process is more complex than that found even in traditional federal states. This means at one level increased bureaucratization even while there are increased calls for increased accountability for actors who often seem unaccountable.

The difficulty is to make the supranational institutions accountable directly to the people of Europe without increasing the authority and perhaps power of the supranational institutions at the expense of the national institutions. Can it be done? There are perhaps three possible answers to this question. They are briefly: create a traditional federal state, maintain the status quo, or look for a new source of accountability. It is not likely that a traditional federal state is an option. This would entail making the Commission responsible to the Parliament or, since the present structures are more congressional than parliamentarian, having the Commission or at least its president elected by the people of Europe. This is clearly not going to happen. Another alternative is the status quo. Theoretically members of the Council of Ministers are accountable to the national parliaments because all of them are members of national parliaments. Yet in reality the accountability is not very great. The proposal that national parliaments adopt a more aggressive oversight role might make a difference, but there is little evidence that this is going to happen. The third alternative is to build on the multiple levels of governance already established.[26] Nation-states are at least accountable through elections to the members of the society, who make up the political community. But what the EU continues to lack is a political community. There is as yet no evidence that most individuals in Europe are going to identify with the idea of Europe or a European supranational state. In some instances, groups in the states of Europe are identifying with units below the nation-state, not above it.

Nevertheless, there is the possibility of finding new methods of ensuring accountability of institutions of government and governance. One solution to this conundrum is to be found in the community framework associated with the patchwork quilt of loyalties and allegiances associated with medieval Europe. The advantage of such a system lies in the source of ultimate authority in the system. In medieval Europe authority and sovereignty was derived from God and moved downward, but in contemporary Europe authority is derived from the people and moves upwards from local to regional, national, and supranational governments. The source of executive, legislative, and judicial authority is the people.[27] This approach to accountability and sovereignty possesses the potential to allow the diffusion of power throughout a whole series of layered institutions. This could result in the revamping of power and authority among these institutions. The medieval system has been described as a "complex and rather loose structure of contractual or mutual obligations existing throughout a complex social hierarchy." The medieval society was "crisscrossed with overlapping groups and conflicting loyalties and bodies of rules."[28] While David Held, the quoted author, rejects the idea of a medieval state because it lacked a central sovereign authority, the argument about a single source of loyalty and authority to be found in the people provides a framework for future discussions about the underlying basis of a European political community. In the modern EU, the single source of loyalty among the overlapping bodies could well be the EU, with the source of authority found in the people of Europe. This is far from being a reality however. It is hard at least at this stage to think of the people of Europe being able to have that type of loyalty to the EU.[29]

Another possibility for establishing future loyalty to the EU may also come through the concept of EU citizenship. The Maastricht Agreement established the concept of European citizenship, which is premised on the individual holding citizenship in one of the member-states. It does not provide for the creation of a separate European citizenship however. Moreover, the ECJ ruled that the decisions on defining citizenship was a prerogative of the member-states and not of the Community. At the same time there is the possibility of creating a multilevel form of citizenship. However the process of accomplishing such a feat is difficult. Moreover, it is something that will take time. There are many ways that a common citizenship can be promoted, including increased exchanges among university students and other work programs. But the larger question of how individuals identify more with Europe than with say France or Sweden is still not answered. It is a problem even in truly federal states. The major issue is that there is not an European citizenship without, for example, a French or Irish or British citizenship. Therefore the issue of loyalty to Europe comes secondarily to loyalty to the state that does provide citizenship.[30]

This is, of course, one of the major distinctions between the EU and more traditionally federal states. There is evidence that the broad concept of American citizenship and loyalty emerged at the end of the nineteenth century when the United States absorbed millions of immigrants. Americanization was the process by which they were assimilated into their new country.

For these new citizens their loyalty was to the United States and not to New York or Massachusetts. Moreover, while they might be residents of New York or Massachusetts they were not asked to become citizens of the state before they became American citizens. This is the reverse of the European situation. Immigrants if they are allowed to become citizens at all become citizens of one of the member-states and then acquire European citizenship. The result is that loyalty is given to the state that confers citizenship. Until this changes, the problems of establishing loyalty to Europe will remain.

Conclusions

The supranational state of fifteen member-states and more numerous subnational units of federal subunits, regions, and devolved governmental structures requires both executive dominance and intergovernmentalism to keep it together. At the same time the concept of sovereignty of the people which is widely accepted—if sometimes more in theory than in practice—allows a wide spectrum of institutional arrangements that are ultimately based in a legal responsibility to the peoples of Europe through the structures of the member-states.

Is the EU a supranational state in the making? On the whole the answer would be positive. The development of the institutional framework under the TEU indicates a clearer delineation over time. EMU and a common currency are almost a reality, and the impact these will have on building a union is likely to be positive (if it does not lead to complete disintegration). Institution building continues and with each stage further integration occurs. The framework of decision making within the EU looks more and more like the intergovernmental relations within federal states. The building of a political community, however, remains elusive and difficult. No single symbol of loyalty has emerged that could serve as a catalyst for the multitiered, multilevel communities and institutions that make up the EU. In part, this is because the institutional framework still has not found a way to make the EU and its institutions sufficiently transparent and accountable.

Notes

1. See G.M. MacMillan, "The European Community: Is it a Supranational State in the Making?" in *Federalism and the New World Order*, ed. S. Randall and R. Gibbins (Calgary, 1994), 215–237.
2. See A. Vincent, *Theories of the State* (Oxford, 1987), for a review of theories of the state.
3. For a brief but excellent overview, see C. Massucelli, *France and Germany at Maastricht: Politics and Negotiations to Create the European Union* (New York, 1997), 6–15. See also N. Winn, "Who Gets What, When, and How? The Contested Conceptual and Disciplinary Nature of Governance and Policy-Making in the European Union," *Politics* 18, no. 2 (1998): 119–132.
4. See G.M. MacMillan, *State, Society and Authority in Ireland: The Foundations of the Modern State* (Dublin, 1993), 5–8.
5. See S. Bulmer, "The Governance of the European Union: A New Institutionalist Approach," *Journal of Public Policy* 13, no. 4 (1994): 351–380. See also P. Pierson, "The Path to European Union: An Historical Institutionalist Approach," *Comparative Political Studies* 29, no. 2 (1996): 123–163.
6. See D. Dunleavy and B. O'Leary, *Theories of the State* (London, 1987), 2.
7. See J. Caporaso, "The European Union and Forms of State: Westphalian, Regulatory or Post-Modern?" *Journal of Common Market Studies* 34 (1996): 29–52. The word "law" is not used, and there are in the treaties four types of legislation outlined (Article 189 of the EC Treaty). The most important are regulations which are directly enforceable laws, applicable and binding on the member states. The states do not need to pass enabling legislation. Many of these regulations are technical and arise out of policy areas, such as the common agricultural policy. The second type are directives which are legally binding and addressed to the states. They lay down broad outlines which are to be filled in by the member states. In theory they are more general and may be addressed to one, several, or all of the states. In practice they have been a mechanism for establishing harmonization of laws in areas of Union activity and as a result are usually addressed to all the states. Further the ECJ has ruled that in some cases directives may, like regulations, be directly applicable to the states without state enabling legislation. The third type are decisions that are usually addressed to member-states or individuals or legal entities (companies). They are often used in competition policy enforcement. Finally there are recommendations and opinions that are not legally binding although they may be influential politically.
8. For the social union and internal market in Canada, see S.A. Kennett, *Securing the Social Union: A Commentary on the Decentralized Approach* (Kingston: Institute of Intergovernmental Relations, 1998); K. Banting, "The Past Speaks to the Future: Lessons from the Postwar Social Union", and R.H. Knox, "Economic Integration in Canada through the Agreement on Internal Trade," both in *Canada: The State of the Federation, 1997, Non-Constitutional Renewal*, ed. H. Lazar (Kingston, 1998).
9. See R. Gibbins, *Conflict and Unity* (Toronto, 1982).
10. Juliet Lodge, "European Political Cooperation towards the 1990s," in *The European Community and the Challenge of the Future*, ed. J. Lodge (London, 1989), 223–240.
11. See J.D. Donahue, *Disunited States* (New York, 1997); A. Sbragia, *Debt Wish: Entrepreneurial Cities: U.S. Federalism and Economic Development* (Pittsburgh, 1996).
12. D. Smiley, *The Federal Condition in Canada* (Toronto, 1987), 83. For a background to Smiley's ideas, see R.L. Watts, "Executive Federalism: The Comparative Context," in *Federalism and Political Community: Essays in Honour of Donald Smiley*, ed. D.P. Shugarman and R. Whitaker (Peterborough, 1989).

13. R. Simeon and I. Robinson, *State, Society and the Development of Canadian Federalism* (Toronto, 1990); see also R. Simeon, *Federal-Provincial Diplomacy: The Making of Recent Policy in Canada* (Toronto, 1970).

14. See P. Fafard, "Green Harmonization: The Success and Failure of Recent Environmental Intergovernmental Relations," and R. Gibbins, "Alberta's Intergovernmental Relations Experience," both in *Canada: The State of the Federation*.

15. See S. Bulmer, "Domestic Politics and European Community Policy Making," *Journal of Common Market Studies* 21 (1982–1983): 349–363.

16. See for instance S. Hoffman, "Reflections on the Nation State in Western Europe Today," *Journal of Common Market Studies* 21 (1982–1983): 21–37.

17. I recognize that this is somewhat different from the use of the term "liberal intergovern-mentalism" in A. Moravcsik, "Negotiating the Single European Act: National Interests and Conventional Statecraft in the European Community," *International Organization* 45, no. 1 (1991): 19–56. See G.M. MacMillan, "Summitry, Legitimacy and Integration: Canada and the European Community Compared," Paper Prepared for Workshop on European Union, European Consortium for Political Research, University of Limerick, 31 March–4 April, 1992.

18. This section is based on an earlier paper G.M. MacMillan, "Intergovernmentalism and Multi-Level Governance in the European Union," Paper Presented at the First Annual Meeting of the European Community Studies Association, Canada, Brock University, June 1996.

19. For similarities and differences between Canadian and EC models of federalism see G.M. MacMillan, "Canadian Executive Federalism and European Community Summitry," in *The European Community, Canada and 1992*, ed. G.M. MacMillan (Calgary, 1994).

20. For a discussion of the codecision and cooperation methods of decision making in the EU, see N. Nugent, *The Government and Politics of the European Union*, 3d ed. (Durham, 1994), 312–323.

21. See W. Wallace, *Regional Integration: The West European Experience* (Washington, 1994), 50.

22. See E. Kirchner, *Decision-Making in the European Community: The Council Presidency and European Integration* (Manchester, 1992).

23. S. Bulmer, and W. Wessels, *The European Council* (London, 1987).

24. D. Cameron and R. Simeon, "Intergovernmental Relations and Multilevel Governance: A Citizens' Perspective," Paper Presented at a Joint Session of the Canadian Political Science Association and the European Community Studies Association, University of Ottawa, June 1998.

25. While it is true that federal states such as Canada and the United States can claim that the people are represented at the center in ways that are not true in the EU, the practical issues of democratic accountability as opposed to the legal nature of responsibility are often the same.

26. Some of this is based on earlier work. See G. MacMillan, "Is the EC a supranational state?" in *Federalism and the New World Order*.

27. It is this argument that the people are the source of all executive, legislative and judicial authority and that only the people can in the end decide on how it is distributed that led the Irish Supreme Court to rule that the Irish government and parliament could not ratify the Single European Act without the permission of the Irish people through their assent to changes in the constitution. The Irish Supreme Court ruled that the people could distribute this authority in any way they wished even to the supranational institutions of the EU.

28. D. Held, *Political Theory and the Modern State* (Cambridge, 1984), 11.

29. The EU itself does provide an alternative mechanism in which some groups and regions (such as Scotland in the United Kingdom and Catalonia in Spain) feel they might be able to protect their own distinctive culture and language while sharing in the greater wealth and security provided by an institution like the Community. It comes down to the source of authority of the institutions of government. The source of the sovereignty the state can exercise over society in democracies has come to be seen as deriving from the people, although in some democracies it is centered in specific institutions, such as parliament.

30. For a discussion of the problems of EU citizenship see Edward Moxon-Browne, "Citizens and Parliaments," in *Constitution Building in the European Union*, ed., Brigid Laffan (Dublin, 1996).

Chapter 4

THE EUROPEAN UNION AND THE DEMOCRATIC DEFICIT

The Emergence of an International Rechtsstaat?

———— ∞∞∞ ————

James A. Caporaso

Introduction

The European Union (EU) is an international state without a centralized and recognizable international government. However, it is neither a Westphalian state nor a social democratic state. The political system of the EU is not easily assimilated into models of federalism cast at the international level, though admittedly the German model of federalism provides a better fit to the European experience than that of the United States. Most pointedly, the difference between the EU and federal systems at the nation-state level does not lie in the amount of power given to the component territorial units. Nevertheless, a central claim of this chapter is that the EU qualifies as a state in the most general sense. While this claim that the EU is a state will be met with skepticism and objections, I anticipate that some of the resistance will be due to the equation of "state" with "Westphalian state." In this chapter I draw the main outlines of the EU as a regulatory-technocratic state and I go on to use this as a basis for trying to understand the role of law in the development of the Euro-

---

Notes for this section begin on page 99.

pean polity. In so doing, I downplay the traditional importance accorded to the status of parliaments and representation, political parties and organized competition, and growth of an active civil society in the democratic evolution of the Union. I do so not because I believe these institutions are unimportant for democracy, but because I think there is another aspect of democratic development that is also important, is often given short shrift, and is in some ways more suited to the overall character of EU institutions.

As the EU has grown as a political system, it has expanded its competence to many areas not covered by the original Rome Treaty. It has moved from commercial policy and agriculture to environmental policy (about which nothing at all is said in the Rome Treaty), industrial policy, transport policy, competition and merger policy, regional policy, and even social policy. At the same time, the EU has amended its founding documents several times (the Single European Act, the Maastricht Treaty, and the Amsterdam Treaty), has added nine new members, and has strengthened its institutions through constitutional rewriting and through the jurisprudence of the European Court of Justice (ECJ). While the EU has developed, it has also created and intensified the democratic deficit, a deficit that has become visible because of the contrast between the role of democratic institutions and procedures at the national and the international levels. However, for the first several decades of the EU's existence, it had not yet become a crucial center for policy making; hence, its nondemocratic nature mattered little. In addition, as long as the Luxembourg compromise preserved the veto for each Member state (until the mid-eighties), few could argue that European institutions had enough autonomy to worry about. The significance of the democratic deficit arises in part from the historical transfer of competencies from the national to the supranational level; and in another part from the institutionalization of new layers of transnational civil society outside the control of both national and supranational levels. In short, two different things are going on. The first concerns the increase of policy making "in Brussels" without the "normal" parliamentary checks presumed to exist at the national levels. The second concerns the movement of some activities (business activities, particularly activities of mobile capital) out of arenas where they are subject to political control and into private spaces, in this case transnational spaces. These two movements can conveniently be described as Europeanization of policy making and transnationalization of capital. Most of the attention to the democratic deficit has centered on the first concern, but there is little reason why we should not worry about the second also.

In what follows, I argue that the EU is not best conceived as a Westphalian state. I do not think this is because of developmental immaturity or that "not enough time has elapsed" for the EU to reach the stage characteristic of modern nation-states. Instead, I argue that the emerging political functions and structures of the EU follow a different template, partly captured by the idea of the "regulatory state," and not completely unlike Monnet's functionalist conception of Europe as a scientific state, heavy on problem solving and expertise but short on patriotism and broad, representative political institutions.[1] For Monnet, the best that Europe could hope for was "generalized reciprocity," rather than a collective will or broad political representation. From here I try to show how the political organization of Europe contributes to the democratic deficit at the same time that it makes conventional remedies, such as party government and representative democracy, inappropriate. Finally, I explore the role of the courts, both the European Court of Justice (ECJ) and the domestic courts, in attempting to supply some democratic content to the new Europe.

The Westphalian State and the European Union

By a Westphalian state I simply mean a state with a centralized structure of political authority organized along territorially exclusive lines.[2] Not all states were so organized.[3] In its ideal-typical Weberian form, the state's centralized structure has lines of authority radiating out from the center to periphery, a continuous staff capable of administering the "laws of the land," a specialized bureaucracy capable of extracting taxes, and a legitimate monopoly of violence. Many scholars recognize that the EU is not a Westphalian state at the same time that they accept many of its standards for statehood. Some do this more or less explicitly as many lawyers do,[4] when they see the emergence of law governing relations among different "levels" of government as indication that the EU is becoming a federal state. Others do so implicitly for example, when they insist on specific forms of institutionalization as proof that Europe is integrating (becoming a state) or not. Still others agree that the EU does not look much like a state but assert that this is due to its infancy, that is, to the fact that it is still in its very earliest stage of development. The problem we are told, is with the analyst, who expects too much of the EU.

Even if we consider the development of the EU since its birth in 1958, we would only have slightly more than four decades to examine, hardly an adequate interval of time in which to study state-building processes. We need only recall the historic sweep of the work of Deutsch et al. and Tilly, to remind ourselves that the last half of the twentieth century is but a snapshot.[5] Thus, we must put away our old methodological tools—comparative

statics, analysis of short-term events and trends—and put on the methodological lens for the long view. Only by doing so will we be able to take note
of the changes that are slowly but importantly taking place in Europe.

Of course many scholars do not accept the Westphalian state as a realistic model for EU integration and may even consider it a straw man to build
a case against it. Indeed, the Westphalian model may not even accurately
capture the historic essentials of the older nation states.[6] The problem here
is quite simply that the general antipathy to the Westphalian idea is rarely
matched with the development of qualitatively different alternatives. Few
have taken seriously new conceptual models of the "new medievalism" and
the "post-modern polity." Quite the contrary, as I have argued, the Westphalian model has often been honored even in the breach.

The Westphalian model is important, indeed it may be reinforced, even
when it is rejected because we tend to envision most of the "alternatives" as
attempts to overcome the shortfalls between model and reality. Thus, the EU
is understood to be integrating only when it can transcend the sovereignties
of the individual states and reassemble those competencies and sovereignties
at a higher level. This requires that we see the EU as an emerging political
structure, which acquires its distinctive sovereign status by draining those
powers and authorities from the constituent member states. Some have
escaped this tendency.[7] Nevertheless, the polarities with which we work—
interstate system versus federal state, intergovernmentalism versus supranationalism—suggest that the state system, and its alternatives, are defined by
reference to the Westphalian model. Conceptually, we are virtually in the
same position where we began, except that we must adjust our expectations
for the "fact" that we are in the prehistory of European state development.

The EU as a Regulatory State

During the early stages of the European integration process, students could
be excused for expecting the EU to parallel the processes of nation and state
building exemplified by earlier states. But as the EU evolved, one could see
that the basic political template of the EU was qualitatively different from
that of the member states. The EU's portfolio of functions and responsibilities differs radically from that of the member states and these differences are
not explicable in terms of its less advanced position on a continuum of
development. The EU is weak in terms of the traditional taxing and spending functions of government. The extractive capacity of the EU institutions
is nearly zero, reflecting a stalemate going back to Hallstein's failed "own

resources" initiative in 1965. The EU spends very little on its own accord, about 1.3 percent of the gross domestic product (GDP) of its member states and about 4 percent of government spending.[8] The European Commission, Europe's chief administrative and regulatory apparatus, is modestly staffed by approximately 20,000 people, of whom about one-third are translators. Despite occasional predawn raids by the Commission, the EU is not a supranational Leviathan. Before the institution of a European Monetary Union, the EU also did very little by way of stabilization policy: countercyclical policy, demand management, inflation, and unemployment. This leaves regulatory policy as the chief area in which the EU specializes.

Despite these structural weaknesses of the EU when judged in light of Westphalian indicators, the EU is normally accorded an important status. Is this just due to sentimentality on the part of international relations theorists on behalf of international institutions? Do liberal institutionalists have a stake in arguing the importance of the EU? Effective international institutions, always a rare commodity, are interpreted by neorealists as a gloss on power relations, from which they are barely once removed. In this war of the paradigms, institutionalists and realists have a stake in inflating or deflating the success of the EU. It is true that the EU is a rare, perhaps endangered species. It is a highly effective international governmental organization, which makes policy across a large number of areas and has moved beyond the universal veto. But there are sound reasons for the attention given to the EU, reasons that go beyond disciplinary curiosity. One answer to the puzzle of "marginal spending along with generally recognized importance" lies in (re)conceiving the EU as a regulatory state. This reconceptualization frees the EU of the onerous requirements that only increased spending and expanding staff and budgets qualify as state development.

The regulatory state is essentially a state specializing in the control and management of international externalities. Because this state does not engage substantially in the classic functions of government—redistribution, stabilization, and provision of symbolic meaning—and because this state does not create its own security umbrella, tax structures, and administrative structures, it can "get by" with very little resources. It specializes, strictly speaking in rule making. In delegating this task to an international institution, the member states hope to overcome crucial problems of collective action, the strategic use of regulatory policy, information failures, and lack of credibility of national commitments. To implement its rules, the EU relies on the administrative structures of the member states, and on the self-enforcing action that derives from individuals and firms litigating before the European Court of Justice, as well as infringement actions brought by the

Commission. How well the EU works according to the above model is controversial. Furthermore, it is doubtful that the Rome Treaty envisioned its political architecture to work this way. Without the doctrine of "direct effect," which did not come about until 1963, the idea of decentralized enforcement based on litigation by individuals and firms was not conceivable, let alone a practical vehicle for interpreting and enforcing the law.

If we accept the basic idea of the regulatory state as a useful description of the EU, a number of implications follow. The first is that we should not expect the EU to look like a traditional nation-state at all, nor for the future course of European integration to follow the familiar path from decentralized state system to loose confederation, to federation. Instead, we should expect a political division of labor among member states, who will continue to focus on security, social, and redistributive policy, and the EU, focusing on international regulatory policy. From this vantage point, it would be misplaced to equate the development of the EU with the growth of its tax and spending powers. The regulatory state is not the Westphalian state, the extractive state, the night watchman state, or the social democratic state. Its future shape is not likely to resemble these older state forms more than at present.

Implications of Regulatory State for the Democratic Deficit

In contrast to the model based on the Westphalian state, the regulatory state posits a different relationship between constituent nation states and emerging supranational polity. The regulatory state is a kind of scientific state, drawing heavily on scientific, management, and technical advice of experts. This new polity, modest as the claims set forth here suggest, can be very important, and not just in finding efficient, Pareto-improving advances to transnational market failures. The making of regulations has always been a central function of government and the move to privatization enhances the importance of this task. While more and more bodies privatize, the tasks of constructing the framework within which these bodies operate multiply. Businesses, factories, scientific organizations, and pharmaceutical companies, just to name a few, require technical standards, uniform measures of reporting and labeling, agreement on environmental goals, and guidelines for public safety and public morality. While the exact line distinguishing regulatory and redistributive functions is cloudy, we nevertheless expect a rough political division of labor between member states, focusing on social and redistributional politics (and of course stabilization and symbolic politics), and the EU, which will increasingly focus on regulatory policy.

This new specialization (new by historical standards at least) has a number of implications for the democratic deficit and the yet to be discussed role of the courts. First, the huge increase in the number of regulations, intensified as a result of the passage of the Single European Act (SEA), has meant a transfer of policy making competencies to the European level, where such policy making is less checked by democratic forces than at the national level. This can be said without romanticizing the extent of democracy at the domestic level. The shift of powers to Europe means that most decisions are taken by the Council of Ministers, whose members are part of the national executives of the respective countries, on proposal by the Commission, and with only weak supervision by the European Parliament. The relatively stronger control and oversight exercised by national parliaments is simply lost in the European arena, unless, as in Denmark, there are national parliamentary committees that will extend their deliberative and oversight functions to European legislation. In addition, and not as a simple extension of the above point about the outflanking of parliamentary control, we should note, following Moravcsik, that the process of decision making in Europe may involve substantial shifts of domestic institutional power from the legislature to the executive.[9] Since decision making in Brussels is often done by the Ministers of Foreign Affairs, or by heads of state in the European Council, delegation of power from legislative to executive institutions may be expected. While there is no certainty that this shift to executives implies any necessary relationship for the democratic deficit, it does imply a decline of influence for parliamentary institutions. Representative institutions may or may not produce policies that are closer to the median voter.[10] However, we should also keep in mind that parliamentary representation is a process as much as a set of policy outputs, a set of procedures and rules about how to legislate even more than what to legislate. Parliaments engage in oversight, they review spending activities, decide on finances, and sometimes subject executives to difficult question and answer sessions. Thus, to be democratic means in part to engage in these processes, quite apart from the results.

A second implication of the regulatory turn for the democratic deficit centers on the way in which the undeveloped political institutions of the EU accentuate the harmful effects of the emphasis on regulatory standards and scientific expertise. Students of political parties come together with theorists of regulation in their agreement that political parties are weak at the European level. Political parties have been, and remain, primarily national in terms of organization, funding, constituent support, candidates, and the targets of their programs. Mass political parties do not offer alternative candidates and programs to address problems of Europe as a whole. Candidates are not voted on by a European constituency but rather by national constituencies. The members of the European Parliament are elected by national constituencies and, once in the European Parliament, they have little association with their national parties. This structural defect is of course not the "fault" of the regulatory state, but recognition of the nature of this state makes the weaknesses of political parties seem even more important. At their best, political parties serve as vehicles to mobilize interest and make people aware of their common predicaments. They facilitate broad coalitions of diverse interests, raise the level of public discussion, and forge programs that allow broad social choices to be made by politicians. The alternative is a kind of interest-group hedonism, according to which hundreds of interest groups present their demands directly to policy makers, without any prior sifting, editing, compromise, and coalition formation. Ad-hoc policy making may occur in this fashion, but policy externalities are likely to be ignored, and public authority is not likely to grow in this infertile environment.

Much is made of the fact that members of the European Parliament sit according to political affiliation, with a socialist from Italy sitting next to a French socialist and a Christian Democrat from Germany more likely to sit next to a Christian Democrat from Belgium or the Netherlands. Very little is said about something more fundamental, which is that what the Christian Democratic, Liberal, or Socialist parties do at the national level has little to do with what these corresponding party members do in the EP. If this accusation is true, it amounts to a fundamental disconnection between the national level, where candidates are selected and political issues are formulated, and the European level, where (presumably) policies are made for Europe as a whole. As Andeweg puts it: "For citizens to choose in elections, they must be offered a choice. The menu from which voters may choose is the party system. But for this choice to be meaningful, and for elections to serve as an instrument of political representation, the party system in the parliamentary arena must reflect the party system in the electoral arena. It is this crucial link that is missing in the context of the Euro-elections."[11]

A third connection between the regulatory state and the democratic deficit looks to the growth of the European market. There is a natural affinity between the expansion and perfection of the market and the growth of regulations. While the Single European Act was hailed as a deregulatory achievement, liberalization in fact quickly spawned reregulation. Indeed, there is a close link between liberalization (privatization, easing of regulations) and the growth of regulations. According to Majone, Europe is today experiencing the tremendous pressure for regulatory laws and regulatory bodies that the United States. experienced a half century earlier. The last decade-and-a-half has witnessed a proliferation of regulatory committees, peopled by experts, and possessed of unclear public status. While the work of these committees is not well known, and the very mention of the word "comitology" [12] is certain to make eyes glaze over, we have reason to be skeptical of their impact in terms of democracy. This is not a critique of specialized commissions per se, but more of a warning of their possible effects when placed inside a truncated political system, particularly one lacking in strong political parties and representative institutions. Even in the United States, the proliferation of such agencies has been attacked as increasing nontransparency, lack of accountability, and confusion of powers.

The democratic failings of the EU should not be surprising to us. According to Guiseppe Federico Mancini and David Keeling, the undemocratic nature of the EU is not an accident; indeed, it was designed in just this way.[13] First, the EU began its life as a standard international organization and was founded on a treaty among sovereign states. Treaties are compacts among states, that is to say, agreements entered into by states and creating binding obligations only on states. People were given no rights at all because they were given no legal status. They were not parties to the original agreement. Second, and closely related, the signatory states were anxious to control the exercise of power and to circumscribe as carefully as possible their own sovereignty. Thus, they created a weak and unpopular European Assembly and represented the states in the most important of all legislative institutions, namely the Council of Ministers, institutionally entrenching the use of the veto for all member states in this institution. This integration of supranational legislative power with national executive personnel and institutions was to provide the ultimate check against supranational tendencies in other European institutions and in transnational civil society. The institutional message seems very clear, indeed transparent. States are the only legitimate actors for it is only they who are popularly elected or appointed by elected officials. Each state, no matter how large or small, could bring the entire EU system to a halt. With each state able to cast a veto, the presumptive burden was placed on those who wanted to change policies.

Sovereign States, Transnational Markets, and Individual Rights: The ECJ as an International Rechtsstaat

Periodic elections, broad, encompassing political parties, representative legislatures, and a healthy society in terms of interest groups and civic associations are what we normally focus on when we think of democracy. However, the extension of rights to individuals, guaranteed by the state, even against the fluctuating tides of public opinion, can also be seen as an important part of the democratic process. When we focus on the spread of rights, we implicitly raise questions about citizenship, that is, EU citizenship. This concept has been disparaged by some as an empty shell and held out by others as offering great promise for involving the individual in the European polis. A citizen is not just a participant in a market. A citizen is by definition a member of a political community, an organized community with a specific political charter. Citizens are members in the state, as the German word *Staatsangehörige* suggests. Members of a state have rights and responsibilities by virtue of their membership. The challenge is to give some meaningful content to these rights and responsibilities. The operational content of rights is to some extent a result of various efforts to rewrite the Rome Treaty, but the day-to-day meaning has a great deal to do with the activities of the European Court of Justice (ECJ). The spread of rights and their entrenchment in constitutions, so that their enforcement depends not just on the whim of the ruler but on some more deeply institutionalized process, is not necessarily related to other dimensions of democracy in a one-for-one manner. A ruler could be responsive to democratic participation (to votes, to preferences for certain policies) and not be tightly constrained by a system of laws and a dictator could be very undemocratic and still work within a framework of laws. In other words, there is a difference between sheer personal rule no matter how democratic, and rule by law, no matter how undemocratic. The idea of the modern democratic state is one in which there is both impersonal rule (a nation of laws and not of people) and democracy, in the sense of institutionalized connections between rulers and ruled.

This focus on the procedural aspect of democracy suggests that strengthening the powers of Parliament and organizing political parties at the European level are not the only ways to deepen European democracy. While the right of individuals to participate in a democracy through their elected representatives is important, so is the capacity of individuals to "vindicate their rights in judicial proceedings."[14] Yet the European Court of Justice (ECJ) might seem the least likely candidate for the expansion of democracy. It is a small body (currently fifteen judges), it conducts its proceedings in secret, does not publish its vote or dissenting opinions, and is not elected. In comparison to the expansion of the electorate and the rise of legislatures publicly deliberating and making laws, the role of the Court would seem limited. In addition, before the ECJ could hold a meaningful place in the lives of ordinary citizens, there are two rather large obstacles to overcome. The first obstacle is simply that the basic documents of the EU, the legal texts that the

Court is to interpret, are international treaties, not constitutions outlining a series of basic rights and obligations for people. The Rome Treaty is a classic compact among states, a legal agreement entered into by sovereign powers to secure certain ends, and for the purpose of which states accepted certain constraints. As a result, individuals and firms had no legal status. The "Community" of which the Rome Treaty speaks is a community of states, not of individuals.[15] The second obstacle concerns the relationship between domestic and community law. In the event that domestic and community law conflict, which legal order is superior? While this question has no simple answer, in parliamentary systems acts of parliament are supreme and the latter of any two laws holds sway. The metanorm that the more recent rule applies can work to the favor of domestic parliaments in that the force of treaty law can be overturned by an act of parliament. So, at the very least, no clear hierarchy exists in the relationship between domestic and international law.

The process by which the ECJ altered this compact among states is today referred to as "constitutionalization."[16] Constitutionalization describes a process by which an international treaty becomes relevant for individuals within those states. In more elaborate terms, it "refers to the process by which the EC treaties have evolved from a set of legal arrangements binding upon sovereign states, into a vertically integrated regime conferring judicially enforceable rights and obligations on all legal persons and entities, public and private, within EC territory."[17] If this process of constitutionalization accurately describes what has taken place, the EC has been transformed from a traditional international organization into "a multi-tiered system of governance founded on higher law constitutionalism."[18]

How did this process of constitutionalization take place? Simplifying greatly, the Court of Justice progressively made the treaties relevant to individuals, firms, and other private actors. The historic case came in 1963. In Van Gend en Loos, the ECJ established the doctrine of direct effect. That is to say, the Court asserted that provisions of the Rome Treaty created rights and responsibilities for individuals even without supplementary actions by national institutions to translate treaty doctrine into domestic law. The Court propounded a radical doctrine, broke down a standing partition between international and domestic law, and created a mechanism by which individuals could claim judicial remedies before international courts. Before the Van Gend case, it was possible for member states to sue one another. In addition, the Commission could bring infringement proceedings against individual member states for noncompliance with Community law. But individuals had no legal standing. They could not sue other individuals for breaches of Community law, or sue their employer, or bring legal proceedings against a public authority in their home country. It is precisely this gap which the Van Gend case addressed. It provided individuals with a set of rights and responsibilities that could be invoked in domestic courts. Domestic courts could then invoke Community law through the preliminary reference procedure (Article 177).

Since the Van Gend case, the Court has thickened its jurisprudence of direct effect by extending this doctrine from treaty provisions to directives (the Van Duyn case in 1974) and other classes of secondary legislation. When domestic laws were out of line with European law, the Court imposed an obligation on national courts to interpret national law "in light of the wording and purpose of the directive."[19] Since directives are only binding as to their desired effect, and not as to the means by which such effects are brought about, possibilities for slippage were considerable. Thus, the Court narrowed a considerable gap in the implementation of legislation across the member states and provided greater uniformity in judicial remedies across countries. In subsequent cases, the Court prescribed that if the intent of the directive cannot be achieved by way of interpretation, damages done to individuals owing to failure to implement a directive had to be compensated. Thus, what started out as a thin wedge of constitutional jurisprudence enlarged and extended to other areas.

Important as the doctrine of direct effect is, it could not very well work by itself in the face of contrary domestic law. It is not surprising that in the year following the direct effect doctrine, the Court of Justice grasped the nettle and confronted the issue of the relationship between municipal and international law. In Costa versus ENEL, the Italian courts first heard the case of an Italian citizen who refused to pay his electricity bill because he asserted his rights under the Rome Treaty had been violated. Since Italian law governing the case came into existence after the Rome Treaty, the Italian Constitutional Court decided against Mr. Costa, citing lex posteriori. The case then was appealed under the Article 177 procedure, and the ECJ, while agreeing that Mr. Costa had to pay his $3.00 electricity bill, quietly added that Community law was supreme. Of course, national governments, particularly legislatures, did not passively accept this doctrine of supremacy of European law. But in varying degrees, and with varying time schedules, this is precisely what has happened, or is still happening. Even in countries hostile to European law, such as the United Kingdom, the supremacy of European law has been accepted as a practical matter, even if legal reservations are posed about the "ultimate right to take its ultimate authority back."

It is difficult to exaggerate the importance of direct effect and supremacy. Indeed, they make up what many now think of as the constitutional pillars of the EU system. In announcing direct effect, the Court provided individuals with legal standing under an international Treaty, and by so doing, it considerably closed the gap between treaty law and municipal law. A transnational legal space was created within which individuals could seek redress for complaints before domestic courts relying on Community law. The ECJ's coup can be partly understood only by comprehending that it co-opted domestic courts in the process through use of the preliminary reference procedure. According to this procedure, domestic courts may, and supreme courts must, ask the ECJ for a preliminary ruling when the issue at hand involves matters of European law. Once the ECJ hands down its judgement, the domestic court applies it to the facts of the case.

The Changes Brought by the ECJ

While the role of the Court and its liberating and protective potential are often exaggerated, it is important to bring out the full impact of the ECJ's jurisprudence. Individuals have acquired legal status in front of an international tribunal, as well as a status in front of domestic courts appealing to Community law. The range of Community law is not as broad as that of a national constitution but it is significant nevertheless. As Mancini and Keeling put it:

> And let there be no mistaking the impact of Community law on the citizens of Europe. Natural and legal persons are intimately involved in the application of the Treaty by Community institutions and the Member States. They are the ones who profit directly by an unhindered flow of goods, services, and capital, they are the beneficiaries of the rules on labour mobility and the right to share, on a par with local workers, the social advantages available in the country to which they move. By the same token, their jobs and their investments may be wiped out by the abolition of a State aid found incompatible with the Treaty; the protection of their health, working conditions and environment may be impaired by a harmonising directive if it imposes a lower standard than national law; and even their fundamental rights may be encroached upon by a Community normative or administrative measure.[20]

The doctrines of direct effect and supremacy, if applied seriously in practice, could lead to an erosion of two constitutional pillars of the Westphalian system: first, that states are the subjects of international law; second, that when a domestic and international law conflict, no clear hierarchy of norms exists. The first pillar puts a firewall between the individual and international law. The second makes the relationship between international and domestic law unclear at best. The firewall is at least leaky, and perhaps it is completely porous today. The expansion of direct effect opens a transnational space for individuals and groups to seek redress for ordinary wrongs, where they might not have had judicial recourse previously. Indeed, the more expansive reading of international law compared to domestic law and the implied amendments of domestic laws resulting therefrom, tell us that there is some value-added in European law. It is not a simple extension and projection to the regional level of domestic laws already in place. And the content of litigation is not trivial: workplace discrimination, social security, unemployment insurance, equal pay for equal work, maternity rights, job safety, and so on are all issues that have arisen.

A second important change has to do with the relationship between supremacy and judicial review. If Community laws are supreme, there must be a hierarchy of norms. A hierarchy of norms does not simply exist (or not); someone or some body must interpret this hierarchy. Thus, when the ECJ declared that Community law was and is supreme, it also declared that it would be the body that would judge the relationship between domestic and Community law. For a judiciary to assess the validity of the laws of a government constitutes judicial review. Since many (if not most) of the member states did not have judicial review to start with, that is since they often had legislatures whose will was considered sovereign, the evolution of judicial review was not simply a trivial extension of a well-known process from the domestic to the international level. In the Costa case, the ECJ not only declared Community law supreme; it also declared an Italian parliamentary law invalid, thus exercising a capacity that the Italian Constitutional Court did not have. In the United Kingdom, which can be regarded as a hard case (because of the sanctity of parliamentary sovereignty), the parliament accepts judicial review as a practical matter, even though the issue is ultimately fudged by arguing that the parliament has decided, through the European Communities Act of 1972, to delegate to the European Court of Justice the authority to review its own legislation. Should the Parliament decide otherwise tomorrow, they could take this right back. Thus, exercising its sovereign powers, the Parliament has given to others the right to overrule them, temporarily at least.

Finally, the process of constitutionalization described here entails more than a victory on behalf of a Community institution over the institutions of the member states. This process also involves changes in interinstitutional relations within member states, particularly changes in the balances of power and rights between parliaments and courts in the member states. There can be no doubt that, to the extent that the ECJ has advanced its jurisprudence it has done so not by conquering domestic courts, but rather by co-opting those courts and by enhancing their power at the expense of national parliaments. Individuals do not go directly to the ECJ. Instead, they take their case to a domestic court and when there is an aspect of European law that is relevant, the domestic court asks for a preliminary ruling on the matter. Domestic courts then write the opinion, using the judgements of the ECJ in so doing. Domestic courts enhance their own power in the process, exercising something like judicial review even where they may not have done so before.

Conclusion

The European Union has often been misconceived as a budding Westphalian state. As such it is expected to grow according to a genetic blueprint that emphasizes growth of a national security apparatus, a well-defined hierarchical bureaucracy, and substantial capacity to tax and transfer large amounts of the (inter)national product. During the brief life course of the EU, it has not tracked these older historical grooves very closely. Instead, the emerging European state appears to be closer to a regulatory state, one designed not to perform the full range of functions of extant nation states, but rather tailored more closely to specialize in rule making and management of international externalities. To some extent, this form of European state suits well the vision of those who see Europe as a market-perfection project, that is, as a project whose chief goal is to facilitate the transition of capitalism from a domestic to a regional level. Nevertheless, the ECJ has succeeded in identifying a set of rights within this framework. Whether these rights will be narrowly attached to the expanding market, or grow more broadly than the efficiency concerns that initially animated these rights, remains to be seen.

The movement toward a rights-based state, an international *Rechtsstaat*, has several implications. First, the jurisprudence of the Court of Justice has created a transnational space for individual rights, an arena within which individuals can press for judicial remedies that did not previously exist. The process by which this has occurred is called "constitutionalization." This term describes the transition from a decentralized, treaty-based system governed by international law to a vertically integrated system of norms conferring judicially enforceable rights on all legal persons, public and private, with EU territory. While this process is far from complete, what it involves is a historic shift from a classic international organization based on state-to-state relations into a partly domesticated system of governance founded on law applicable to individuals. Second, the Europeanization of social policy has influenced domestic structures of greatest importance, including the definition of economic citizenship. These changes in citizenship are not always in the nature of extensions to the regional level of well-established national rights, nor are they simply coordination gestures, that is, attempts to deal with the lacunae that result from the emergence of the transnational labor market. The logic of many situations faced by the member states has resulted in a common authority (the EC) deciding what the rules should be, thus undermining the territorial logic of rules. Westphalian sovereignty, in the sense of exclusion of external authority structures, has been weakened.

The enforcement of European rights has suggested several things. Article 119 regarding "Equal Pay for Equal Work and the Equal Pay and Equal Treatment" directives adopted by the Council of Ministers have been interpreted as providing a higher and more encompassing standard, by providing rights and remedies not available under (interpretations of) domestic legislation. In many, if not most cases, the discrimination claims made would have failed without the benefit of EC law. The ECJ's interpretations in the area of equal pay and equal treatment have provided remedies against discrimination where none existed under U.K. law and have incited not only the rewriting of domestic legislation but also increased activity by the Council and Commission. Subsequent to the "Equal Pay and Equal Treatment" directives, the Council passed directives on social security, equal treatment in social security schemes, and equal treatment for self-employed workers. The Commission has proposed numerous directives (e.g., on reversing burden of proof in discrimination cases) but the United Kingdom has blocked most of them in the Council of Ministers.[21] The ECJ, as most courts, proceeds slowly and cautiously. The limitations of European Union democracy, the so-called democratic deficit, provide an accurate description of the EU today. The gap between legislative oversight and representation on the one hand and executive power on the other has been widened by the process of European integration. But there are many components of democracy: representation, political competition (especially competition in the party system), separation of powers, a free press, and a widespread system of rights according to which all officials and private persons must conform. A democratic political system implies that certain assets, for example, rights, must be universally distributed. Votes, free speech, the right to associate, to own property, and to practice one's religious beliefs are to be held by all and may not be bought and sold. Thus the extension of rights to individuals according to European law, over and above the rights citizens hold nationally, is an important part of the democratic process. Where this process will end is difficult to say, but the mix of judges and experts provides the political skeleton that describes the evolving European state.

Notes

1. G. Majone, "The European Community Between Social Policy and Social Regulation," *Journal of Common Market Studies* 31, no. 2 (1993): 153–170.
2. In this section, I rely heavily on my article, "The European Union and Forms of State: Westphalian, Regulatory, or Post-Modern?" *Journal of Common Market Studies* 34, no. 1 (1996): 29–52.
3. J.G. Ruggie, "Territoriality and Beyond: Problematizing Modernity in International Relations," *International Organization* 47, no. 1 (1993): 139–174.
4. J.H. Weiler "The Transformation of Europe," *Yale Law Journal* 100, no. 8 (June 1991): 2403–83.
5. K.W. Deutsch, et al., *Political Community and the North Atlantic Area* (Princeton, (1957); C. Tilly, ed., *The Formation of National States in Western Europe* (Princeton, 1975).
6. S.D. Krasner, "Westphalia and All That," in *Ideas and Foreign Policy*, ed., J. Goldstein and R.O. Keohane (Ithaca, 1993), 235–264.
7. W. Wessels, "Staat und (westeuropaische) Integration: Die Fusionthese," *Politische Vierteljahreschrift, Sonderheft Die Integration Europas* (1992): 36–61; G. Marks, "Comparing European Integration and Nation-Building," Paper prepared for a Conference on "Markets, States, and Social Citizenship" at the New York School for Social Research, 1994, 1–17.
8. G. Majone, "The European Community: An 'Independent Fourth Branch of Government'?," in *Verfassungen für ein ziviles Europa*, ed., G. Bruggemeier (Baden-Baden, 1994), 23–43.
9. A. Moravcsik, *Does International Cooperation Strengthen National Executives? The Case of Monetary Policy in the European Union*, Center for European Studies, Harvard University (1998), 1–43.
10. Ibid.
11. R. Andeweg, "The Reshaping of National Party Systems," in *The Crisis of Representation in Europe*, ed. J. Hayward (London, 1995), 60.
12. Indeed, as I write this sentence, my PC, ever alert to the misuse of language, flags the word "comitology" in red.
13. G.F. Mancini and D.T. Keeling, "Democracy and the European Court of Justice," *The Modern Law Review* 57, no. 2 (1994): 175–190.
14. Ibid., 184.
15. Ibid., 183.
16. A. Stone Sweet, "Constitutional Dialogues in the European Community," European University Institute Working Paper 95/38, Robert Schuman Centre, San Domenico di Fiesole (Florence, 1995), 1.
17. A. Stone Sweet and J.A. Caporaso, "From Free Trade to Supranational Polity: The European Court and Integration," in *European Integration and Supranational Governance*, ed. W. Sandholtz and A. Stone Sweet (Oxford, 1998), 102.
18. Ibid., 102.
19. D. O'Keefe, "Judicial Protection of the Individual by the European Court of Justice," *Fordham International Law Journal* 19, no. 3 (1996): 905.
20. Mancini and Keeling, *Democracy and the European Court of Justice*, 182.
21. S.J. Kenney, *"For Whose Protection"* (Ann Arbor, 1992), 80–81.

Section II

LESSONS FROM FAILED FEDERATIONS

Chapter 5

The Demise of Socialist Federations

Developmental Effects and Institutional Flaws of the Soviet Union, Yugoslavia, and Czechoslovakia

—⊱⊰—

Jim Seroka

Introduction

It would be tempting, but inaccurate, to state that federalism was abandoned in East Central Europe because it was never a powerful symbol of unity, or that it did not hold strong emotive attractions to large segments of the population. If this view had been accurate, it would be easy to conclude that federalism was an alien concept imposed by outside forces and without any cultural roots. Instead, we need to note that the Pittsburgh Agreement of 1918 establishing a federal Czechoslovakia was the modern fundamental act of statehood for the linked nations of Slovakia and Bohemia/Moravia. The Yugoslav federation had deep historical roots tied to Bishop Strossmeyer's nineteenth century vision for a south-Slav or Illyrian federation; and the mythology of the formation of the Soviet Union closely paralleled the ideals of the panslavic movement of the nineteenth century nationalists. While it is true that the socialist regimes did not always argue that their federal institutions were direct manifestations or descendants of these national

Notes for this section begin on page 114.

historical movements, the concept of federalism itself was certainly congruent with national aspirations in each of the three socialist federations.

In order to understand the collapse of the socialist federations, one cannot rely exclusively on historical speculation about the supposed incompatibility of the East European political culture to the federal idea. Rather, it is necessary to analyze and appraise the structural, behavioral, and normative weakness of the socialist model as applied to the federal idea. Towards this end, the first requirement is to pinpoint the common factors in the socialist experiences of Czechoslovakia, Soviet Union and Yugoslavia that contributed to the mass abandonment of federalism and the federal institutions. A second requirement is to identify and analyze how socialism weakened the processes, institutional patterns, and public and elite linkages with the federal idea and federal-level institutions so that there were few defenders of the federal idea following the collapse of the communist regimes.

Commonalties Among the Former Socialist Federal Systems

Each of the communist federal regimes shared many common features. Among the most prominent were an asymmetric federal structure, a foundation based on ethnic federalism, and a legacy of centralized and nondemocratic decision making. Separately, each of these factors weakened the capacity of federal institutions to prosper or survive. When considered together, they dealt a fatal blow to the continuance of the federal idea in each of these states.

Asymmetry

There are a number of characteristics that the socialist federal systems have in common with one another. First, each of the socialist federations were asymmetric.[1] The Soviet Union was dominated by Russia. Czechs were the asymmetric nation in Czechoslovakia; and Serbs were dominant in the Yugoslav federation. Despite protestations to the contrary and formal constitutional arrangements pledging equality among socialist federal members, the dominant member tended to exercise disproportionate influence over decision making, particularly when critical redistributive issues were involved.[2]

According to the perceptions of the nondominant members of the federation, the socialist federal system implied second class citizenship and permanent assignment to a minority status within the federal compact. From the perspective of the dominant member, constant acknowledgment or accommodation to the "second tier" member republics provided an irritant to that member's national pride. The centrally mandated policy of ethnic quotas and privileges satisfied no group and often served only to heighten ethnic differentiation. Thus, as the discipline imposed by communism began to crumble, leaders from nondominant republics pushed for the adoption of new arrangements that would guarantee them a greater and more autonomous role. The dominant republic leaders, on the other hand, argued for an arrangement that would reduce the frictions associated with ethnic autonomy and quotas.

The fact that the dominant power in each of our three cases acquiesced to the abandonment of the federation, despite a reduction in its international standing, clearly illustrates the importance of this conflict between dominant and nondominant federal members. Even in Yugoslavia, the most violent case of dissolution, the dominant power (i.e., Serbs) chose to battle initially for a Serbian dominated state and secondarily for the inclusion of all Serbs in its new rump state borders. Russian and Czech leaders respectively chose not to contest the breakup at all, and there was no concerted campaign to maintain the "union" at all costs. For nondominant federal republic leaders, continuance of the federal system implied the replacement of party hegemony with hegemony by the dominant federal republic. The politics of compromise and concession associated with federal decision making ran against the popular current of national ethnic renaissance, and the emerging ethnic-based leaderships chafed under the prospects of voluntary suppression of the popular will to the discipline of federal accommodations.[3] Slovak leaders, for example, perceived that agreement with the economic shock therapy espoused by Czech leaders would weaken their base of support and would be perceived as a betrayal of the Slovak public interest.[4] Slovene leaders perceived Serb dominance as an impediment to eventual membership in European institutions. Ukrainian leaders, and the Slovaks, perceived their public's interest to be best served with an even slower transition from a socialist planned economy.

Ethnic Federalism

Complicating the survival potential of the socialist federations even further was the fact that each of the federations were founded on ethnic national principles, and that the socialist federal systems institutionalized ethnic federalism at the expense of territorial federalism. Unlike Germany, the United States, Australia, and Austria, the constituent republics of the socialist federations were also ethnic homelands with distinctive cultures, histories, languages, and so on. In addition, each of the former socialist ethnic republics could lay claim to sovereignty and the right to secede. In many republics the new democratic leadership had strong roots with the cultural intelligentsia of the originating ethnic group (e.g., Czech, Croat, Estonian) and had used their claim to ethnic heritage as a primary instrument in the contest for power with communist authorities.

Second, in many of the smaller ethnic republics, rapid modernization and urbanization diluted the identity and demographic power of the dominant ethnic groups. In republics such as Latvia, Ukraine, and even Slovakia and Croatia, the federation was perceived as endangering the very survival of the nation. For these and other nations with long historical identities, the potential for assimilation was a bitter pill to swallow. It is very difficult to engender a spirit of compromise in the context of ethnic-based federalism.[5] Whenever an issue is defined in symbolic or ethnic terms, accommodation and concessions become highly conflictual and almost impossible to obtain. In addition, as Lijphart and others have indicated, the politics of accommodation depend heavily on the existence of cross-cutting cleavages, avoidance of ethnic-based political issues, and an understanding among the elite to defuse and avoid attempts to force a resolution of issues that are perceived in ethnic terms.[6] Under normal circumstances, such an accommodation may take generations to achieve and is always a delicate arrangement. In the socialist federations, there was no time and little willingness on the part of the newly enfranchised elites to attempt such an accommodation.[7] Of critical importance was that the end of the cold war and absence of a national security threat eliminated any international incentive to compromise and accommodate an ethnic group's core political interest to a broader collective good. Thus, under conditions when there is no necessity for parties to agree, negotiations to achieve an agreement will often fail.

In the case of Yugoslavia, it was fervently believed that neither Croatian nor Slovenian interests would be served by continued membership in a struggling and weak federation. In the case of Czechoslovakia, both Czech and Slovak leaders accepted that their respective national identity would be enhanced with separation.[8] In the case of the Union Republics, independence was portrayed by the ethnic leaders as a historic opportunity for national affirmation, while the continued instability in Russia was seen as a potential threat to national survival.

In each of the three federations, any leadership defense of the federal arrangement would easily be portrayed by their political opponents as national treason. Considering the fact that some of the nations involved have histories that extended longer than a millennium, any leader who "betrayed" his nation in its "historical moment" of opportunity could take a place in infamy for countless generations. Thus, while membership in the federation could mean substantive economic and pragmatic gains, it could also be perceived as national betrayal, given that continued federal association in the post-cold war environment did not assist national survival. Throughout east central Europe, continuation of ethnic-based federalism offered a leader few advantages, but numerous significant risks.

Legacy of Democratic Centralism

A third factor that mitigated against the survivability of socialist federations was their common and debilitating experience under Communist one-party authoritarian rule accompanied by varying intrafederal transitional experiences in the post-Communist period. Even in its benign form, democratic centralism mandated strict discipline among the political leaders, repressed the free and open articulation of political needs, severed linkages between particular interests and political demands, and relied on validation by Party leaders in place of public support.[9]

During the forty to seventy-five year period of Communist rule, the authoritarian systems of the communist world had bred an extremely cautious and rigidly ideological political leadership cadre. This group was also opposed by a politically naive, but ideologically rigid opposition. As a consequence, both Communists and opposition leaders in the early years of the transition viewed politics as an extremely serious political struggle between two irreconcilable camps. Trust across the political spectrum was incredibly low, undercurrents for revenge were very strong, and understanding of the role of a loyal opposition was very rare. In many cases, for both democratic and authoritarian leaders, support for a new territorial-based federation to supplant the former ethnic-based federation offered few, if any, political advantages and attracted few adherents. The mutual trust and confidence, which a territorial-based federalism implied, simply did not have time to develop. Under socialist federalism, the multilayered network of intergovernmental relations and shared authority was used to maintain authoritarian control. However, under the transitional regimes, this same network of overlapping and diffused authority engendered the fear of chaos and anarchy. Because no group could hope to control each and every institution at each and every level of the federation, each group labored to prevent the other from governing effectively. Underlying all this was the fear by the new non-Communist leadership that the political chaos could facilitate the return of the communists, and the recognition by the communists that their sole hope of survival depended upon reducing the parameters of political life (i.e., building upon a subfederal level friendly base of support).

In Czechoslovakia, the victory in 1992 of a strong free market coalition of parties in the Czech lands and the mirror opposite victory of the neo-communist groups in Slovakia paralyzed federal decision making.[10] In Yugoslavia, the victory of a pluralist liberal coalition in Slovenia, an embittered right wing party in Croatia, and the continuance of communist rule in Serbia created enormous dissonance, mutual antagonisms, and a determination by each side to avoid collaboration, negotiation, and compromise with any other. Within the Soviet Union, enormous disparities in political outlooks and variations in the power of local Communist cadres prohibited any serious political discussions across federal lines. It also quickly highlighted that continuance of the Soviet Union under the Union Treaty would strain not only federal decision-making processes, but might invite intervention from outside the republics (e.g., Russians). In the new political dynamic, the specter of possible fraternal socialist assistance chilled any enthusiasm for strengthening federal institutions.

Finally, the shared experience of one- party Communist rule meant that the opposition to Communists in federal systems were invariably republic-centered. While in power, Communist authorities never permitted competing federal institutions to form, and also never permitted the articulation of competitive federal national interest platforms. As an unintended consequence, therefore, the only all-union or federal parties and interest groups to emerge in the multiparty elections had links to the Communists, and the sad result was that support for federalism often became indistinguishable from support for the communists.[11]

Communism and Its Role in the Destruction of the Federal Idea

Our second challenge is to identify and analyze how socialism weakened the processes, institutional patterns, and public and elite linkages with the federal idea and federal institutions so that there were few, if any, defenders of the federal idea following the collapse of the communist regimes. In realization of this goal, we will examine how the structure and process of political socialization, political economy, and political institutionalization interacted with the federal concept and contributed to this result.

Political Socialization

One of the most pervasive characteristics of communist rule was its simultaneous fetish in creating enormously complex, multilevel political institutions that were then later ignored or misused. In all three socialist federations, the federal-level structures fell into this category of highly complex but essentially irrelevant organizations, and party organizations and leaders, not constitutionally sanctioned political institutions, held the loci of real decision making.

In the grand scheme of things, committed Communists believed in socialism first, internationalism second, and state building third. Communists rarely identified themselves as federalists, but they did characterize themselves and their movement as anti-imperialist. This meant that Communist support for federalism was essentially passive and was viewed as a pragmatic alternative to imperialism. Consequently, when constructing a federal institution, Communist officials tended to devise it as an expression of socialist internationalism. Federal institutions existed primarily, therefore, as a mechanism to illustrate socialist unity and brotherhood. Where such unity did not exist, Communist authorities choreographed a virtual international brotherhood through the federal institutions. Socialist federalism represented an acknowledgment that the brotherhood of nations had not yet been perfected. National-based representation in the federal institutions was a political convenience to the "temporary" political realities and became an additional means to exercise party unity and control. Under socialism, federalism was a bureaucratic-administrative tool, not a political idea, and it had no theoretical or legal link to the protection of individual and minority group rights that served as the foundation for federal systems in the West. Furthermore, in the socialist federation, political power flowed from party institutions to federal structures, which meant that the communication-authority flow among federal institutional levels had little significance for policy and that intergovernmental relations among federal levels were irrelevant.

Prior to the first multiparty elections, republic-level governmental leaders echoed the party platform, and the role of ethnic or republic representatives/delegates at the national level was to enthusiastically endorse and support the party program. Within federal institutions, expressions of republic or ethnic positions were severely repressed, and federal bodies took pride in being labeled simultaneously as anti-Czech and anti-Slovak, anti-Serb and anti-Croat, anti-Russian and anti-Armenian. In short, unanimity, not diversity, was the celebrated value; and each and every nonparty ethnic manifestation was repressed. The Communist embrace of class consciousness and rejection of ethnic diversity clashed fundamentally with their support for ethnofederal institutions within the republics, and this contradiction, which the communist dogmatists practiced regarding national diversity, had significant impacts following the collapse of their regimes. Because Communism was inherently internationalist and intolerant towards national expressions as an article of dogma, Communists could not initially seek common cause with the nationalists. Simultaneously, the existence of a wide array of ethnic-based institutions meant that there were built-in institutional avenues for secession once communist party discipline and power collapsed. When multiparty elections occurred in the socialist federations, nationalist groups led the opposition to the Communists at the ethnic/national level, organized to isolate the Communists as enemies of the nation or ethnic group, and labeled the Communists and federal institutions as enemies of national expression. Some Communists at the ethnic level such as Serbia's Milosevic and Slovakia's Meciar also reinvented themselves, preempted the nationalist program, and divorced themselves from the federal Communist party. Thus, following their victory at the elections, the numerous newly empowered nationalists at the federal level had to switch the locus of politics from the federal level to the national republic in order to achieve real political power. Among these incredibly diverse political groups, there was only one point of agreement; namely, the destruction of the federation.[12]

The Communist socialization experience had other implications for federalism as well. From the public's perspective during the transition period, the long-term subordination of federal institutions to party control meant that a break with Communism also meant a break with federalism. Federal institutions were perceived as the Trojan Horse through which the Communists could plot and conspire to return to power.[13] Since continuation of the Communist structure was non-negotiable, choices then included full dissolution of the federal system, radical restructuring and renegotiation of the federal compact, or a return to unitarism and imposition of a colonial type rule on the junior members of the federation. Viewed from this perspective, it is not surprising that with the exception of rump Yugoslavia and its occupation of Kosovo, political leaders in all three federations chose secession as the easiest and least risky alternative. In summary, federalism was not particularly important to the Communist movement and Communist dogma. Nevertheless, Communist political socialization, in its quest for total control of the political environment, linked federalism and Communism so closely together that anti-Communists in the transition period viewed maintenance of the federal system as a major impediment to the liberation from Communist control.

Political Economy

A second major factor in the wholesale abandonment of federalism throughout the former Communist world was its extremely close identification with the planned economy and the increasingly intrusive and ineffective redistributive policies of national economic development.[14] While many in the West argued for keeping the rational economic benefits of the larger market and interdependent productive capacities in existing federations, on-site reformers perceived that the essential problem for growth and productivity was the current inflexible, inefficient, and exploitative market and highly irrational pattern of economic interdependencies. Abandoning market access and economic ties offered risks, but also provided an opportunity to eradicate the suffocating tentacles of economic control, which the communist authorities had monopolized.[15] To illustrate the point, the Baltic republics endeavored to integrate themselves more closely in the economies of the Nordic countries both as a way of integrating into the much richer European market, and as a way of achieving economic independence from Russia. The Czechs and Slovenes argued that independence from their respective federations would facilitate entry into the European Union which they felt was blocked by their Slovak and Serb federal partners. Even many Russians argued that the breakup of the socialist network of economic linkages freed them from continued subsidization of the Asian republics.

Since the early 1980s, the socialist economies had been in an era of stagnation or decline. Within the socialist federations, this economic atrophy was often viewed through narrow, regionally based lenses so that each group within the federation perceived, often irrationally, that other members of the federation suffered less or benefited from their exploitation and misery. An excellent illustration is socialist Yugoslavia, in which it was a common perception that every republic suffered at the hands of every other republic. In this case, Slovenes perceived that their investment capital, which had been involuntarily extracted from them, had been wasted by the Bosnian, Macedonian, and Kosovan recipients. Bosnians and Macedonians conversely perceived that the Slovenes were exploiting their natural resources or agricultural products without returning a fair rate of return. Croatians perceived that federal (i.e., Serb) authorities were appropriating their tourism hard currency earnings to prop up inefficient and corrupt Belgrade firms. Bosnians resented Croats who had dominated their energy resources. Finally, even the Serbs, in the highly inflammatory draft memorandum by the Serbian Academy of Sciences, asserted their grievances of economic exploitation by Croats, Bosnians, Slovenes, and others.

Although all the socialist economies suffered in the 1980s, the scapegoat for the economic reversals differed markedly between the unitary and federal socialist states. Unitary states such as Romania, Hungary, and Poland identified their Party bureaucrats as the primary villains and the collapse of the Communist regime meant an opportunity to reverse the tide. In Yugoslavia, Czechoslovakia, and the Soviet Union, however, the villains were the party functionaries from other republics who allegedly siphoned off scarce resources to their republics at the expense of the others. The typical perception of an Estonian, for example, was that while Estonia had electrical brownouts, Muscovites reveled in electricity and warmth. Thus, a change in leaders at the top would not be sufficient to reverse the exploitative relationship—there had to be a change in the system. Both the communists and the federal system had to go.[16]

Political Institutionalization

Any discussion of political institutionalization in communist regimes must begin from the vantage point that institutions exist for political control, not political expression or interest articulation. As discussed by Dorff, the Communist federations were the product of social engineering, not a reflection of a true federal process.[17] Federal institutions did not behave as federal consultative bodies, rather they were mechanisms for party control. As institutions, the federal structures in Czechoslovakia, the Soviet Union, and Yugoslavia served to deprive ethnic groups of the ability to mobilize, and they tended to divide rather than unite a named ethnic group. Political institutions in the federal hierarchy did not communicate up the hierarchy and did not leave a legacy for compromise and agreement. Furthermore, under the guise of anticareerism, membership within legislative bodies at all levels changed repeatedly so that it became very rare for members of the political institutions to garner enough political experience or develop federal contacts that would facilitate understanding and empathy for federal problems.[18]

Institutionally, since federal structures were designed to express support for the party program, they never developed mechanisms for conflict resolution.[19] Thus, when multiparty elections introduced political conflict and debate within the federation, there were no precedents, no procedures, and no structures to facilitate conflict resolution. Further, many of the new non-Communist parliamentary deputies emerged from ethnic-based mass movement organizations and shared the same myopic and polarized view of politics as the communists. For these delegates, debate was perceived as a battle between good and evil or as a struggle for national survival. Within the socialist federations following multiparty elections, the federal parliamentary bodies quickly became paralyzed and incapable of action. The lack of a tradition of compromise and political debate was one dimension of the problem. The insecurity that ethnic groups felt about being swallowed up in an asymmetric federation was a second dimension of the problem. The legacy of distrust towards other nations was a third dimension of the problem, while different languages, cultures, histories and political platforms contributed to a fourth dimension of the problem.[20] Under the best of circumstances, the newly emerging political institutions from the socialist experience had serious difficulties. Under federal systems, the difficulties were compounded and became unmanageable.

Conclusion

In each of the three socialist federations there was, initially, little support for secession, and the dissolutions appeared to have been engineered almost by accident by the political elite seeking a complete break with the past and searching for an easy solution to their problems. Appearances, however, can be deceptive. While there may have been little support for secession, there was almost no deep support for continuance of the federal system. In addition, following the multiparty elections, the demands of the various federal constituencies for autonomy and the redress of grievances could not be accommodated by the inexperienced and newly evolving democratic institutions.[21]

The socialist federations suffered from an entire series of crippling weaknesses. In particular, they had never been a mass-directed political arrangement. They never created a Soviet, Yugoslav, or Czechoslovak citizen base, and they never engendered much public enthusiasm and identity separate from the Communist party. Following the multiparty elections, both the public and elite had assumed that the centralized Communist-dominated federations would give rise to some form of confederation, and it was a given that the federal structures could not survive without fundamental change. In the final days, the Slovenes attempted to promote a confederal Yugoslavia. In the Soviet Union, Gorbachev had attempted to implement a new union treaty, and Havel in Czechoslovakia attempted to broker a new confederal Czech-Slovak confederation. None of these attempts offered many positive inducements, and none ever came close to fruition.

The fact that federalism was abandoned throughout the post-Communist period is not a coincidence. The socialist federations' asymmetric structures exacerbated conflict among the existing federal units; its ethnic foundation heightened differentiation and political conflict; and the legacy of democratic centralism alienated reforms and ethnic elites from cooperating within the system. In addition, the socialist federations had, at best, weak emotional links to the population; did not engender flexibility for democratic change; and were comparatively inefficient in resolving basic political conflicts. Finally, in the post-Communist world, the federal systems did not offer marked efficiency in governance nor much protection from outside threats. For many, federalism served more as an impediment to economic growth and entry into Europe. For Czechs and Slovaks, the absorption of

Germany in the new Europe nullified the original rationale for the construction of the Czechoslovakian state. In Yugoslavia, the end of the cold war eliminated any threat to national survival. In the USSR, the evident cost of holding on to the empire became so high that Russia preferred to go it alone. With all three socialist federations, the federal-level institutions played no positive role in the transformation, and did not provide a significant portion of the new democratic leadership. In retrospect it should not be a surprise that federalism did not survive the collapse of Communist rule. Indeed, we should have been surprised if it did.

Notes

1. One member of the federation holds a disproportionate amount of power, resources and/or population within the federation.
2. V. Vujacic, "Institutional Origins of Contemporary Serbian Nationalism," *East European Constitutional Review 5*, no. 4 (1996): 51–61.
3. J. Seroka, "The Dissolution of Federalism in East and Central Europe," in *Evaluating Federal Systems*, ed., B. de Villiers (Dordrecht, 1994), 208–224.
4. A. Stanger, "Czechoslovakia's Dissolution as an Unintended Consequence of the Velvet Constitutional Revolution," *East European Constitutional Review 5*, no. 4 (1996): 40–46.
5. R. Lukic and A. Lynch, *Europe from the Balkans to the Urals: The Disintegration of Yugoslavia and the Soviet Union* (Oxford, 1996).
6. A. Lijphart, *The Politics of Accommodation: Pluralism and Democracy in the Netherlands* (Berkeley, 1976).
7. T. Snyder and M. Vachundova, "Are Transitions Transitory? Two Types of Political Change in Eastern Europe Since 1989," *East European Politics and Societies 11*, no. 1 (1997): 1–35.
8. J. Elster, "Consenting Adults or the Sorcerer's Apprentice?" *East European Constitutional Review 4*, no. 1 (1995): 36–41.
9. The essence of democratic centralism was that once party policy was agreed upon by the relevant party decision makers, there could be no open or covert opposition to the policy. Thus, federal republic leaders were obligated to support policy that could be opposed to the vital interests of their interest group/republic.
10. M.F. Goldman, *Revolution and Change in Central and Eastern Europe: Political, Economic, and Social Challenges* (Armonk, 1996).
11. P.G. Roeder, "Soviet Federalism and Ethnic Mobilization," *World Politics 43*, no. 2 (1991): 196–232.
12. A. Innes, "The Breakup of Czechoslovakia: The Impact of Party Development on the Separation of the State," *East European Politics and Societies 11*, no. 3 (1997): 393–435.

13. The problem continues today in the Russian Federation. See I. Liubimtsev, "Russian Federalism: Problems and Solutions," *Problems of Economic Transition* 38, no. 12 (1996): 73–89.

14. R. Sharlet, "The Prospects for Federalism in Russian Constitutional Politics," *Publius: The Journal of Federalism* 24, no. 2 (1994): 115–127.

15. Goldman, *Revolution and Change in Central and Eastern Europe.*

16. K. Verdery, "Nationalism and National Sentiment in the Post-socialist Romania," *Slavic Review* 52, no. 2 (1993): 179–204.

17. R.H. Dorff, "Federalism in Eastern Europe: Part of the Solution of Part of the Problem?" *Publius: The Journal of Federalism* 24, no. 2 (1994): 99–114.

18. J. Seroka, "Jugoslovenski federalizam danas: nuznost stvaranja i jacanja medurepublickih komunikacija," in *Federacija i Federalizam*, ed. J. Dordevic and M. Jovicic (Nis, 1987), 321–327.

19. A. Bebler, "Yugoslavia's Variety of Communist Federalism and Her Demise," *Communist and Post-Communist Studies* 26, no. 1 (1993): 72–86.

20. P. Pithart, "The Division of Czechoslovakia: A Preliminary Balance Sheet for the End of a Respectable Country," *Canadian Slavonic Papers* 38, nos. 3–4 (1995): 321–338.

21. A good example is the Russian Federation today. See G.M. Easter, "Redefining Centre-Regional Relations in the Russian Federation: Sverdlovsk Oblast," *Europe-Asia Studies* 49, no. 4 (1997): 617–635.

Chapter 6

FABRICATING FEDERALISM IN "DAYTON BOSNIA"

Recent Political Development and Future Options

❧

Lenard J. Cohen

Our job is to turn a province into a country—sometimes whether the people like it or not. Forget about [an] exit strategy. There is no exit strategy. We're not walking away from this. This place is healing not dying. But we are the life support system.

Jacques Klein, Deputy High Representative
(of the International Community in Bosnia), August 1998

Bosnia is what we [in the country] agree it is. That part is a bit difficult now because we have the High Representative, but some day we will be left on our own, and we will then talk about that.

Milorad Dodik, Serb Republic Prime Minister, August 1998

Notes for this section begin on page 140.

Power-Sharing and Federalism in Bosnian Political Culture:
The Pre-Dayton Context

Even in a region of Europe renowned for its diverse pattern of subcultural identities, Bosnia-Herzegovina has been notable for its unique pattern of kaleidoscopically intermingled and religiously-based ethnic communities. Indeed, historically, Bosnia-Herzegovina's three major ethnoconfessional groups—the Eastern Orthodox Serbs, the Catholic Croats, and the Islamic Bosniaks (Bosnjaci or Muslims)—have exhibited an impressive, though hardly spotless, record of being able to blend their respective separate identities with a pancultural or overarching regional notion of "Bosnianness." Thus, although interethnic relations among the three groups has always been delicate, and sometimes even violent, the overwhelming majority of citizens in Bosnia-Herzegovina historically saw themselves as not only Serb, Croat, or Muslim, but also as Bosnian.

At the same time, however, the notion of political power-sharing among different territorial units and levels of political authority in federal-like fashion has not been part of the Bosnian political legacy. The successive regimes that have ruled Bosnia over the past millennium—medieval, Ottoman, Austro-Hungarian, Royalist Yugoslav, Fascist Croatian, and communist (Titoist)—all governed Bosnia's ethnic communities in a substantially unitary or centralized manner, though at times leaving considerable scope for religious and cultural autonomy by the region's different ethnoconfessional groups. For comparative purposes, most such nonfederal modes of governance in Bosnia-Herzegovina's history (the ethnocide during World War II is a notable exception) correspond to a regime model which may be termed *unitary multiculturalism* (see Figure 6.1).

Granted, for forty-five years within Titoist Yugoslavia, Bosnia-Herzegovina as a whole was a republic within a broader six-republic, two-province, socialist federation. However, for the first two decades of the Titoist period that federation was largely spurious, and even after the Communist system became more regionally pluralistic, one-party governance in each republic remained highly centralized.[1] The main point is that federal institutions and values during this period were not a prominent part of Bosnia-Herzegovina's internal political culture and subcultures. Thus, while plural community coexistence—within a politically centralized framework providing for the nonpolitical autonomy of religious groups, and some multigroup representation in top political structures—was part of Bosnian tradition, federal-type distribution of sovereign authority was historically absent.

Figure 6.1 Interethnic Dynamics and the Distribution of
Sovereign Authority

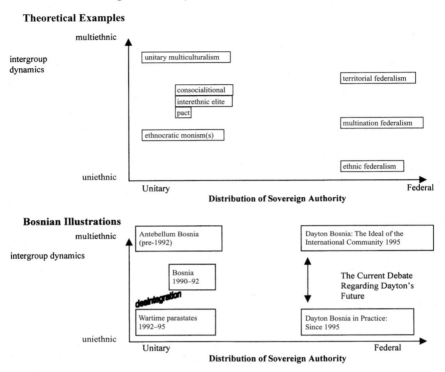

Theoretical Examples

Bosnian Illustrations

When the monopolistic control of the Yugoslav League of Communists finally collapsed at the end of the 1980s, the most vocal and successful political actors who emerged on the still unsettled political landscape were leaders of new parties advancing exclusivist nationalistic ideologies. In Bosnia, for example, most citizens—who were extremely anxious about Yugoslavia's impending collapse, and also the growing nationalism exhibited by many of their ethnic neighbors—cast their votes for one of the three strongly nationalistic party organizations (the Serbian Democratic Party/SDS, the Croatian Democratic Alliance/HDZ, and the (Muslim) Party of Democratic Action/SDA).[2] However, owing to the ethnically intermingled pattern of Bosnia's population, such ethnically based party pluralization was not accompanied by the internal territorial federalization of the republic (that still remained within the Yugoslav federation). Rather an ad hoc and unstable consociational-like system of power-sharing and patronage distribution developed among the principal nationalist party elites.

During this first short-lived phase of Bosnian post-Communist political history (December 1990 to April 1992), tensions among the three main ethnic groups intensified as the republic was buffeted by external regional and international influences relating to the violent disintegration of socialist Yugoslavia, and was destabilized by the internal ethnopolitical "homogenization" and mobilization of each ethnic community. Fighting among military forces associated with each of the three major ethnic communities broke out soon after the leaders of the republic's Muslim and Croat communities decided to declare Bosnia-Herzegovina as an independent state. Violent initiatives by Bosnian Serb forces were supported and closely directed by the Milosevic regime in Belgrade, while the Bosnian Croats (initially allied to the Muslims) received the military backing of the Tudjman regime in Croatia. Meanwhile, Bosnian Muslim leaders turned to their friends in the Islamic world for moral and economic assistance. In the savage warfare and forced relocation of the civilian population that followed—the notorious pattern of so-called "ethnic cleansing" from which citizens of all groups suffered to varying extents—large tracts of Bosnia-Herzegovina, which had been demographically multiethnic, became essentially homogeneous. Indeed during the war, Bosnia-Herzegovina became de facto partitioned into three ethnocratic and politically monolithic parastates.

Paradoxically, it was this tragic pattern of areal and demographic partition that first provoked serious discussion about the utility of federalism as a viable framework for peacemaking, and a possible model for the future Bosnian state. Thus, prior to the war in Bosnia, federalism was viewed as inappropriate to Bosnia's configuration of ethnically interwoven or mixed communities, and also its political traditions (unless such a new political arrangement would be preceded by politically unpalatable and very costly measures for peaceful population transfer). But once ethnic cleansing had occurred—motivated by plans for partition, not federalization—it seemed more realistic to some observers that a federal arrangement might prove helpful in securing a peace settlement.[3]

While schemes for reconfiguring Bosnia-Herzegovina along loose federal or confederal lines were most acceptable to Bosnian Serb and Bosnian Croat leaders—whose respective foreign patrons (Slobodan Milosevic and Franjo Tudjman) had already discussed Bosnia's eventual partition—such ideas were anathema to the Bosnian Muslims. This latter group had not only borne the brunt of ethnic cleansing, but their leaders also wished to provide survivors with the right to return to their former homes. Bosnian Muslim policy aimed at reestablishing the intermingled multicultural fabric of the country. Any form of territorial segmentation along ethnic lines was viewed by the Muslims as virtual capitulation to the strategy of partition.[4]

For example, Bosnia's president, the conservative Muslim leader, Alija Izetbegovic, strongly advocated a unified and fundamentally centralized state. In such a state, which would ostensibly be organized on a civic basis, Muslims would play a salient political role commensurate with their proportional status as the largest group in prewar Bosnia (44 percent in the 1991 census). Izetbegovic was keenly aware that unless Bosnia had a strong central government, it would be difficult for the state to resist the strong traditional irredentist pressures from Croatia and Serbia-Montenegro. Moreover, he strenuously opposed any international community plans for recognizing aspirations by the Serbs and Croats of Bosnia to maintain and expand the sovereignty of the parastate formations they had erected before and during the war—the so-called Republika Srpska for the Serbs, and Herceg-Bosna for the Croats. For the Bosnian Serbs, who by early 1993 controlled roughly 70 percent of Bosnia-Herzegovina's territory, any idea of establishing a centralized state, or even federal-like power-sharing with the Muslims, was out of the question. Indeed, interethnic coexistence was no longer an acceptable option for the ultranationalists leading the Bosnian Serbs. Meanwhile by early 1994, the Croats, who had earlier supported the idea of an independent Bosnia, and had initially been allied with the Muslims against the Serbs, had decided to pursue their separate territorial aspirations through a partitioned state. The intense fighting during 1993 between the formerly allied Croats and Muslims (including ethnic cleansing and other atrocities), would leave a bitter legacy of distrust and mutual fear of domination that would severely complicate future efforts at peaceful coexistence between those two groups. Thus, by early 1994, when the United States became more actively involved in efforts to find a peace settlement in Bosnia, major conceptual, political, and psychological divisions regarding the value and character of intergroup power-sharing had already become deeply entrenched among Bosnia-Herzegovina's principal ethnopolitical antagonists.

Federalizing Muslim-Croat Relations

In early 1994, in a major breakthrough designed to end the war in Bosnia, the United States orchestrated an agreement between the Bosnian Muslims and Bosnian Croats to establish a "Federation" on the territory controlled by those two groups. Although there was little love lost between the two new federal partners, their common vulnerabilities as a result of Serb military and territorial gains, provided an impetus for the new arrangement. Considering the context of the Bosnian war, the importance of the agreement was not in its structural details, which would remain substantially unimplemented for the next several years, but the fact that it ended Muslim-Croat fighting and reunited the two groups in the military struggle against the Bosnian Serbs.[5]

For purposes of the present discussion regarding federal dynamics and political development in Bosnia, a number of aspects concerning the origins and features of the Muslim-Croat federal agreement are worth noting. For example, the agreement was substantially designed by American lawyers, not the major actors from Bosnia. Thus, the Bosnian Muslims and Bosnian Croats viewed their new federal alliance as a necessary expedient, not a constitutional model in which they had a major stake.[6] Washington hoped that the new federation would facilitate an all-Bosnian resolution to the war; a framework that could eventually be broadened to include territory under Serbian control (albeit, after the Serbs would voluntarily or involuntarily withdraw from territory they had seized during the war). For their part, Muslim political leaders, such as President Izetbegovic, who had become very suspicious about Croatian motives in Bosnia-Herzegovina, saw the Federation as having several advantages: a major first step in reversing the tide of Serbian success, returning Muslim refugees and displaced persons to their homes, and reintegrating Bosnia-Herzegovina as a unified, centralized, and multiethnic state. For President Tudjman of Croatia and his Bosnian Croat clients, however, the Federation was regarded as a very abstract design necessary to advance Croat goals (e.g., to obtain U.S. support for help in dealing with the Serb rebellion in Croatia, and ending Muslim military pressure on the Bosnian Croat community) and, at most, a loose decentralized framework in which Croats would be accorded equal status with their more numerous Muslim neighbors. President Tudjman, who had long believed that Bosnia belonged squarely within Croatia's sphere of influence, was also pleased that the Muslims had agreed to sign a parallel "preliminary" agreement for an eventual "confederation" between the new Muslim-Croat Federation and the Republic of Croatia.

The different perceptions of what the new Federation implied essentially continued the ongoing conceptual debate about how Bosnia should be governed, or indeed whether it should exist at all as an independent state. In terms of the future of the new Federation, such divisions would plague Muslim-Croat relations in Bosnia throughout the second half of the 1990s. Moreover, the fact that the new federal framework, at least on paper, created a biethnic union that was totally separate from the Bosnian Serb zone of control (the Republika Srpska parastate), did not provide an auspicious beginning for the future of any conceivable pan-Bosnian federal framework.

Indeed, the Bosnian Serbs correctly perceived that the Muslim-Croat Federation was designed primarily to reverse Serb military and territorial gains. Equally significant, though Bosnian Serbs constituted approximately 17 percent of the Federation's population (Muslims were roughly 52 percent, Croats 24 percent, and other minorities 7 percent) the political unit's constitution only named Muslims and Croats as constituent nations. A catch-all category, "others," was used to refer to Serbs and other ethnic communities in the Federation.[7] Future efforts to encourage Bosnian Serb cooperation with the Federation would, not surprisingly, prove to be just as difficult as convincing the Muslim and Croat federal partners to cooperate with one another.

Designing the Dayton Accord: A Medley of Compromises

The war in Bosnia would continue for another year and a half following the creation of the Muslim-Croat Federation before any serious progress would be made in the realm of institution-building and political development. Driven in large part by the imminent presidential election in the United States, and also by public and international outrage with the ongoing bloodletting in the Balkans, Washington accelerated efforts to deal with the Bosnian crisis. Mandated by President Clinton to bring about an end to the war, U.S. Undersecretary of State, Richard Holbrooke, would skillfully employ a formidable array of diplomatic and military techniques to force the sides in Bosnia to reach a peace agreement. The story of Holbrooke's efforts in this regard is now relatively well-known. Indeed, he has provided his own fascinating personal account of the coercive diplomacy that eventually produced a cease-fire in Bosnia, and the subsequent peace settlement reached in Dayton, Ohio.[8] Briefly, the new constitution designed at Dayton in November 1995 (and which came into force on 14 December 1995), provides that Bosnia and Herzegovina would be a unified state consisting of two entities—the Federation of Bosniaks and Croats (made up of ten cantons), and the Republika Srpska—and three "constituent peoples" (Muslims or "Bosniaks," Croats, and Serbs). Bosnia and Herzegovina, as conceptualized by the negotiators at Dayton, is a unified and sovereign state with subcentral units (entities, cantons, and municipalities), but the Dayton-inspired state model is not explicitly a federation, or a "union," or a confederation.

In his recent retrospective on Dayton, Holbrooke admits that in 1995 the distinction between the two levels of government—the central government and the entities—"was still confusing, even to my people at Dayton." Regional entities were included as a second governmental tier for Bosnia, but Holbrooke emphasizes that this was "minus any claims to sovereignty"[9] by that level of the political structure. Significantly for the future implementation of the Dayton accord, the perspective of Holbrooke and his team of constitution-makers regarding the entities was completely at odds with what the Bosnian Serbs and Bosnian Croats had been led to believe in the weeks of diplomatic preparation leading up to Dayton. For example, in talks at Ankara on Labor Day 1995, Holbrooke persuaded President Izetbegovic that a draft agreement for the Peace Conference must include the reference to "Republika Srpska" because Serbia's president, Slobodan Milosevic, had insisted that such a concession be offered to the Bosnian Serb side. After all, one of Holbrooke's colleagues told Izetbegovic, in the United States "some states including Texas and Massachusetts, call themselves 'republics' or 'commonwealths.' It doesn't matter as long as they acknowledge that they are part of one country." And, Holbrooke added in order to convince Izetbegovic on this matter: "it is the best we can do with Milosevic at this time."[10] Pressured to go along, Izetbegovic grudgingly accepted the designation "Republika Srpska."

But for the Bosnian Serbs, the inclusion of their political and military creation, the Republika Srpska (RS), as one of the cosignatories to the agreements leading up to Dayton (e.g., the Geneva Agreement on basic constitutional principles for Bosnia on 8 September 1995, and the New York Agreement "Further Agreed Basic Principles" on 26 September 1995), and also to the Dayton constitutional framework itself, was tantamount to full recognition of their entity as a sovereign state, or at the least, an associated state unit in what they perceived to be a new bistate "union." Indeed in retrospect, Holbrooke concedes that the use of the name "Republika Srpska" by his negotiating team was "more of a concession than we realized."[11] Similarly, president Tudjman and the Bosnian Croat leaders saw the federation entity—in which Croats were one of the two constituent peoples, and held a constitutionally predominant position in three cantons out of ten, and which, under the 1994 Washington Agreement, was slated for eventual confederal linkage to Croatia—as being endowed with sufficient sovereignty to allow ethnic Croats to resist any encroachment by the central state authorities constituted at Dayton. Indeed because the Croat side showed no intention of quickly dismantling their parastate of Herceg-Bosna, as mandated by Dayton, they believed that they possessed several buffers (their parastate, the cantons, and the federation itself), to maintain Croat autonomy from central, that is, predominantly Muslim, control.

Thus, confusion over what was being agreed to at Dayton—a single state, two entity-states, or perhaps even three ethnic states—was benignly ignored by Holbrooke and his team when they fashioned Bosnia's future governmental structure. Briefly, at Dayton, and in the discussions leading up to the peace conference, the United States assured the Muslim side that Bosnia would be reintegrated as a cohesive and unified state (along the lines of the prewar republic). However, the compromises necessary to get the Serb and Croat sides on board resulted in a bientity state arrangement (which on the Federation side was multicantonal in order to divide control between Muslims and Croats) that left Bosnia considerably decentralized. Two of the country's constituent peoples (Serbs and Croats) felt strongly that they enjoyed substantial "sovereignty" over the territory they controlled. This decentralized arrangement constitutionalized at Dayton essentially reflected the situation that had developed during the war. However, what was lacking was a political culture of power-sharing between the two entities and three constituent "peoples" of the new country, or even between the two ethnic groups that shared control of the Federation. De jure, Dayton Bosnia did include some features which might be construed as federal-like. For example, a new two chamber central legislature included a House of People for entity and ethnic representation (the Federation entity's five Muslim and five Croat delegates to that chamber would be selected from ten cantonal assemblies; the Republika Srpska's five Serb delegates by that entity's National Assembly). Other major institutions, such as the three-member presidency and the constitutional court also incorporated such ethnic/entity representative features. Constitutional scholars described the country's political architecture as a contradictory mix of institutions, including facets that resembled some federations, but, within the Bosnian context did not constitute federalism.[12] For international officials, the "spirit" of Dayton mandated a "unified," "pluralistic," state and society with constitutional provisions for ethnic and territorial power-sharing. But de facto the country was deeply segmented along ethnic lines, had no federal political culture, and there was no commitment to countrywide federal practices among the signatories to the peace agreement.

Contending Mindsets and Lost Momentum: 1995-1997

Sharply different perceptions on the part of Bosnia's three dominant national party elites and their followers regarding what kind of state had been established under the Dayton Accord would prove highly detrimental to the implementation of the agreement during the initial period of Bosnia's postwar development. As expected, for the Muslim political elite, the Republic of Bosnia and Herzegovina conceived at Dayton envisaged the formation of a relatively strong centralized state—an integrated Bosnia and Herzegovina—in which the citizen's of all ethnic groups would share a common "Bosnian consciousness." From that perspective, the country's two-entity configuration was simply a Dayton-inspired political expedient to end the war. For the majority of Muslims, any effort to treat the entities as independent state units, or to strengthen the power of those units at the expense of the central government's powers, was considered unconstitutional.

In sharp contrast, for most of the Bosnian Serb elite and citizenry, the Republic of Bosnia-Herzegovina was an illegitimate and artificial creation. The Bosnian Serb leadership maintained that Republika Srpska already enjoyed a kind of semi-independent status (with new interentity boundary lines considered tantamount to state borders), or at least a prestate transitional arrangement pending Republika Srpska's eventual secession from Bosnia, and its unification with Serbia-Montenegro (in the rump Yugoslavia). The goal of Serb leaders was to preserve and expand entity "sovereignty." In their view, the Muslims and their supporters in the international community, were insidiously revising Dayton and attempting to expand the power of the country's central authorities.[13]

Meanwhile, the Bosnian Croats, who were constitutionally linked to the Muslims through the Federation entity, generally took a more flexible position than the Serbs regarding the question of central versus entity powers, and also interentity cooperation. Nevertheless, the Croats staunchly opposed the idea of "unitarism," that is, efforts by the Muslim side to assert political domination through Bosnia's central institutions. Most of Bosnia's territory with a predominantly Croat population was already under the control of the Bosnian Croats, or more accurately their sponsors in the Zagreb regime. Thus, the Croat strategy of statebuilding in Bosnia and Herzegovina was to largely ignore the central government in Sarajevo, and to emphasize their rights and claims to equal representation in the Muslim-Croat Federation. The Croats also favored an expansion of the cantonal powers within the Federation (three of the ten cantons were exclusively under Croat control, while in two, Croats and Muslims had roughly parity power). Bosnia's Croat leaders particularly objected to what they perceived as the Muslims' dual basis for power, that is, through central institutions, and their strong position in the federation. Prepared to postpone any final judgment concerning the question of whether Bosnia would survive as a viable state composed of three ethnic groups, or would eventually be partitioned, the Croats were willing to settle for the side-by-side coexistence of three relatively homogeneous ethnic enclaves. Interestingly, surveys conducted by the United States Information

Agency (USIA) in Bosnia during July 1997, revealed that 83 percent of the
Muslim respondents believed that all three major nationalities could live
peacefully together, but that 81 percent of the Croats and 95 percent of the
Serbs interviewed thought that partition of the country was inevitable.[14]

Opportunity Knocks: The Intra-Serb Conflict and Embryonic Cohesion

The cohesion of Bosnia and Herzegovina remained so tenuous during the
fall 1996 American presidential election campaign that the Clinton administration downplayed the situation in Bosnia, except to mention that the
country was at peace and elections had "been held." By early 1997, the dangers of such benign drift were becoming increasingly apparent. At Sintra,
Portugal in May 1997, the Peace Implementation Council's Steering Committee, which guided Dayton's civilian side, took some limited steps to rein-
vigorate the badly stalled efforts in Bosnia. For example, specific deadlines
were set, and pressure was applied for fulfillment of a number of Dayton's
civilian goals (appointment of new ambassadors, delivery of indicted war
criminals, passage of citizenship laws, reform of property laws, police
restructuring measures, etc.). Measures were to be taken if the leaders of
Bosnia's three ethnic groups failed to reach scheduled agreement on these
issues. A new policy of "conditionality" was adopted, whereby those political forces in Bosnia that resisted full compliance with Dayton were to be
denied external assistance.

Both during and after the conclusion of the war in Bosnia, the Bosnian
Serb political leadership had been the most obstreperous party in negotiations with the international community. In the summer of 1996, Dayton's
chief architect, Richard Holbrooke, had brokered a deal providing that the
president of Republika Srpska, Dr. Radovan Karadzic, who was under
indictment by the war crimes tribunal, would retire from political life. But,
to the frustration of his designated successor, Serbian Democratic Party
(SDS) leader, Biljana Plavsic, and the international community, Karadzic
continued to direct the course of Republika Srpska development from the
shadows.[15] But Plavsic set the stage for a major turnabout in the course of
Bosnian Serb political life, and in a broader sense, the prospects for Dayton's
success. Despite fierce pressure and threats from hard-liners loyal to the
Karadzic faction, many SDS activists declared their allegiance to Plavsic's
emerging program of anticorruption and "pragmatic nationalism." Plavsic
had gambled and won. Having previously looked in vain for a cooperative
Bosnian Serb leader, the international community rushed to embrace her

professed pragmatism and new pluralist impulses. Interestingly, both when negotiating and trying to implement the Dayton accord, the international community had relied primarily on Serbian President Slobodan Milosevic in Belgrade to put pressure on the Bosnian Serbs. However, during the late fall of 1996 and the first part of 1997, Milosevic had been preoccupied with a serious domestic political crisis. With confusion in Serbia, Plavsic's defection from the Pale Serb clique seemed to offer Washington a fresh point of leverage to advance the Dayton model of a unified Bosnia. However, the obstacles to interethnic and interentity cooperation remained formidable. During August 1997, the Clinton administration sent top Dayton architect Richard Holbrooke back to Bosnia, together with Ambassador Robert Gelbard (the Assistant Secretary of State for the implementation of the Dayton accords). The achievements of their mission were rather modest, and revealed Bosnia's deep internal divisions. For example, the members of Bosnia's presidency were finally pressed into reaching an agreement for the appointment of ambassadors from their country. Each of the country's ethnic groups would be accorded an equal number of positions in the diplomatic corps, with the appointment of each ethnic contingent of ambassadors made by the presidency member from the corresponding ethnic community. Agreement on telephone lines between the entities was also finalized, including provision of a common telephone code for Bosnia (with three subcodes for the Republika Srpska, Sarajevo, and the rest of the Federation). Leaving Bosnia, special envoy Holbrooke naturally accentuated the positive aspect of his mission— "We picked up some steam, and we closed the gap"[16]—but he was very aware of the deep divisions remaining in the country, and the many unfulfilled aspects of his Dayton agreement.[17]

Problems in the Fragile Federation

For international officials entrusted with Dayton's implementation, the power struggle within the Bosnian Serb leadership offered an excellent opportunity to establish closer links between Bosnia's two hostile entities. But building such ties was constrained by the very chilly relations between the Muslims and Croats within the Federation entity. That negative climate derived mainly from Croatian President Tudjman's decidedly anti-Muslim sentiments and his longstanding belief that Bosnia and Herzegovina would eventually prove unworkable as a unified state. Tudjman's preference for partitioning Bosnia accounted for Zagreb's lukewarm support for the Dayton project. Meanwhile, Bosnia-Herzegovina's president, Alija Izetbegovic, and the more radical Islamic members of the Bosnian Muslim political and security establishment were anxious to advance their own political interests through the Dayton process, and highly skeptical about the political intentions of their Croatian allies in the Federation. After all, the Muslims remained the largest ethnic group in Bosnia, had suffered greatly in the recent war, and were desperately trying to assert their nationhood within Bosnia's fragmented political architecture.

In attempting to reduce Muslim-Croat enmity, Washington focused on two contentious areas of Muslim-Croat interaction: the attempt to forge a new military structure for the Federation (from forces of the Croat Defense Council and the predominantly Muslim Army of Bosnia-Herzegovina), and relations between Croats and Muslims in Mostar. The creation of an integrated military structure in the Federation was closely linked to the Dayton goal of achieving an overall military balance in Bosnia. That plan called for both a program of regional arms control,[18] and a military buildup of unified Muslim-Croat forces under the U.S. Train and Equip program. During 1996, the United States had successfully pressured President Izetbegovic into removing his close friend and radical Muslim minister of defense, Hasan Cengic, before military hardware earmarked for the Federation was delivered. Thus, though notable progress was made during 1997 in forming a joint Muslim-Croat command structure (including a limit of twenty Muslim generals and ten Croat generals) and also in initiating combined Muslim-Croat schooling for officers at new military schools, the goal of creating a genuinely unified Federation Army remained unfulfilled. The conscripts are still trained in ethnically segregated brigades.[19] The Zagreb regime and its Croat allies in Bosnia were also equally responsible for obstructing the Federation's development as a cohesive political unit. Notwithstanding those problems, some progress was made during 1997 in establishing a joint police force for the Federation. Thus, by the end of the year, joint Croat-Bosniak police units were patrolling in Mostar, and about 5,000 Federation police officers had gone through a one-week "human dignity" course concerning the role of the police officer in a democratic society.[20] It was only in the fall of 1997, after intense U.S. lobbying in Zagreb—including blocking World Bank and IMF loans to Croatia, and threatening to cut off military aid to the country—that Tudjman was finally induced to adopt some measures to improve Bosnian Croat compliance with Dayton.[21] For example, in September, Tudjman ordered Bosnian-Croat leaders to rescind their planned boycott of the OSCE-run municipal elections. Washington's most high profile success in Zagreb occurred in October 1997, when Tudjman allowed ten Bosnian Croats indicted for war crimes to be sent to the Hague for trial.[22]

Croatian authorities explained that they had only agreed to send the indicted individuals to The Hague after assurances that the proceedings against the accused would proceed fairly and quickly. Limited Croatian cooperation was also reflected in the resignation of several hard-line Bosnian Croat politicians in Mostar. But over the next year, the Federation remained bifurcated between areas of Muslim and Croat control, and hard-line Croatian resistance to the international community's interpretation of Dayton's requirements was undiminished.[23]

Emergent Party Pluralism: The Municipal and RS Elections

The electoral recruitment of pluralist and nonnationalist politicians is an important component of the Dayton peace-building project. The elections held in September 1996 were somewhat of a letdown in that endeavor, but substantially more progress was made the following fall. In September 1997, municipal OSCE-managed elections were held in Bosnia's 136 municipalities, nearly 5,000 candidates were elected, representing 79 parties. Though the absence of a free media and free movement across interentity boundary lines seriously undermined the democratic character of the election, the voting was an impressive exercise in electoral logistics, including absentee ballot participation of refugees from around the world, and displaced persons from all over Bosnia. Not surprisingly, given their organizational resources and grip on power since 1990, the three ruling nationalist parties won approximately two-thirds of the council seats throughout the country. Non-nationalistic parties, that is, those that do not exclusively represent the rights of one ethnic group, won only about 6 percent of council seats in Bosnia; about 12 percent in the Muslim-Croat Federation, and 2 percent in the Republika Srpska. Nonethnic parties were only able to capture a majority of the council seats in one municipality (Tuzla, already renowned for its support for ethnic pluralism and civic democracy). Despite the continued political dominance of the old nationalist parties, there were some significant changes that emerged from the election. In the Republika Srpska, where the intra-Serb power struggle had become very intense, the ruling SDS lost considerable ground, particularly in the West Bosnian municipalities supporting Biljana Plavsic. Plavsic (who had only been expelled from the SDS in July, and had formed her own party in August, the Serbian People's Alliance, SNS) was still organizationally unprepared to benefit from voters' dissatisfaction with the pro-Karadzic SDS loyalists. Thus, a good deal of the vote lost by the SDS was picked up by the equally, if not more, nationalistic Serbian Radical Party (SRS), that is, the Bosnian branch of the party, which, in Serbia, is led by the extremist, Vojislav Seselj. Many Bosnian voters regarded the SRS candidates as honest nationalists, as opposed to the discredited Karadzic group headquartered at Pale. However, many other Bosnian Serbs voted for the Serb Radicals simply to thumb their noses at the international community.

Though the ruling or nonruling nationalist parties carried the day in the local elections, parties representing refugee and displaced persons, and urging the right of such uprooted citizens to return to their prewar municipalities, fared quite well. Interestingly, survey data collected only a month and a half before the local elections revealed that a large majority of Bosnian Muslims (81 percent), believed that elections could not really be "free" unless the issues of refugee returns, and the arrest of war criminals, were resolved. On the other hand, less than a majority of Croats expressed the same opinion, and less than 15 percent of Bosnian Serbs worried about the impact of these matters on the electoral process. Unlike international supporters of the Dayton agreement, and most Bosnian Muslims, Bosnian Croats and Serbs saw the political future of their respective ethnic enclaves as substantially unrelated to issues such as reversing the consequences of ethnic cleansing, or establishing individual responsibility for war crimes.[24]

Notwithstanding continued difficulties with the Dayton peace process, the tentative signs of pluralization and minority political mobilization in the September 1997 countrywide municipal elections were impressive. Progress in democratization was also substantial considering the relatively short period the country had been at peace, the overall poor economic situation, and the continuing strength of incumbent nationalist parties. The parliamentary elections held during November 1997 for the Republika Srpska National Assembly went a small step further in delegitimizing the SDS hardliners. The nationalist/patriotic mindset of the political class in the Republika Srpska remained substantial, but the pragmatic and reformist bent of nationalism now had the upper hand, and the Serb entity had become substantially more pluralistic.

Governing a Semi-Protectorate

During the last few months of 1997, international officials in Bosnia appreciably stepped up their offensive to impede forces perceived as "anti-Dayton," and to fortifying the civilian side of the Dayton project. It had been clear for some time that the high representative (HR), entrusted with Dayton's civilian implementation (Carl Bildt until June 1997 and then Carlos Westendorp), had been unable to persuade the divided Bosnian leaders to reach decisions on fundamental issues for state development (e.g., citizenship rights, common currency, common flag and symbols, common license plates, and tariff rules, etc.). In order to expedite the decision-making process in Bosnia's central government institutions, the meeting of the "Peace Implementation Council" held in Bonn on 9 December 1997, endorsed a broadened interpretation of provisions in the Dayton agreement that would allow the HR to utilize a process of "binding arbitration," and to adopt "interim measures" for the implementation of pending decisions. Such authority included removing officials or persons occupying public posts who were not cooperating with Dayton. Strict deadlines were also set for the implementation of various measures, as well as an inventory of major problems that needed to be addressed.[25] HR Westendorp lost no time in implementing his expanded authority and within a week of the Bonn meeting he instituted the first of what were being called "interim arbitral decisions," effectively ordering that a law on citizenship in Bosnia would become effective on 1 January 1998. The procedure, which was subsequently utilized to deal with other matters (for example, on 15 January, when the presidency could not reach agreement on the design of Bosnia's currency, Westendorp said he would make a decision on the matter), envisions that the parliament of Bosnia will eventually pass a specific law on each matter, but that the country's Council of Ministers can legally implement the interim decisions made by the high representative. Under the new Bonn guidelines, the High Representative, if not yet the proconsul of a protectorate, has in essence become the grand arbitrator of Bosnia. HR Westendorp referred to himself as a "friendly arbitrator." "In the future," he observed, "I will put an end to all that endless decision-making ... If the parties do not agree, I will tell them, no problem. I will make the decision for them. And I will ... and if they systematically block Dayton I will ask those who are not cooperating to resign."[26] Near the end of January 1998, Westendorp decided on a common currency for Bosnia—the *Marka*—with separate designs for each entity (this became operational in June 1998). Shortly afterwards, the three members of the Bosnian presidency were finally able to decide among themselves on a common license plate for the country. But when agreement could not be reached on a flag for the country, Westendorp again intervened and decided on the appropriate design. Westendorp persistently rejected the idea that the Bonn meeting had established a protectorate.[27] However, during 1998, the HR and his deputies had clearly adopted a more imperatorial brand of civilian implementation. As the high representative put it in one interview:

Bosnia suffers from the same phenomena we experienced in Spain. The church
bears a large responsibility for the war. But Bosnians are the same people. They
are all Slavs. Religious identity is simply the raison d'etre for these nationalist
leaders to hold on to power, like animals who cling to their turf. We need to
build a new set of values, new traditions, new political parties to present competing ideas and culture to overcome these nationalist movements.[28]

Westendorp's colleagues were even more emphatic and emboldened
about their nation-building methodology for remaking Bosnia. "We dictate
what will be done," claimed senior deputy HR Hanns Schumacher, when
asked whether the Bosniak side was obstructing the Federation. "We simply
do not pay attention to those who obstruct! I think we have already proved
that we can use the authorities that Dayton gives us and all those who resist
will have to fact the consequences."[29] Christian Clages, the head of the HR's
political department, remarked that his office had "become deeply involved
in the functioning of the state. We may not run essential functions from start
to finish, but at all levels we must monitor to make sure the work is being
done. We have an unprecedented amount of control on the legislative and
executive branches of government." But Clages also expressed some concern
about the future: "We do not know, however, how we will exit, how we will
not perpetuate Bosnia's culture of dependency."[30]

Whether or not the very proactive approach taken by Westendorp and
his colleagues in carrying out their tasks constitutes appropriate behavior for
international officials implementing a peace agreement is a matter that may
be viewed differently by fair-minded observers of Bosnian development. But
it is worth considering the broader issue of whether decisions, symbols, and
personnel imposed by international diktat in Bosnia can engender the kind
of cross-ethnic legitimacy that will allow Bosnia's political institutions and
political leaders to effectively govern a unified state after the eventual departure of foreign military and civilian authorities. The fabric of stable statehood, leave alone democracy, cannot be easily tailored. Over the long run
the real measure of Dayton's success may not be how many of the international community's goals are reached, and how quickly, but the question of
how the goals are obtained, and even more importantly, the degree of support such goals enjoy within Bosnia's indigenous elite and general population. Thus, politicians can be prodded to hold meetings, and animate
dormant governmental structures, and can also be pressured to reach decisions that have been persistently postponed. But such induced governmental
activity cannot guarantee that political structures will become institutionalized, that is, develop value and deep-seated support in society at large, or
that decisions will actually be implemented, or not quickly reversed, when

external pressure is no longer present. Reading the interviews with representatives of the international community in Bosnia, it is fair to ask whether or not their considerable optimism at both state building and nation building have outstripped their actual achievements to date (which when compared to the warfare of the early 1990s are undoubtedly impressive), and whether the members of Bosnian society will support such externally fabricated successes over the long haul.

By the fall of 1998, the strongly U.S. backed semi-protectorate in Bosnia and Herzegovina had made significant progress in achieving a number of key Dayton goals. Indeed, more progress was made during the spring and summer of 1998 than during the entire prior two years. But Bosnia and Herzegovina remained profoundly segmented in terms of its political and governmental structures. Most important from the vantage point of this study, the only progress made in the area of power sharing between the two entities, and between those entities and the central government, occurred as a result of measures imposed by the international community through the office of the HR. Thus, near the close of 1998, the central government in Sarajevo still enjoyed primarily only the allegiance of the Muslims (Bosniaks), while central government support in the other ethnic communities remained quite shallow. While the concentration of power on the entity level, and within the Federation's two ethnic enclaves, suited most Bosnian Serb and Bosnian Croat politicians, Muslim political leaders in the central government complained bitterly that the situation was totally unacceptable. "I will be very precise," remarked Haris Silajdzic, the Muslim cochairman of the Council of Ministers, "the existence in Bosnia and Herzegovina of different constitutions has resulted in legal chaos. [Several] legal systems overlap, the two entity constitutions are not harmonized with the country's constitution, and as a result the laws of the entities are not harmonized. If the state isn't above the entities then there are really two states ... my concept is that Bosnia is one state."[31] Siladjzic's concerns were echoed by the Peace Implementation Council (PIC), which monitors the progress of Dayton's implementation. In a June 1998 meeting in Luxembourg, the PIC reported that the central institutions of the state, parliament, the presidency, and the Council of Ministers, do not function as "sustainable and efficient common structures."[32] The PIC placed blame squarely on Bosnia's political leaders. "Too many of the current leaders continue to use the politics of domination and ethnic separatism to advance their own positions at the expense of the Bosnian people, thereby condemning the country to stagnation and isolation from the European family of nations." The country's institutional noncohesiveness was compounded by the fact that formally Bosnia also has two entity based armies (indeed, de facto, three ethnic armies), as well as two police forces and two judiciaries. Moreover, two-and-a-half years after the Dayton agreement was signed, the interentity boundary line (IEBL) continued to operate as a statelike border between the entities, which impeded the internal movement of goods and people on a countrywide basis.

Considerable entity and ethnic segmentation also characterizes the party system in Bosnia and Herzegovina. Granted, by mid-1998, the country's party system had become substantially more pluralistic than when the Dayton agreement was first adopted. For example, moderate pro-Dayton politicians and party organizations had begun to challenge the grip of the previously dominant nationalist parties, particularly in the Republika Srpska. A similar process was also underway in the Croat portions of the Federation. But it is noteworthy that the pluralization of Bosnia's party system has been significantly assisted, and remains very dependent on, the encouragement and tangible support of international agencies in Bosnia.[33] Moreover, it is equally important that the new group of moderate nationalists, who are now ostensibly prepared to cooperate with the international community in carrying out the Dayton accords, are still operating within an essentially uniethnic context: Bosnian Serb moderates are mobilizing Serb voters, and Bosnian Croats mobilizing Croat voters.[34] Thus, the pattern that is emerging may be termed *multiparty ethnic pluralism*. Such pluralism contrasts sharply with the one-party ethnic pluralism of the Communist period, and also the pattern of domination by hegemonic nationalist parties of the 1990–1997 period. Thus, the current party pluralism that exists within the three major ethnically segmented communities of Bosnia and Herzegovina is not yet the *multiethnic party pluralism* (consisting of countrywide parties with a civic orientation that enjoy substantial support in more than one ethnic group), which is the goal of the Dayton accord. Moreover, while some major parties, such as the powerful and predominantly Muslim SDA, evince a civic orientation in theory, in practice they are uniethnic organizations appealing to a uniethnic voting base. Indeed, the Bosnian Muslim areas, where support for the ruling SDA and President Izetbegovic remained substantial through the early autumn of 1998, were the least politically pluralized regions of Bosnia and Herzegovina.

Throughout 1998, the international community offered considerable support to the moderate nationalist parties and leaders among the Bosnian Serbs and Croats, and also to the small nonethnically oriented parties in the country. Largely as a result, the hard-line nationalist parties suffered a further erosion of support in the September 1998 elections.[35] But the results of the election were mixed. The strongest showing in the election was by party organizations in both entities that are substantially uniethnic in composition, and whose candidates represent only one ethnic community. Nevertheless, non-national or multiethnic parties did expand their representation in Bosnia legislative bodies in the 1998 election, and thus it is fair to say that pluralism had made an incremental advance.[36]

The Future of Federalism in Bosnia: Looking Beyond Dayton

Certain extremists want a minimum dose of a state, while on the other hand there are extremists who support a kind of unitary Bosnia and Herzegovina ... the over-dosed state. We must find some kind of medium.

Carlos Westendorp, 31 July 1998

The deep bientity and triethnic segmentation that currently characterizes the political landscape of Bosnia and Herzegovina, including the country's evolving party system, has severely impeded the implementation of the Dayton agreement. Indeed, the same conceptual divisions about how Bosnia should be governed that emerged in the early 1990s and continued during the war, have obstructed interentity and intergroup power sharing within the hastily improvised institutional structures adopted at Dayton. For some citizens and leaders in Bosnia and Herzegovina—mainly but not entirely on the Muslim side—the country should be a cohesive state with weak entities in which all citizens have a common Bosnian consciousness. Others, mainly Serbs and Croats, prefer a decentralized union of the existing two (and potentially even three) statelike entities; each of which has a distinctly ethnic orientation. Moreover, most Bosnian Serbs hope that their entity will be closely associated with neighboring Serb-Montenegro (the rump Yugoslavia), while Bosnia's Croats—even those who prefer to live in a unified Bosnia and Herzegovina—want to maintain their existing close ties with Croatia.

During 1998 and early 1999, political divisions deepened in the country regarding the proper manner of implementing the Dayton agreement, and with respect to the question of whether the institutions established by that agreement should be altered. The most revisionist forces were found in nationalist circles of the Bosnian Croat political leadership, supported by the Tudjman regime, who advocated a completely new three-entity model of Bosnia and Herzegovina.[37] In its most audacious form, this proposal contemplated the dismantling of the Muslim-Croat Federation and included measures for the internal territorial reorganization of the areas currently assigned to the Federation entity. Thus, the plan envisioned that the existing mixed Croat-Muslim cantons would be reconfigured, and a more ethnically homogeneous national-cantonal arrangement (more along the lines of the Swiss model) would be established. Such Croat proposals, which harkened back to political models for the country advanced during the war, were immediately rejected by the Muslim leadership and the international community, as well as pro-Dayton moderate Croat leaders.

Meanwhile, most Bosnian Serb political leaders, whether of the soft or hard nationalist variety, largely ignored the debate in the Federation, and indeed the Federation itself. Thus, the Serb side remained firmly committed to the idea that the existing "entity sovereignty" was the bedrock of the Dayton agreement.[38] Faced with Croat advocacy of a new entity, and Serbian intransigence about transferring any entity prerogatives to the central authorities, Muslim leaders, such as President Izetbegovic, threatened to call for a complete revision of Dayton following the election. Muslim leaders continued to emphasize the need to establish a more "integrated" country along the lines of "one-man one vote." Such revision would give less prominence to measures for ethnic representation, and would also attempt to overcome the existing paralysis within the central governmental structure. For example, Izetbegovic claimed to be unimpressed with the widely praised moderation and pluralization within the Republika Srpska under the Plavsic-Dodik team. Though suggesting that the end of hard-line, ultranationalist control in the predominantly Serb entity was a welcome development, Izetbegovic nevertheless pointed out that such evolution had occurred in a uninational setting. Until Muslim and Croat refugees and displaced persons would be able to return to the Republika Srpska in larger numbers, and a more multiethnic political leadership in that entity would adopt a civic rather than ethnic mindset—not to mention cooperate more extensively with the central government—Izetbegovic believed that the spirit of the Dayton accords were being subverted.[39] Meanwhile, moderate Serb leaders such as Biljana Plavsic emphasized that they wanted the "letter not spirit" of Dayton to be upheld.[40] She also objected to the fact that despite Muslim statements about the return of refugees to their homes, Izetbegovic and his supporters had done little to facilitate the return of refugee Serbs to the Federation entity.

At the core of the political difficulties in Bosnia concerning Dayton's implementation, and the tension between centralized governance and entity prerogatives (and even more broadly integration versus partition), lies the thorny question of how much political autonomy a modern democratic state can or should grant to subcultural communities and regional units of governance. Too much autonomy can be harmful to state cohesion; too much concentration of power at the center may prove stifling to cultural and regional diversity, not to mention also fostering politically destabilizing ethno-political grievances and secessionist tensions. Because federal-type institutions that create a divided power structure can help with the difficult challenge of blending and balancing state cohesion and cultural-regional autonomy, and thus also address the larger issue of establishing a viable democratic state, federalism is a pertinent framework for addressing political difficulties in Bosnia and Herzegovina. The Dayton agreement did not explicitly establish a federal system, though the governmental structure includes one entity (the Federation), which formally has federal-like features. Moreover, de facto, over the last three and a half years (1995–1999), Bosnia and Herzegovina has functioned along lines that resemble aspects of *ethnic federalism*, that is, a system where the central government is relatively weak, and power is concentrated in very segmented subunits of governance, each of which is politically controlled by a hegemonic ethnic community (see Figure 6.1).

Up to the spring of 1999, however, the representatives of the international community in Bosnia energetically rejected such ethnic federalism. In contrast, they have interpreted the Dayton agreement as aiming at a model of governance that approximates what might be called *territorial federalism*, that is, in which citizens of each federal or federal-like "entity," or subunit, share, and give their primary allegiance to, an overarching transethnic state nationality or national identity (along the lines of countries such as the United States, Germany, and Australia). Accordingly, international bureaucrats in Bosnia have placed enormous emphasis on such goals as reestablishing Bosnia's traditional multiethnic structure in all regions of the country through the return of refugees and displaced persons, diluting the power of ethnically based parties through electoral engineering, as well as discouraging any aspects of ethnopolitical activity in the media and other sectors of society. The underlying premise of such international efforts is that the institutions of the new Bosnia must be "ethnically neutral" (although, interestingly, such neutrality is hardly in accord with functioning territorial federal models found outside the Balkan region).[41] In any case, as shown in the present analysis, such efforts in Bosnia have only been partially successful,[42] and whatever progress has been made is due almost entirely to pressure and political manipulation by international representatives operating what has become a de facto international protectorate. Those efforts, however, have created the danger of a dependency culture, in which the political actors and citizens of Bosnia depend significantly on the guidance and support of the international community.

Anxious to avoid a resumption of violence and to move ahead with the implementation of the Dayton agreement—by keeping all political forces in

Bosnia reasonably happy, or equally unhappy, with the compromises
achieved at Dayton—the international community has strenuously refused
to consider any major political reorganization of the framework developed
by Holbrooke and his colleagues in 1995. As HR Westendorp remarked in
June 1998, the "Dayton Agreement cannot change, and everything that
seems to be a step out of the Dayton Agreement represents an error of interpretation."[43] Regrettably, as a result of the perspective advanced by Westendorp and the international community, no serious consideration has been
given to the idea of explicitly reconfiguring Bosnia on the basis of a federal
model that, although less segmented and ethnically grounded than ethnic
federalism, is also not as ambitiously civic oriented as the model of territorial federalism. Under such a system (see Figure 61.) of *multination federalism* (found, for examples, in India, Switzerland, and Canada), designated
federal units may be composed predominantly of distinct nations, but
minorities in each federal unit enjoy full human rights protections. Citizen
allegiance, within the multination federal model, can include both relatively
strong ethnoregional identities, and also commitments to a pan-national or
civic identity.[44] Federalism understood in that manner, would not require
that the leaders and citizens of Bosnia and Herzegovina accommodate themselves to notions of pluralism, assimilation, and multiethnicity elaborated in
Boston, Berlin, or Brisbane—which is currently promoted by well-intentioned, but rather naive international officials currently urging the unvar-
nished implementation of the Dayton model. The multination federal
structure would be appropriately designed for creatively blending federal
principles with ethnically based rights and identities within the unique, but
now tragically changed, Bosnian environment.

A number of changes in Bosnia's current constitutional and political
structure might help facilitate the country's reconfiguration in accordance
with the principles and practices of multination federalism. First it would be
helpful for the constitution of Bosnia and Herzegovina, and also the entity
and cantonal constitutions, to be harmonized, and to stipulate that all three
of the country's constituent peoples enjoy complete equality in both entities.
Strengthening constitutional provisions to that effect, and also judicial
enforcement of countrywide ethnic equality would help ensure minority
rights within the entities and the subentity units (cantons and municipalities). An initiative to carry out such changes was put forward by the government of Bosnia and Herzegovina early in 1998, but had not been adopted
a year later due to opposition by Croat and Serb nationalists.

Second, the federalization of the entire country on a three, rather than
two-entity basis, might also prove fruitful. The new entity would respond to

the demand of some Croats for a distinct self-governing unit that would express their own standing as a constituent "group" in Bosnia. As noted here, such a change is not intended to encourage partition or "ethnic territorialization," but to realistically respond to persistent Croat complaints over Bosniak "domination," which have undermined the functioning of the present Muslim-Croat Federation. Many Croats genuinely feel that owing to their reduced demographic size in postwar Bosnia they have become a "small nation in jeopardy," and there is "no identity without sovereignty."[45] Another helpful measure that could facilitate linkages among the entities would be to adopt electoral reform measures to encourage cross-ethnic voting behavior; changes which would combine incentives for supporting multiethnic parties with feelings of ethnic security.[46] Strong Bosnia-wide equality rights, three entity federalism, and the growth of parties with a multinational composition that have popular support in more than one entity, are all measures that could help create a more democratic and decentralized, albeit still cohesive, state. The best solution for Bosnia is to develop institutions that facilitate power sharing and protect civic rights, but also provide considerable space for the expression of ethnic sentiments and identity politics. Any effort to institutionally engineer the disappearance of ethnic attachments, and fabricate a panethnic identity at this point, will prove counterproductive.

Territorial federalism, with a decidedly civic or multiethnic focus, whereby Serbs, Croats, and Muslims are pressured to share a common or shared notion of Bosnian nationality or identity, and Bosnian symbols—as is currently urged and interpreted by many international officials and their present local allies in Bosnia—is not likely to prove a sustainable formula for the citizens of Bosnia and Herzegovina following the departure of foreign (SFOR) troops. Granted, any effort to renegotiate, amend, or reinterpret Dayton will not be an easy task. Presently, Dayton is "like the Bible," as one American official put it, "it should be read as it was written."[47] Moreover, developing a new federal model for Bosnia and Herzegovina must overcome the negative legacy created by the unfortunate experience with spurious one-party federalism in communist Yugoslavia. There is also always the danger that a relatively decentralized multination federalism might founder in Bosnia due to irredentist forces from neighboring kin states. Legitimately fearing such a potential breakup—and not wanting to recognize the demographic changes which occurred in Bosnia during the recent war—Muslim commentators vigorously oppose moves towards what they perceive as the "territorialization of sovereignty." But tragically, Bosnia has changed enormously with respect to its ethnic configuration, and well-intentioned efforts to recreate the pre-1992 unitary multiculturalism, or an assimilative territorial federalism à la

Dayton, are very problematic indeed. In 1992, President Izetbegovic referred to the intermingled ethnic composition of his country "as a living breathing Jackson Pollack painting." Unfortunately, that reality exists no longer.

Proposals for developing a new federalism must be pertinent to the current realities in Bosnia. The international community can nurture federal-like institutions in order to bridge the current divisions in Bosnia and Herzegovina, but should not attempt to facilitate or dictate a political model that does not enjoy widespread elite and citizen support within that country. Externally fabricated federalism that is weakly legitimated will not prove stable or sustainable. Admittedly, in historical terms, multination federalism is rather foreign to Bosnia. But such a model seems far more suitable to present conditions in that country than the ostensibly neutral, or civic, brand of territorial federalism currently espoused by those advocating the unadulterated implementation of Dayton's provisions. Foreign officials in Bosnia find the present difficulties manageable, and the international community now seems ready to remain involved in the country for a generation, or even longer. But, ignoring alternative models of power sharing, and blindly promoting Dayton as presently conceived, is a recipe for chronic political instability and potential violence in Bosnia and Herzegovina.

Notes

1. In post-World War II Bosnia-Herzegovina, Serbs wielded a disproportionately high degree of influence within the republic's communist elite, although formal provisions for ethnically balanced political representation ensured that Croats and Muslims were represented in the one-party political leadership.
2. In the election of 1990, the SDS, HDZ and SDA respectively received 29.6, 18.3, and 33.8 percent of the 240 seats in the republic's legislature. Smaller parties shared the remaining 18 percent of the seats.
3. Daniel Elazar has emphasized that the "effective use of federal solutions is enhanced if the ethnic groups are territorially separate and weakened, if they are intermixed." And he adds, "there are political cultures that will never be able to sustain federal solutions ... nevertheless introduced at the proper time and in the proper manner, federal arrangements, and at times even federal principles, can be of great help in moving an interethnic conflict the next step towards resolution." See D. Elazar, *Constitutionalizing Globalization: The Postmodern Revival of Confederal Arrangements* (Boulder, 1998), 207, 211.
4. As one Muslim official describing the prewar situation put it: "Bosnia is so intermingled that it is impossible to divide it. You only have three municipalities where 90% of the population is [from] one ethnic group, and that is in Western Herzegovina where all the

Croats live." Avdo Campara, "Washington Agreements." *The Modern Concept of Confederation* (Strasbourg, 1994), 89.

5. The agreement to establish a federation was reached in Washington on 18 March 1994. Muslim and Croat officials elaborated the Washington Agreement between 7 and 11 May 1994 in Vienna where agreements were signed on criteria for the territorial division of cantons in the Federation, principles of cantonal organization, and so on. According to its constitution, the new Federation was given control of foreign affairs, defense, monetary policy, and other macro functions, while remaining matters were to be managed by the cantons. Initially, the Washington Agreement had envisioned a federation of fifteen cantons, but at Vienna in May, the cantonal structure was reduced to eight units: four cantons were substantially areas of Muslim control, two were Croatian, and two were ethnically "mixed" (in 1995, the Federation would be reorganized into ten canotns). Some commentators objected that the ethnic delineation of cantons would prove an obstacle to reintegrating Bosnia. See, for example, Senad Pecanin, "Kontradiktorna definicija kantona," in *Federacija Bosna i Hercegovina: Drzava i civilno drustvo* (Zagreb, 1995), 21–23.

6. Bosnian Muslim general, Mehmed Alijac, took a very pragmatic view of the agreement: "The Federation means open roads. Open roads mean guns. And that means my men can go home." *International Herald Tribune*, 30 May 1994.

7. The Republika Srpska entity constitution would also give one ethnic side special political status. Thus, Article 1 as replaced by Amendment 44 of the Constitution of the RS provides that the "Republika Srpska shall be the state of the Serb people," and then adds "and all of its citizens. " *Ustavi Bosne i Hercegovine*, ed. Federalno Ministarstvo Pravde (Sarajevo, 1997), 129. Such constitutional provisions have reflected and influenced ethnic political realities in the country.

8. R. Holbrooke, *To End A War* (New York, 1998).

9. Ibid., 240–241.

10. Ibid., 130–131.

11. Ibid., 361.

12. Serb and Muslim constitutional lawyers in Bosnia differ on how to technically characterize the state in which they live, but both perceive elements that could potentially become the basis for federal development. For example, for Serb experts Bosnia "is a complex state community," a "state of states," in which "confederal elements predominate." In that view, "statehood or sovereignty resides neither in the entity nor in Bosnia-Herzegovina," making the country a unique case that is not a "classical state," and certainly not a federal state. At most, for the Serbs, the country is a "union" with some "specific federal elements" that are "not classical federal units and can't be compared to the federal units in the former Yugoslavia." For Muslim experts, the entities have very "restricted sovereignty inside the unified state of Bosnia-Herzegovina." But in this view, the entities "resemble all federal units in the world," although the country is not a federal state. The only thing the two sides agree upon is that there are clear contradictions between various elements in the Dayton agreement. "Bosna i Herzegovina: Konfederacija ili klasicna federacija," *Radio-Most*, 14 June 1998.

13. Under the Dayton agreement, the Republika Srpska comprises 49 percent of Bosnia's territory, and the Federation entity, 51 percent (split between areas of Croat control, roughly 23 percent, and Muslim control, 28 percent). The September 1996 elections in Bosnia, in which the three major nationalist parties consolidated their positions, tended to reinforce both interentity and interethnic segmentation in the country.

14. *Opinion Analysis*, United States Information Agency (7 August 1997), N-127-97; (21 August 1997), M-141-97; (27 August 1997), M-145-97.

15. Plavsic had been a politically independent botany professor during the Communist regime (though never a member of the League of Communists), who joined the SDS in 1990 and became well-known for her strident Serbian nationalism and anti-Muslim views. Elected in 1990 as a member of Bosnia's multiparty and multiethnic "collective presidency," Plavsic participated in the Bosnian Serb secession from the newly independent Bosnia-Herzegovina. Throughout the war she served in the top executive *echelons* of the RS (as a member of the presidency from May–December 1992, and subsequently as one of the two vice-presidents), and earned the nom-de-guerre, "Pale's iron lady."

16. *CNN Interactive World News,* 9 August 1997.

17. Very little progress was still being made, for instance, on the problem of returning refugees and displaced persons to their former homes. The situation was particularly disappointing with regard to "minority returns," that is, the return of uprooted citizens to areas where they had been, or had come to be—because of the war and ethnic cleansing by one side or another—a minority of the population. USIA survey data revealed that while a large majority of the Muslim population (89 percent) expressed support for the return of refugees, such a perspective was substantially less apparent among Bosnian Croats (59 percent), and very weak among Bosnian Serbs (17 percent). Moreover, while Muslims mostly (47 percent) preferred SFOR or some other component of the international peacekeeping effort (the International Police Task Force, UNHCR, etc.) to take responsibility for minority returns, less than a quarter of the Croats and Serbs interviewed felt the same way. Bosnian Serbs in particular showed a strong preference (71 percent) for this matter to be left to local political and police authorities. *Opinion Analysis,* United States Information Agency (2 August 1997), M-141-97.

18. By November 1997, some 6,700 heavy weapons were destroyed by the Republika Srpska military and the Federation Army.

19. During June 1998, after eighteen months of attention to this matter, the United States briefly suspended the Equip and Train program because lack of progress in the use of common military insignia and Federation flags by Muslim and Croat units of the Federation army obstructed the ethnic integration of the armed forces.

20. A more difficult organizational sector impeding the Federation was its Ministry of the Interior, which members of the UN mission unsuccessfully attempted to restructure. UN officials suggested that more responsibility fell on the Muslim side, that is "Bosniak" secret police, who acted as an arm of the ruling party, the Muslim Party of Democratic Action.

21. Surveys conducted by the USIA among Bosnian Croats during 1996 and 1997 consistently revealed much less support for the Muslim-Croat Federation than for the confederation of that entity with Croatia. Efforts in 1997 and early 1998 by the Zagreb regime to elaborate the idea of confederative links (or "special relations") between Croatia and the Federation, and also to demilitarize Bosnia, were rebuffed by the Muslims, and the international authorities in Bosnia (foreign officials also rejected closer RS links to Yugoslavia). However, in March 1998, a Council for Cooperation was established between the two countries to resolve mutual problems. For the nonimplementation of the Federation constitution and the mistrust between Muslims and Croats during 1997, see *Report on the Human Rights Situation in the Federation Central Bosnia Municipalities With a Special Emphasis on the Situation of Minority Groups* (Sarajevo, 4 April 1997).

22. The International Criminal Tribunal for the Former Yugoslavia was established in 1993, and by 1997 had publicly indicted 78 suspects (an undisclosed number were the subject of sealed indictments). During the second half of 1997, the number of indictees held at The Hague tripled from 7 to 21 (mostly Croats). Public indictments reached 80 by the end of August 1998 (of whom 26 persons were in custody, 1 person was on bail awaiting trial, several had died, 30 remained at large, and 17 had been acquitted). But Yugoslavia and

the RS continued to resist cooperation with the tribunal. By the fall of 1998, only two low level suspects, a Bosnian Serb and a Croat, had been convicted.

23. For example, international officials observed that "although officially disbanded, illegal structures of the former (pre-Dayton) 'Croat Republic of Herceg-Bosna' and 'Republic of Bosnia-Hercegovina' continue to exist at different levels, preventing the full establishment of the Federation of Bosnia and Herzegovina. These parallel structures include, for example, separate intelligence services, judicial systems, public activities, and financial institutions, which need to be integrated, dissolved or privatized." *Chairman's Conclusions,* Federation Forum (Mostar, 16 April 1998).

24. *Opinion Analysis,* United States Information Agency (4 August 1997), M-123-97; (6 August 1997), M-126-97; (15 August 1997), M-135-97; (22 August 1997), M-143-97. Indeed, even if such responsibility is established, many citizens may persist in attributing "collective guilt" for war criminality to neighboring ethnic communities. Thus, only a third of the Bosnian Croats surveyed even felt that suspected war criminals could get a fair trial at The Hague tribunal, a figure that is only slightly higher among the Bosnian Serbs. In the RS, the popularity levels of top Bosnian Serb leaders indicted for war crimes, including Radovan Karadzic and Ratko Mladic, remained extremely high in 1997. And even after the Bosnian Serb power struggle had been underway for several months, Bosnian Serbs in roughly similar proportions viewed both Radovan Karadzic and Biljana Plavsic as highly trusted politicians. However, Plavsic supporters who were interviewed were significantly more likely than supporters of the Karadzic-Krajisnik clique to favor sending Bosnian Serb war criminals to The Hague for prosecution.

25. The Muslim political leader of the Federation, Ejup Ganic, took a cynical view of what was accomplished: "These conferences don't bring much. The fact is we Bosnians are getting stronger, and the Serbs and the Croats are getting weaker." *Guardian,* 11 December 1997, p.13. Less than two weeks after the Bonn meeting, President Clinton publicly announced that once SFOR's mandate terminated in mid-1998, U.S. troops would participate in a downsized follow-on force. But unlike the earlier IFOR and SFOR deployments no specific deadline was provided for ending the mission. The emphasis had shifted from finding an "exit strategy" to formulating a more open-ended "transition strategy," which anticipates long-term NATO involvement in the Balkans.

26. *Slobodna Dalmacija,* 30 November 1997.

27. Westendorp's spokesman, Simon Haselock, claimed that the HR was "not looking for a protectorate ... when there is, if you like a proconsul in charge, in a colonial fashion and actively runs the whole country ... where an international or external authority has control of all the mechanisms, and in fact governs the country de facto." Haselock was implying that the citizens of Bosnia still govern themselves, but he added that "those individuals at any level who are seen as being anti-Dayton ... can be removed from office." Meanwhile, early in 1998, Westendorp observed that "it is bad when you have to democratize a country with the use of force, but in this case when you have such an abnormal mentality in the leadership, then you have to do that." *SFOR Transcript: Joint Press Conference,* Sarajevo, 12 December 1997.

28. *New York Times,* 10 April 1998, p.A10.

29. *Dani,* 11 April 1998.

30. *New York Times,* 10 April 1998, p.A10. In the late summer of 1998, there were approximately 35,000 foreign soldiers serving in Bosnia and 50,000 civilian "foreign nation-builders" (including 10,000 persons located in Sarajevo alone). *Wall Street Journal,* 26 August 1998, p.A1.

31. *Globus,* No. 375 (13 February 1998), pp.24.

32. *Declaration of the Ministerial Meeting of the Steering Board of the Peace Implementation Council* (Luxembourg, 9 June 1998). During early 1998, Bosnia's Council of Ministers had two cochairmen, a Serb and a Bosniak, and the deputy chairman was a Croat. The twelve members of the Council included four Serbs, four Croats, and four Bosniaks. The Serb co-chairman at the time, Boro Bosic, remarked that Bosnia is not a "standard state," and the Council of Ministers was not a "classic government." "If we were to create a government, we would probably have to transfer certain entity authority to the level of B-H (Bosnia and Herzegovina) institutions, which would be absolutely wrong." *Banja Luka Srpska Televizija*, 27 February 1998. On the question of central versus entity power see also Jens Reuter, "Die politische Entwicklung in Bosnien-Herzegowina. Zusammenwachsen der Entitaten oder nationale Abkapselung," *Südosteuropa* 3–4 (1998): 97–116.

33. In May 1998, Deputy High Representative Klein promised: "I do intend to create a more pluralistic model of voting ... to give a chance to women and smaller parties...we will force some candidates ... I want people to vote on the basis of their ideology. ... We have gathered experts from all the famous institutes all over Europe, and they are holding lectures in villages, in cantons, on how to form a political party, how to train political candidates, how to prepare the electoral body. That takes time." *Oslobodjenje*, 7 May 1998, p.4. When Klein eulogized Croatia's recently deceased Defense Minister, Gojko Susak, and suggested that the bulk of Bosnia's politicians were "self-interested," and could not see the "larger picture," President Izetbegovic attacked Klein's remarks as "arrogant" and "insulting" intervention in Bosnian affairs. *Los Angeles Times*, 12 May 1998, p.6. Izetbegovic also warned Klein "our people like foreigners as friends, but they do not like them as tutors ... The Dayton agreement does not establish a protectorate over Bosnia and you are not a protector." On a later occasion Izetbegovic explained, "our people are not xenophobic but they do not like foreigners who establish the authorities in Bosnia and Herzegovina." "Drzava to sam ja," *Dani*, 13 August 1998, pp.24–25.

34. For example, Zubak's new NHI is moderate and pro-Dayton, but is oriented to serving the interests of the ethnic Croat community in Bosnia and Herzegovina. Thus, while Zubak has committed himself to working within the Dayton framework, he intends to do so primarily on behalf of the country's Croats. Indeed, Zubak told an interviewer earlier in 1998 that from his perspective, as the Bosnian Croat member of the country's three-person presidency, he often finds it easier to deal with the Serb presidential representative because the Muslims are trying to dominate the country. *Globus*, 22 January 1998, pp.17–19.

35. A total of eighty-three political parties, coalitions, and independent candidates were registered for the September 1998 elections, and overall, more than 5,900 candidates were competing.

36. The merger in December 1998 of the two major left-oriented nonethnically oriented parties to form a new Social Democratic Party, held out the promise that the big three nationalist party organizations would face even stronger competition in subsequent elections.

37. Jozo Pavkovic, "BiH–Jedna drzava, tri entiteta, tri naroda," *Vecernji list*, 20 April 1998, p.6.

38. In July 1998, President Plavsic claimed that the Serb republic (RS) enjoyed "75 percent sovereignty." Earlier visiting the United States, Plavsic maintained that "two-thirds of sovereign functions" provided to the Serb republic under the Dayton agreement provided a "sound basis for the realization of basic Serb national interests." *Bosnian Serb Television*, 20 May 1998. During the same visit she asserted: "we have given up on the objective of unification with Serbia and Montenegro, and she observed that the government of the RS supported a "loose union of entities ... centralized Bosnia is an oxymoron." *The Plain Dealer*, 21 May 1998, p.9B.

39. *Dani*, No. 72 (3 March 1998).
40. *Antenna News*, 18 June 1998.
41. See, for example, Will Kymlicka, "Ethnic Relations and Western Political Theory," in *Managing Diversity in Plural Societies*, ed. Magda Opalski (Nepean, Ontario, 1998), 278–283.
42. It is estimated that over two million people were uprooted from their homes and became refugees or displaced persons during the war in Bosnia. By mid-1998 international efforts to recreate Bosnia's prewar demographic and multiethnic structure, had met with only limited success. For example, international officials estimated that by mid-August 1998, close to 243,000 refugees and 230,000 displaced persons had returned home. But only approximately 10 percent of those returnees constituted so-called "minority returns," that is, individuals returning to locations where they now constituted a minority. Moreover, 96 percent of minority returns had occurred in the Federation (11,000 of whom were Muslims returning to Croat areas, and 26,000 Croats returning to Muslim areas). Less than 1,900 Croats and Muslims had returned to the Serbian republic. *SFOR LAND-CENT Joint Press Conference Transcript*, 14 August 1998. Such data underlined the substantial bientity and ethnic segmentation in post-Dayton Bosnia. Survey research conducted for the U.S. government during July 1998 indicated that roughly 91 percent of the Muslim respondents (a nonelite sample) supported the return of minority individuals to their areas, but there was considerably less support for such resettlement by Serbs (37 percent), and substantially less enthusiasm on the part of Croats (54 percent). *European Opinion Alert*, USIA, Office of Research and Media Reaction, (3 and 7 August 1998), L48-98, L43-98, L46-98.
43. *AIM*, Banja Luka, 24 June 1998.
44. On this and related concepts of federalism see W. Kymlicka, "Ethnic Relations and Western Political Theory," 289, 309–311, and also W. Kymlicka and J.R. Raviot, "Living Together: International Aspects of Federal Systems," *Canadian Foreign Policy 5*, No. 1 (Fall 1997): 1–51. Advocacy of balancing ethnic interests and civic identity in a democratic Bosnian state does not imply acceptance of the misguided view that interethnic divisions in Bosnia are "ancient hatreds" or primordial constructs. Moreover, many ardent American proponents of Dayton, who attack the international community for being delinquent and timid at enforcing the accord's ostensible "liberal elements," should give closer attention to the variety of ways civic nationalism has been reconciled with the expression of ethnic interests in multinational states.
45. Some of the smaller Croat parties in Bosnia regard the three entity idea as a HDZ effort to further divide the country into ethnic ghettos as a precursor to partition. See "Treci entitet u Bosni i Hercegovini," *Radio-Most*, 3 May 1998. Deputy High Representative Klein recently commented that "the Croats joined in [the] Federation before Dayton took place. That is why they do not have the right to entity status. They are probably looking towards Banja Luka [in RS] now and saying 'how come the Serbs can have their own symbols, a flag, and the like?' ... It would be easier to work with the Croat population in Bosnia if they had their own entity, as they would have their own identity and culture." *Vecernji list*, 27 January 1999, p.7. High Representative Westendorp's staff quickly disavowed Klein's remarks.
46. C. Bennett and A. Husarska, "Let Bosnians Vote a Rainbow Ticket," *Los Angeles Times*, 16 October 1997 and more fully in *Doing Democracy a Disservice: 1998 Elections in Bosnia and Herzegovina*, ed., International Crisis Group (Washington, D.C., 9 September 1998).
47. *Dnevni Avaz*, 8 May 1998, p.3.

Chapter 7

WHY DID RUSSIA NOT BREAK APART?

Legacies, Actors, and Institutions in Russia's Federalism

———— ∞∞∞ ————

Andreas Heinemann-Grüder

Among those observing Russia's state building after the collapse of the Soviet Union we find more pessimists than optimists. Pessimists stress the lack of a civic culture, the ailing economy, a miserable record of obedience to law, legacies of authoritarianism, rampant corruption, crony capitalism, dangers of disintegration, the strength of former communists joining ranks with nationalists, and the overwhelming incapacity of the central state to provide basic services. The optimists, far fewer in number, highlight the progress made in constitution building, the traits of civil society evident in Russia's history and contemporary politics, the prevention of major interethnic strife—at least compared to former Yugoslavia—the sketchy but still cooperative relationship with the West, and the seemingly limitless patience of Russia's people while enduring transformational hardships.[1] Pessimists sometimes get tired of alarmism and turn into optimists, but it is mostly the optimists who get tired and turn into pessimists. Whereas both sides can make legitimate claims and provide ample empirical evidence, the differing approaches to Russia are deeply informed by opposite understandings of what Russia was, is, and should be. Interpretations of historical legacies, assessments of transition achievements, and normative prescriptions for the future diverge substantially. The criteria for such assessments are mostly derived from perceived essentials of the established Western democracies. Elements of consolidation that are highly disputable even in the case of Western democracies are often taken as prerequisites of a successful system change. Any assessment of Russia's final outcome—a consolidated democracy, viable constitutionalism, and an institutionalized market—is premature.

I want to address the impact of federalism on center-periphery relations in Russia as one of the key concerns of Russia's system change. In trying to develop criteria for an informed judgment about forces of disintegration or integration, I have become particularly interested in three aspects of the current regime: the role of legacies of the past, actor preferences during transformation, and the impact of federal institution building. Social scientists analyzing the potential for Russia's disintegration tend to be either students of nationalism or disciples of transitology. Both groups engage in discourses usually isolated from the other; there is, however, a third discourse that is mostly out of the picture—comparative federalism. I will try to combine insights from all three approaches. My argument focuses on state-centered perspectives. In the case of Russia, a state-centered perspective is frequently criticized as overly formalistic: the constitutional and institutional settings exist only on paper, many authors declaim, the normative salience of constitutional provisions is said to be close to zero, with actors' preferences neither shaped nor constrained by constitutional arrangements.[2] If we were to take at face value the claim that institutional arrangements do not matter we can stop talking about federalism in Russia from the outset and invest instead in the booming (and almost addictive) market of catastrophic forecasts. Denying the relevance of emerging state institutions and norms from the outset is simply a nonacademic assertion; instead of analyzing institutional effects, such statements take their absence for granted. But it is more than personal distaste for alarmism that justifies a state-centered approach. While society-centered approaches should not be dismissed as irrelevant; they simply address a different set of questions. If we want to understand the influences of state institutions on actors' behavior in center-periphery conflicts, we have to study these institutions first. Institutions may rely on stronger or weaker sanctioning capacities, and enforcement of norms may be weak or strong. The self-interest in obeying norms may vary, depending on time, context, and the costs of defection. But institutions clearly affect politics, though often with unintended side-effects.

It is useful to start with a counterintuitive yet fact-related question that may challenge those that dismiss a state-centered approach. If institutions (and norms) do not matter, why did Russia not fall apart immediately after the demise of the Soviet Union? All causes commonly attributed to the dissolution of the Soviet Union, Yugoslavia, and Czechoslovakia could be extended to Russia: the lack of genuine federalism, a weak center, and the power of nationalism. The central state in the late Soviet Union as well as in Russia in the 1990s showed a growing incapacity to perform elementary functions such as properly collecting taxes, ensuring the supremacy of the constitution and federal laws, providing social and physical security, and protecting the socially weak. As in other Eastern European federations, federalism in the former Soviet Union was identified with concentration of power in the ruling communist party. Nondominant groups often perceived Soviet federalism as a mere smoke-screen for centralist political practices. The Soviet Union and the RSFSR certainly lacked a civic, federalist culture (whatever its concrete features might be). Instead of a sense of partnership in intergovernmental relations, constitutionalism, and a voluntary and internalized agreement on shared federal norms and values, political practices featured the centralism of the Communist party and executive command chains, the hierarchical structure of the central planning apparatus, and the dominance of Russian elites and their culture over non-Russians. Minority groups therefore feared domination by the core ethnic group—the Russians. As in other Eastern European federations, the Soviet Union subsequently failed in its attempt to establish an overarching, "internationalist," purely politically defined identity as a lasting basis for statehood. External threats and shared perceptions of the outside world—World War II and the cold war—that had played a key role in creating a sense of belonging within the Soviet Union had also faded as circumstances fostering integration. Additionally, with the transformation to a postsocialist regime, former Communist elites as well as anticommunist counterelites often began to legitimize different transition strategies by embracing ideas of ethnic "self-determination." Compared to nationalism, federalism therefore rarely ranked high on the agenda of post-Communist reformers.

The Soviet Union's institutionalization of ethnicity—its ethnofederalism—is often seen in recent literature as the key trigger for nationalist mobilization.[3] Contrary to the integrationist intentions of its founders, ethnofederalism supposedly provided the institutions, resources, and skills for belated nation-state building. Eastern European federalism thus functioned not simply as a facade for Communist party politics but also became a resource for minority mobilization. Simply asserting that Eastern European federations were not genuinely federal is obviously insufficient, because ethnofederalism made it at the very least easy to dissolve three Eastern European countries.

Nevertheless, the legacy of Soviet ethnofederalism did not lead in the Russian case to uncompromising quests for statehood among the non-Russians, Chechnya being the exception. Although Russia was not immune to secession, as the Chechnyan separatism amply demonstrates, the overall diminution of separatist activism compared to the early 1990s is nevertheless striking. Given the commonalties between Yugoslavia, Czechoslovakia, the Soviet Union, and Russia, how can we explain the different effects of ethnofederalism in Russia and the failed Eastern European federations? Ethnofederal institutions alone do not seem adequately to explain differences in outcomes. The demographic dominance of ethnic Russians and the duration of coexistence of multiple ethnicities in the Russian empire since the sixteenth century evidently mark points of difference from Yugoslavia and Czechoslovakia. Nevertheless, these different legacies of the past do not explain why Russia's experience in the 1990s contrasts with the rejection of both socialism and federalism in Eastern Europe. Even minor non-Russian groups could have opted for secession if assimilation and incorporation had failed and resources for secession had become available. As I will argue, the Russian situation is, compared with the failed federations in Eastern Europe, characterized by three specifics: a particular legacy of centralism and ethnofederalism; distinct actor configurations during transformation; and the integrative effects of federal institution building.

Legacies of the Past

In terms of its historical legacy, Russia failed in the nineteenth century to develop an assimilative, homogenizing nation-state. Similarly, the Soviet Union's "internationalism" did not succeed in its attempt to overcome national attachments. How could the successive failures of nation-state building become a prerequisite for Russia's contemporary federalization? Historically, non-Russians did not voluntarily opt for a merger with ethnic Russians—the propositions to the contrary are evidently a colonialist and Soviet-Marxist myth. Soviet ethnofederalism was originally designed as a mechanism to regain territories lost during the civil war, not as an aim in itself. It nevertheless unintentionally contributed over time to the preservation and even development of national consciousness among non-Russian ethnic groups. Soviet ethnofederalism thus, as a legitimizing ideology, erected barriers against the ideal of national homogenization so typical of Western European nation-state building. Russia's historical failure in developing a nation-state in the nineteenth century and the Soviet Union's inability to

engineer a supranational, internationalist state in the twentieth century dele-
gitimized compulsory assimilation as a means of integration. However, unsuccessful nation building marks the other Eastern European federations,
too. The proposition that institutionalization of ethnicity by means of ethnofederalism contributed to belated nation-state building among minority
groups—once the center could not effectively sanction their quests—finds
ample support in the death throes of Eastern European federations. How
can we explain why the ethnofederal preservation of ethnic diversity did not
lead in the case of Russia to mass-scale separatism as in other Eastern European federations? Why did ethnofederalism contribute to the spread of federal ideas instead of solely stimulating nationalism? Although the centralist
practices of the Soviet Union had contradicted the federal camouflage, federal ideas have laid the foundations for institution building after the end of
the Soviet Union.

Suggesting answers to the riddle of Russia's distinctive multiethnic
legacy might still be premature, but I would like nevertheless to suggest
three tentative explanations. First, regardless of repeated attempts to Russify
and assimilate non-Russians into the core culture, Russia's ruling elites never
developed a coherent or hegemonic idea of collective self. The potential to
develop a hegemonic idea was hampered by rifts among the Russian elites—
especially within its intellectual circles—over what Russia's mission should
be. Among the ideas put forward were, first, a religiously defined and missionary "Third Rome" embedded in its orthodoxy; second, a supranational
pan-Slavism; third, Russia as an empire circumscribed by its territorial
expansionism and absolutist center; and fourth, Russia as merely a Great
Power. In addition there were such ideas as Russia being a civilizational
bridge between Europe and Asia (Eurasianism), of spiritual communalism
grounded in a collectivist way of life, and finally, the concept of an ethnically
based nation-state.[4] There has never been a consensus among Russia's elites
about the essence of the "Russian idea." Russian nationalists in the late
nineteenth century as well as their counterparts in the late twentieth century
remained deeply divided over their links to the Western European political
and cultural heritage. The only shared view seems to consist of highly
ambiguous assertions of Russia's mystical distinctiveness. To put it briefly, as
long as the hegemonic potential of any version of Russian nationalism
remained unrealized, any attempt to impose assimilation on non-Russians
was ultimately doomed to failure.

My second hypothesis refers to the incorporative and developmental
effects of ethnofederalism in twentieth-century Russia. There was a comparatively high degree of "integral incorporation" of non-Russian elites into

decision making, and into the administration of their respective subnational units. These provided incentives for acculturation and assimilation instead of outright secession.[5] Wherever indigenous elites formaly loyal to the CPSU participated extensively in subnational decision making, a shift to secessionism could have undermined their very power basis.[6] Ethnofederalism in the former Soviet Union advanced the incorporation of indigenous elites to varying degrees. The differential intensity of secessionist ventures among ethnofederal units with comparable degrees of "institutionalization of ethnicity" seems to be a function of successful or unsuccessful elite incorporation. The more subnational elites could advance by using opportunities provided by ethnofederal institutions, the less attractive secessionism became. If this premise holds true, ethnofederalism would then only promote nationalism up to the point of secessionism if elite incorporation permanently fails or is at least expected to do so both on the central and the subnational levels.

Thirdly, ethnofederalism in Soviet Russia clearly set limits to the privileges exercised by titular ethnic groups in the second-order autonomous units (the autonomies inside the union republics).[7] Under the rule of the CPSU, the ethnofederal assignment of privileges could, as a rule, not evolve into an "ethnocracy" of the titular ethnic group in the autonomous republics. Soviet "matryoshka federalism" made second-order titular ethnic groups dependent on the Soviet center. In order not to be taken over by the core ethnic group, second-order titular groups within union republics had to rely on the center's protection against domination by the first-order titular group. In the case of Russia, this explains why most of the leaders in autonomous republics preferred a renewed Soviet federation instead of its dissolution. The dissolution of the Soviet Union would have brought these second-order titular groups under the sole tutelage of the first-order titular group of the union republics. Federalism was thus embraced as a strategy to forestall a possible imposition of first-order titular group norms.

The Transition Context

Apart from these historically different legacies in the case of Russia, the context of transition played a conducive role in fostering federalization after the demise of the Soviet Union. In contrast to the failed federations in Eastern Europe, system change in Russia was combined with federalization. One obvious difference between Yugoslavia and Russia is the antagonistic split within the central power in the latter case—first between the Soviet and

Russian governments over control of Moscow, and afterwards between Russia's executive and legislative branches (the president and the Supreme Soviet). Internal splits in the center therefore overlapped the center-periphery cleavage, consequently, the center could not proceed as a unified actor. Some of the center's clashing actor groups depended on the support from and cooperation of regional actors. The bargaining power of regional actors vis-à-vis the center was therefore strong as long as the splits in the center could be used for advancing regional interests. Russia was therefore different from the failed federations of Eastern Europe in one important respect. There was much greater regional participation in politics at the center in the early 1990s. In Yugoslavia, by comparison, nondominant groups identified Serbian dominance with the Communist party; antifederal, anti-Communist, and anti-Serbian cleavages subsequently reinforced each other.

Additionally, federal institution building in Russia after the demise of the Soviet Union altered the content and structure of center-periphery conflicts. Whereas sovereignty claims vis-à-vis the Soviet center were high on the initial agenda, they lost urgency. The conflicts emerging during the negotiations over a renewed Russian federation assured central and regional actors that they could attain their long-term interests. During these negotiations and the ensuing learning processes, actor groups at the center and in the regions tested maximalist strategies. They soon began to recognize the limits of their strategies. President Yeltsin, whose approach to federal power division in Russia remained a function of power conflicts in the center and who strove primarily to enhance the presidential portion of executive power, reluctantly recognized the limits of presidential rule because residual powers remained with the regions. As a result, center-periphery conflicts lost their antagonistic character for regional elites, because of their involvement in central decision making and the growth of independent decision-making autonomy. Learning processes and institution building contributed to the exclusion of maximalist strategies and merely instrumental, gain-maximizing approaches to federal adherence. After 1993, the primacy of federal institutions has been in principle recognized by all relevant actor groups. Among these were the Federation Council, regional equality in national representation, the coexistence of ethnically and territorially defined units, and the concepts of concurrent powers and of regional residual powers—all enshrined in the 1993 constitution. Federal institutions as they have emerged after 1991, and as sanctified in the 1993 constitution, are still deficient in terms of efficiency. But they nevertheless have created a normative context for actor behavior. Beyond a mere utilitarian, instrumentalist approach, core federal institutions are now respected as a legitimate locus and means of interest articulation.[8]

Russia still lacks a broadly accepted federal founding myth. This could have evolved as a result of public discourses among parties, ethnic groups, regional and central elites, and the media. Russia is lacking a federal culture that is the foundation for loyalty to the state and federal society as a whole. Unlike the experience of the United States in framing a constitution, Russia did not engage in a broad federalist discourse at the beginning of its refoundation. Nevertheless, it would be deceptive to ascribe the federalization exclusively to power configurations between the center and regions prevailing at that time. The foundation of the Soviet Union resulted from a tactical adoption of certain federal principles; it represented a federation without federalism. Russia's federalization after 1991 was different. The call for federal power sharing and protection of ethnofederalism clearly was part of the agenda of Russian reformers as well as to those of indigenous party elites. In the course of Russia's refoundation, the concept of federalism began to encompass not only ethnic accommodation but a fundamental principle of vertical power division and constitutionally protected assignments of authority. The constitutional debates showed an early consensus on these principles. It is exactly this combination of ethnofederal legacies with federalization as part of system change that marks the specific path of Russia compared to the failed Eastern European federations.

Paradoxically, a change in the system change "from above"—through the self-transformation of former Communist elites—became a prerequisite of federalization in Russia. A more active civil society would undoubtedly have radicalized the national consciousness among non-Russian groups as well as among ethnic Russians. The relative success of Russia's federalization is instead based upon exclusive elite pacts between Moscow and the regions. The old elites in the center and the regions recognized one other and assured one other of their status. Conflicts over elite change were, compared to other Eastern European countries, far less structured by center-periphery cleavages or ethnic cleavages. With the dissolution of the Russian Supreme Soviet and the regional Soviets in the fall of 1993, a partial elite change occurred. The executives in the center and regions—both largely outgrowths of the old Communist power apparatus—remained unified in their interest in preserving power and strengthening the executives at the expense of legislatures. The center-periphery pact is based upon a marginalization of legislatures, or to put it even more bluntly, on a disjunction between federalism and parliamentary democracy. Presidential federalism in Russia is therefore not only rooted in traditions of accumulating power at the center but in the shared interest of central an.d regional elites in executive power concentration.

After August 1991, decentralization in Russia has proceeded through six distinct stages, each characterized by specific actor preferences and prevailing power distributions. The first, lasting from August to the end of December 1991, featured the instrumental use of regional preferences by Gorbachev and Yeltsin for their struggle over power in the center. Calls for sovereignty among ethnic units of the Soviet Union were deliberately instigated "from above" in order to weaken the competing actor group in the center. In the second stage, immediately following the dissolution of the Soviet Union and lasting from January to March 1992, the Russian government was able to hedge most of the autonomy and sovereignty claims and pacify secessionism. In March 1992, almost all subnational entities signed the Federation Treaties with the Russian government, the notable exceptions being Tatarstan and Chechnya. The ensuing third stage featured debates over the new constitution and the efforts of several subnational units to upgrade their status (from ethnic districts to republics and from administrative regions to republics). This phase concluded with the violent dissolution of the Supreme Soviet and regional soviets in early October 1993. The leverage and mobilization power of the regions was to a large extent reduced with the end of the conflict among the three branches of government in the center and the replacement of the regional Soviets as institutional resources of subnational mobilization by significantly weakened legislatures. The fourth stage—October to December 1993—was distinguished by recentralization through presidential decrees that reestablished a strong administrative hierarchy and the adoption of the constitution with its recentralizing features. The fifth stage, beginning early in 1994, was marked by the contradiction between a formal concentration of power in the presidency and the actual lack of implementing capacity of the central government, resulting in a significant decentralization of authorities and growing socioeconomic discrepancies among the regions. Additionally, tensions between the federal constitutional order and often unregulated economic states of emergency in the regions grew worse. A sixth stage, largely reinforcing patterns of the fifth stage, began in 1996 with direct elections of regional governors, who were until then mostly appointed by the president. With a mandate from regional constituencies independent of the president, regional governors could more vigorously pursue territorial interests through their membership in the Federation Council, through economic policies, and by forming interregional coalitions.

Since 1991, federalization has involved decentralization of economic decision making and the formation of autonomous spheres of action in the regions. Over time, regional (territorial) cleavages have proven more important than ethnic and ideological divides. Cleavages with the center have mainly depended on the availability and mobilization of economic resources.[9] The weakness of the central state resulted in different degrees of decentralization of authorities and the extralegal exercise of competencies by the regions. As regional administrations had to cope with such problems as unemployment, a restricted monetary supply, closure of enterprises, social and welfare policy devised at the center, and nonpayments of federal transfers, it comes almost as a surprise that regional resistance to Moscow's macroeconomic policy did not provoke more coordinated efforts by the regions.[10] While the central state decentralized many competencies in order to stabilize its budget, the subsequent exercise of these competencies in the regions suffered from deficient administrative and material resources. This uncoordinated decentralization promoted inconsistent and ineffective mechanisms for the distribution of competencies. Decentralization did not result from a planned, conceptualized regional policy at the center, but from reaction to the weakness of the central authorities. As a result, the center's ability to collect taxes was reduced, redistributional capacities shrank dramatically, and federal laws were only partially implemented. Recentralization was not an option, an effective recentralization would have required a rigid political repression. The regions were hence faced with three pressures: the decentralization of social and welfare responsibilities without additional funding, the growing expectations of regional constituencies, and a degree of politicoadministrative interference from the office of the president in an attempt to reestablish executive hierarchies.

Institutional Features

Do federal institutions mitigate these pressures on governments? What kind of effects could be ascribed to federal arrangements? Institutional effects can be divided into normative and functional dimensions. An understanding of the functional dimension—efficiency in fulfilling assigned tasks—would require distinct case studies that are mostly not available yet. I therefore concentrate on the normative and identity shaping aspects of institutions. Among the institutional features of Russian federalism we can discern five elements each of which marks a tension between opposite principles. These are (1) the combination of elements of "contractual" and "constitutional" federalism, (2) the unique coexistence of super-presidentialism and federal power sharing, (3) the blending of ethnofederal and territorial-federal principles, (4) the joining of executive and legislative federalism in the formation of the second chamber of the national legislature, and (5) the asymmetry expressed in the jurisdictional inequality of the constituent units.

Because Soviet federalism institutionalized ethnic identities, Russia's federalization could start neither exclusively "from above" (as was the case in Canada, Spain, and Belgium) nor exclusively "from below" (as was the case in the United States). Through contractual federalism Russia institutionalized the idea of a federal "social contract." Since 1992, federalism has been partially understood as contractual, in distinction from a mere decentralization of powers by center. The contractual element became formalized in the Federation Treaties of 1992 and the bilateral treaties signed since 1994. Although these treaties do not constitute the regions as constituent entities, they nevertheless recognize them as partners to a contract. They are therefore protected against unlimited concentration of power in the center. The bilateral treaties additionally led to flexible bargaining mechanisms in the exercise of joint competencies.

On the whole, the inclusion of regional elites into federal decision making and the bilateralization of federal-regional relations contributed barriers to regionalist and secessionist strategies. With the exception of Chechnyan separatism, other separatist movements are in decline. The constitution of 1993 and the bilateral treaties essentially contributed to the reduction of separatist activism. The contractual element of Russia's federalism set boundaries for secessionism through its combination with a constitutional federalism that excluded subnational sovereignty. While a pure contractual federalism would have entailed the possibility of a fundamental revision of the contract, a pure constitutional federalism would have only incompletely protected the multi-ethnic nature of the federation. The facts that Russia's federalism does not correspond to the classical understanding of watertight assignments of authorities in governmental systems, that Russia combines contractual with constitutional elements, and that it has to cope with unresolved sovereignty claims, should evoke concern, at least in principle, as it could undermine external sovereignty and the supremacy of federal law.

If we approach federalism from its Latin root, it encompasses the notion "foedus" (an alliance) as well as "fides" (meaning trust). Compared to a mere contractual, in the end confederal relationship, a federal alliance seems to be sustainable only if all parties share long-term interests and if the knowledge of these interests is shared.[11] The alliance itself should not be in the free disposition of the contracting parties. With the Federation Treaties of 1992, the approximately forty bilateral treaties signed since 1994 (at the time of this writing), and the acceptance of the constitutional order in principle, all parties, with the exception of Chechnya, actually assured each other of their adherence to a common order. The basis of this alliance is the division of authority between different levels of government. The Federation Treaties and the bilateral treaties mark the decisive difference between a mere decentralization of powers. With respect to the exclusive character of essential competencies of the center, the distribution of powers is more or less beyond dispute. Issues of dispute are rather related to the exercise of joint jurisdiction and the highly symbolic sovereignty claimed by some republics. Since the bilateral treaties do not have constitutional standing, the constituent units are in doubt as to whether assigned powers are really permanently protected. In sum, the Russian Federation is best described as "contractual federalism in action." The contractual character and membership of the federation is on the one hand recognized, but essential elements of the federal alliance remain on the other hand subject to continuous renegotiation.

The presidential federalism in Russia is distinguished from parliamentary federations (such as exist in Germany, Canada, Australia) or presidential-legislative federations (as in the United States) by having executive power concentrated in the presidency. The presidency has strong centralist features—rule by decree, veto powers over the legislative, control over regional administrations, and emergency powers. Furthermore, legislative and executive powers are merged in the presidency. Although certain aspects of the federal division of powers, especially the competencies of the Federation Council and the constitutions and statutes in the regions limit presidential powers, nevertheless, concentration of presidential power and federal division of powers represent opposing principles that create permanent tensions. Presidential federalism is a governmental system that entails conflict between centralism and regionalism as a systemic feature. The principal flaws of presidential systems like the Russian—weak incentives for the formation of parliamentary parties, charismatic leaders instead of parties with programs, polarization of the electorate, and the dangers of authoritarianism—disrupt the federal division of powers and diminish the federal potential for conflict solution. The greatest danger for Russian federalism thus seems to flow from a presidentialism that attempts to be strong in implementation of legislation and executive power, but that cannot keep its promise, that is, a formal presidentialism without any corresponding power of redistribution and implementation.

Due to its deficient functional differentiation and the existence of a double executive (the presidential administration and the prime minister/Council of Ministers), the Russian presidential system is overburdened with the tasks of integrating the regions and striking federal bargains. Russian federalism is, as a result, characterized by the mushrooming of extraconstitutional channels of influence, through which regional actors try to get access to decision making in the central ministries and the presidential apparatus. Individually, these channels of influence may appear more efficient than interest aggregation through political parties and the Duma. Nevertheless, they are characterized by one critical flaw—the unpredictability of outcomes. In order to prevent the weak implementation powers of the central government from resulting in an uncontrolled exercise and accumulation of competencies by the regions, the sole solution seems to consist in a clear distribution of functions and the efficient incorporation of regional elites into federal decision making. The approval of a strong presidency by regional executive elites could be relied on so long as these elites were appointed by the president himself. With elections of regional governors after 1996 a structural cause for approval disappeared. Integrative effects thus have to emerge from other mechanisms, for example, the provision of arenas for federal bargaining in the Federation Council and through mutually beneficial bilateral treaties.

Unlike parliamentary federations, with their concentration of legislative power in the first chamber, the power division between the Duma and the Federation Council is comparatively balanced. The unitary elements of the Russian governmental system—the presidency and the Duma—are thus checked and balanced by crucial exclusive competencies and veto powers of the Federation Council. In view of the concentration of constitutional power in the presidency, the division of federal power became a means of vertical power restriction and control. Given that strong intermediary associations, regionally anchored parties, and a potent Duma are still missing, the federal division of powers has become one of the main guarantees against authoritarian regression. The federalization of Russia therefore contributes to the consolidation of democracy insofar as it diminishes the potential of regression to authoritarianism.

One great advantage of Russia's combination of ethnofederal and territorial-federal principles has been the prevention of ethnic hegemony by the core ethnic group, the ethnic Russians, as well as unitary rule over the territorially defined regions. The combination of ethnofederal and territorial-federal principles nevertheless causes some conflict. Russian-dominated regions periodically challenge the privileges of the ethnically defined units, especially in cases where regions belong to the net beneficiaries of federal redistribution. Yet, in comparison to its alternatives—a pure territorial federalism or pure ethnofederalism combined with unitary rule over the non-ethnic territories—the combination of both principles seems to be the best available variant for Russia. The costs for the center and the ethnic Russian majority of having ethnofederalism and territorial federalism combined might be higher than a pure territorial federalism. The costs for opting out, however seem to be even higher. The departure from a pure ethnofederalism and the avoidance of a pure territorial federalism are key achievements of federalization in Russia.

The ethnofederal principle may promote disintegrative forces under two conditions: if nontitular groups are significantly marginalized or disempowered, and if ethnofederalism becomes a pretext for the preservation of predemocratic orders in the regions. Even if political practice in the autonomous regions, especially the republics, clearly shows a notable preference for titular ethnic groups, most of the constitutions and statutes in the autonomous entities protect minority rights in terms of nondiscrimination. Furthermore, nontitular groups often partake in the privileges of ethnic republics. As long as no ethnic group is in a position of territorial dominance—unlike the situation in former Yugoslavia—multiethnicity enhances cooperative incentives.[12] Conversely, an ethnicization of the autonomous entities in favor of the titular ethnic group would weaken incentives to accept federal arrangements, because nation building would become an available alternative. Whether interethnic conflicts will increase in the autonomous entities depends very much upon the protection of minority rights through national and republican constitutions. Conflicts are likely to increase if Russians in the autonomous entities feel constantly marginalized to such an extent that they are led to ask for protection by the central government and the regions dominated by ethnic Russians.

The composition of the Federation Council, which includes representatives of both the regional executives and the legislatures, combines elements of executive and legislative federalism. Russia's "executive-legislative federalism" embodied in the second chamber tries to incorporate the subnational branches of government into federal decision making and to integrate them. From an integrationist point of view, the combination of executive and legislative representation has a distinct advantage: it mitigates collective action pressures of the regions, because the executive and the legislative branch represent distinct interests not necessarily unified in their approach to the center. The mixture of both representational principles provides the central government with the power of indirect control, because a significant barrier for collective action is institutionalized. The fact that delegations from each region in the Federation Council consist of a representative of the region's executive and a member of the regional legislature contributes to the depoliticization of the second chamber: in order to get a mandate for action in the Federation Council, no voters or political parties have to be mobilized. Through the principle of equal representation of all federal units in the Federation Council, ethnic and territorial units have been institutionally equalized vis-à-vis the federation as a whole. While the legislative jurisdiction of the second chamber does not include coparticipatory rights in forming the executive, the Federation Council participates significantly in the enactment of legislation and constitutional amendments. Until recently, party affiliations played only a marginal role in the election of regional executives and regional parliaments. Consequently, the voting behavior in the second chamber was shaped hardly at all by party allegiances. The lack of party coordination in regional interest articulation limits the collective action potential of the regions in the Federation Council.

With respect to the composition of the Federation Council, one serious problem is that regional governors and republican presidents had to double as regional executives and representatives at the federal level. The physical presence of executives in the Federation Council causes such enormous coordination problems that the minimal and irregular participation of the regional executives in its sessions comes as no surprise. The governors and republican presidents usually try to overcome the coordination obstacles by sending vice governors or vice presidents as permanent regional representatives to Moscow to coordinate action in the Federation Council and function as liaison officers vis-à-vis the ministries of the central executive. Almost all regions have opened quasi-embassies in Moscow that lobby before the central government and prepare sessions of the Federation Council. In order to overcome these obstacles and make the second chamber an actual working parliament, president Putin launched in summer 2000 a reform of the Federation Council that will replace the governors with permanent representatives of the regional executive branch.

A final specific of Russian federalism consists in its asymmetry. This is evident in the status hierarchy among subnational units and the bilateral treaties signed between central and regional executives. This asymmetry realizes first of all Russia's constitutional claim to have a "multinational sovereign," because it assigns ethnically based rights to non-Russian titular ethnic groups. This institutionalized asymmetry thus departs from the Western European ideal of homogeneous nation building. The assimilation of non-Russians into the dominant Russian culture is not the aim, but rather the protection and development of ethnic distinctness. In view of the deficiencies in Russia's federal power division, it is important to mention additionally that asymmetry provides insurance against presidential power usurpation and the subjection of the multiethnic people under one "Russian idea." Ethnic homogeneity, for example the Western European archetype of nation building, by no means provides a legitimate model at the beginning of the twenty-first century for national integration, even if many emerging states still strive for ethnic purity. Departing from this model, Russia's federalism recognizes the alternative—institutional protection of heterogeneity.

Juan Linz has defined a consolidated democracy as an order "in which none of the major political actors, parties, organized interests, forces, or institutions consider that there is any alternative to the democratic process to gain power, and that no political institutions or groups have a claim to veto the action of democratically elected decision makers."[13] If we apply this definition to Russia's federalism we immediately realize that asymmetry did not rule out the quest for alternatives to the existing federal order. Asymmetry nevertheless significantly reduced the salience of such a quest: asymmetry became the alternative to secession. Through the bilateral treaties the executives of the center and the regions came to terms in principle over the concrete individual exercise of concurrent powers as well as over mechanisms of conflict regulation and the supremacy of the federal constitution. The bilateral treaties did not represent an "order" that was resistant to fundamental questioning; constitutional conflicts were not replaced by asymmetry but were perpetuated.[14] In lieu of uncompromising "all or nothing" conflicts over the very aims of the federation, procedural and issue-related conflicts prevail. Instead of the traditional European understanding of well-delineated authorities among levels of government, Russia's federalism now exhibits an institutionalized bargaining process over the assignment of governmental responsibilities.

Russia's federalism remains a conflict system, although an institutionally regulated one. Despite the increase of regional powers, the central government still retains a crucial direct and indirect leverage in determining regional policies. The taxation system remains largely centralist. In addition, the overwhelming majority of regions are the net beneficiaries of federal redistribution. Furthermore, since socioeconomic discrepancies among the regions prevent collective action the central government can influence the behavior of regional leaders in the Federation Council. Finally, renegotiating the terms of bilateral treaties offers flexible incentives for individual accommodation. With respect to the preservation of unity and diversity, the division of powers, and conflict regulation, since 1991 Russia has made substantial progress that allows one to rule out at least some of the most feared disintegration scenarios. The central government retains basic elements of state sovereignty: the federal constitution, regulation of citizenship, core elements of a common market, defense, and the representation of the state in foreign affairs. By and large, Russia still has a uniform monetary and federal fiscal system, even if the regional emission of money surrogates and extra-budgetary funds threaten to undermine these federal authorities.

The central flaws in Russia's federalism consist of its unclear distribution of powers resulting from the broad interpretation of concurrent jurisdiction and deficiencies in the constitutionally sanctioned means of conflict regulation. Regional legislation often contradicts the federal constitution: in 1997, the Russian Ministry of Justice reported that 16,000 regional laws adopted in 1995–96 contradicted the constitution.[15] The former prosecutor general, Yuriy Skuratov, reported that through early 1998, approximately 2,000 regional laws had been rejected due to inconsistencies with the constitution. According to estimates by the then justice minister, Sergey Stepashin, the Justice Ministry had to return one third of regional laws after review because of violations of the constitution.[16] However grave and extensive these regional violations of constitutional provisions might be—the differences in the figures given by various sources are astonishing—the cardinal conflict between federal and regional legislation is beyond any doubt. Regions often assume federal authorities in cases where the central government proves unable to exercise its duties effectively. Deficits in implementation then result rather from the weakness of the central government than from conscious disrespect for federal legislation and constitutional provisions on the part of the regions.

The exercise of powers in the regions is only insufficiently protected by the constitution and its implementation by the Constitutional Court. Russian federalism is therefore still far from having institutionalized predictability and law enforcement through an independent "third party" with strong sanctions. Among the institutional deficiencies is the weakness of the Constitutional Court. It is "neutral" insofar as both chambers participate equally in its appointment. The Constitutional Court nevertheless does not act on its own initiative in determining the constitutionality of legislative and administrative acts, but must be called into action by other constitutional organs. Furthermore, political opportunism often prevents constitutional clarification. The implementation of rulings of the Constitutional Court in cases relating to regional violations of constitutional norms remains irregular.

Even if the Constitutional Court were consistent in its ruling, conflict over the exercise of powers is nevertheless inherent in the constitution. The vagueness of the concept of concurrent jurisdiction has blurred the lines of assigned powers. The mutual and institutionally protected trust in territorial assignment of powers therefore remains precarious. Insufficient clarity in the distribution of powers reflects the stalemate between the regions and the central government in the years 1991–93, becoming a feature of the constitution itself. Regardless of Russia's declaration of sovereignty, the RSFSR judicially continued to exist after the collapse of the Soviet Union. The constituent units of the federation did not form a federation in a void. Two principles therefore compete in the unresolved exercise of concurrent powers—the concept of a federation "from below" and the concept of Russia's judicial inheritance of the RSFSR's statehood. The ambiguity of the joint competencies is furthermore a result of the contradiction between the unitary character of the presidential system and the federal principles of power division. The Russian constitution failed to allocate responsibility for elementary public services. In view of the inability of the central government to efficiently exercise joint competencies, it is small wonder that regions unilaterally assume these.

Following the functionalist theory of David Mitrany one could argue that the clear distribution of powers characteristic of nineteenth-century constitutions became obsolete due to changing requirements of a modern economy. Mitrany argued: "The function ... determines the executive instrument suitable for its proper activity, and by the same process provides a need for the reform of that instrument at every stage ... Not only is there in all this no need for any fixed constitutional division of authority and power, prescribed in advance, but anything beyond most general formal rules would embarrass the working of these arrangements."[17] I agree with Mitrany that under conditions of a weak central redistribution capacity an open, functional, flexible, and regionally differentiated bargaining and accommodation of authorities is unavoidable. Yet, predictability is a prerequisite of the functioning of the system as a whole. Without the validity of the "most general rules," each issue tends to become a fundamental conflict. A mere functionalism would reduce the federation to the goal-maximizing and limited aims characteristic of a confederation. Institutional securities are a precondition of functional adaptability. In view of the growing socioeconomic discrepancies between Russia's regions and the simultaneous weakness of the central power, Russia faces the task of striking a balance between its federal system of government and its centralist traditions. Given the fragility of the implementation power of the central executive, a conscious recognition of the subsidiarity principle and a clear distribution of federal and regional competencies, taxes, and incomes would seem to be conducive for both democratization and federal integration. This would involve a dramatic increase of differences in living standards and developmental strategies and contradict the federal idea of equalization of living standards. The geographic vastness of Russia, limited internal migration, and weak interregional communication networks could nevertheless constrain the politicization of these discrepancies.

Regardless of these obvious setbacks, the federalization of Russia since 1991 has provoked salient changes in actor strategies. Regional executives are no longer prefects acting on behalf of the president, even if the president repeatedly tries to reinstall the old dependency pattern. Compared to Soviet times, the central executive is bound by constitutional frameworks. With the Federation Council, the regional elites dispose of veto powers that incorporate them into federal decision making. With the introduction of governorships and presidential posts in the regions, the status of regional elites is strengthened. Gain-maximizing through federal bargaining incorporates regional elites, whereas dissociative strategies remain extremely costly, as was demonstrated not least by the military intervention in Chechnya. On the whole, regional autonomy has been significantly strengthened. Regional executives dispose of independent sources of legitimacy, and regional identities and power claims have found their expression in a vivid and highly differentiated regional constitutionalism. By virtue of recognition of regional autonomy and diversity, and the allowance of asymmetric regulations, the region's readiness to respect federal interests, to participate in the federal process and to use their constitutionally provided institutions has increased. The constituent units have substantially increased their coparticipatory rights in federal decision making. This holds true not only for constitutional amendments but also for the growing role of the Federation Council in drafting legislation. The sphere of autonomy from central intervention has increased with the adoption of the constitution, the signing of bilateral treaties, and the election of governors. Autonomy is nevertheless restricted to regional executives who could, based on executive power concentration, successfully constrain interest articulation by regional parliaments and parties. The price of successful integration of regional elites has been a fundamental democratic deficit in the regions themselves. The bias in favor of executives in both the center and the regions has established a congruence of nondemocratic authority patterns. Whether this congruence actually increases administrative performance, as suggested by "congruence theory," remains a question open for empirical research.[18]

Comparing Russia to other states that federalized after authoritarian and centralist rule, we can strike a positive note in evaluating the 1990s. Russia combined the state-building agenda with federalization and thus profoundly reduced the potential for nationalist center-periphery conflicts. The constitution and political practice are not congruent yet, but one conclusion is beyond any doubt: dissociative and secessionist strategies are discouraged. The asymmetry in Russia's federalism and the unique combination of ethnofederal and territorial-federal principles could mark the beginning of an alternative way of state building. It is precisely these characteristics that represent the general relevance of Russia's federalization.

Notes

1. For optimistic assessments, see N. Petro, *The Rebirth of Russian Democracy: An Interpretation of Political Culture* (Cambridge and London, 1995); A. Aslund, *How Russia Became A Market Economy* (Washington, D.C., 1995); S.M. Fish, *Democracy from Scratch: Opposition and Regime in the New Russian Revolution* (Princeton, 1995).

2. G.A. Almond, "Foreword," in *Can Democracy Take Root in Post-Soviet Russia?* ed. H. Eckstein, F.K. Fleron, E.P. Hoffmann, and W.M. Reisinger (Lanham, Boulder, New York, and Oxford, 1998), viii.

3. R. Brubaker, *Nationalism Reframed: Nationhood and the National Question in the New Europe* (New York, 1996).

4. On the diversity of the "Russian idea" see T. McDaniel, *The Agony of the Russian Idea* (Princeton, 1996).

5. The term "integral incorporation" I borrow from David Laitin, *Identity in Formation. The Russian-Speaking Minority in the Near Abroad* (Ithaca, 1998). Laitin distinguishes between three types of nondominant elite behavior—the "most favored lord" scheme (incorporation into the center), colonial dependence, and "integral incorporation" (into subnational politics).

6. P.G. Roeder, "Soviet Federalism and Ethnic Mobilization," *World Politics* 43 (1991): 196–232.

7. Ian Bremmer distinguishes between first-order titular nationalities in the union republics, second-order titular nationalities in the autonomous units within union republics, and nontitular nationalities. Compared to first-order groups opting for liberation from the center, second-order and non-titular groups opted, according to Bremmer, for integration or assimilation. Ian Bremmer, "Reassessing Soviet Nationalities Theory," in *Nations & Politics in the Soviet Successor States*, ed. I. Bremmer and R. Taras (New York, 1994), 3–26.

8. On normative aspects of institution see R.L. Jepperson, A. Wendt, and P.J. Katzenstein, "Norms, Identity, and Culture in National Security, " in *The Culture of National Security: Norms and Identity in World Politics*, ed., Peter Katzenstein (New York, 1996).

9. A.R. Magomedov, "Politicheskie elity rossiiskoi provintsii, " *Mirovaya ekonomika i mezhdunarodnye otnosheniya* 4 (1994): 72–80.

10. J. Ahrens, "Systemtransformation von unten—Über die Bedeutung der national-staatlichen Ordnung für den russischen Systemwandel," *Osteuropa: Wirtschaft* 1 (1995): 31.

11. On the principal distinction between federalism and mere decentralization see W.H. Riker, "European Federalism: The Lessons of Past Experience," in *Federalizing Europe? The Costs, Benefits, and Preconditions of Federal Political Systems*, ed. J.J. Hesse and V. Wright (Oxford, 1996), 10.

12. Daniel Elazar argued that federal solutions would be fostered if ethnic groups could be territorially divided. In view of the high degree of ethnic intermingling in Russia's autonomous entities a clear-cut ethnic division seems only perceivable as a result of civil

war. The Bosnian case (Dayton Accord), that is, the institutionalization of cooperative pressures among territorially divided ethnic groups, is not an encouraging example supportive of Elazar's thesis. See D. Elazar, *Constitutionalizing Globalization: The Postmodern Revival of Confederal Arrangements* (Boulder, 1998), 207 and 211.

13. J. Linz, "Transitions to Democracy," in *Transitions to Democracy*, ed. Geoffrey Pridham (Dartmouth, 1995), 158.

14. The distinction between "stability" and "order" I borrow from R. Sakwa, *Russian Politics and Society* (London and New York, 1996), 357.

15. D.N. Jensen, "How Russia is Ruled—1998," Radio Free Europe/Radio Liberty Report, section IV. Institutions of government, http://www.rferl.org/nca/special/ruwhorules/culture-1.html.

16. "Constitution Watch," *Eastern European Constitutional Review* 32 (1998), 32.

17. D. Mitrany, *A Working Peace System* (London, 1944), 35.

18. H. Eckstein, "Congruence Theory Explained," in *Can Democracy Take Root*, ed. Eckstein, Fleron, Hoffman, and Reisinger, 3–33.

Chapter 8

A CONFEDERATION IN THE MAKING?

Means, Ends and Prospects of the Commonwealth of Independent States

————— ⊗∞⊗ —————

Mark Webber

The Commonwealth of Independent States (CIS) was created in December 1991 coincident in time with the dissolution of the Soviet Union.[1] Formed by an agreement signed initially by the leaders of Belarus, Russia, and Ukraine, the CIS has come to embrace all the former Soviet republics bar just the three Baltic states of Estonia, Latvia and Lithuania.[2] Despite this comprehensive membership and despite the fact also that the CIS encompasses a once highly integrated geographic area, since its formation the organization has registered only modest results in multilateral interstate cooperation. A number of ostensibly far-reaching projects have been devised within the CIS framework. However, their actual implementation has been, at best, halting and incomplete. Overall, the organization has come to play an increasingly marginal role in the post-Soviet area. Its main achievement may simply have been to survive at a time of profound economic and political transformation. This chapter involves both a description and explanation of the (dis)integrationist tendencies within the CIS. The CIS, it is suggested, is an organizational form which exhibits a limited, politically constituted coordination of activities

---

among sovereign states (and can thus be regarded as approximating a confederation) but which lacks the features of more overt political federation,
and specifically the existence of a sovereign central authority. The reasons
for this state of affairs are explored through a disciplinary frame of reference
derived from International Relations. This approach suggests that the
dynamics of interaction among the CIS member states, coupled with their
peculiar national characteristics, inhibit both the development of efficient
functional cooperation and the delegation of sovereignty to a central body.
More specifically, an absence of federalization within the CIS is seen as a
consequence of inter-state competition, underinstitutionalization, and a
weakness of unifying values within the CIS, alongside incongruities arising
from national elite perceptions, state viability, regime type, and levels of
economic convergence.

The CIS as a Confederation

The CIS conforms pretty accurately to most accepted definitions of confederation. The basic organizing principle of such an arrangement is that its
component units, while united in some limited sense, envisage no surrender
of sovereignty to a common authority. States involved in a confederation do
undertake to coordinate their activities in certain restricted spheres (through
the operation of joint authorities), but such coordination relies heavily on
voluntarism; it is organized on intergovernmental lines rather than imposed
supranationally. Confederations also tend to be constituted by a treaty (or a
comparable interstate document). Such a text, however, does not legitimate
acts over and above states, in fact the reverse. While it might provide the
confederation with a sense of corporate identity, its political-legal significance is as much to stress the limits of joint actions and the sovereign status
of the constituent units.[3]

Two difficulties are apparent in using the term confederation. First it
courts some imprecision. As defined above, confederation can be applied to
a range of different bodies that includes both highly devolved state-type
entities and some regional organizations, principally the European Union
(EU). More specifically functional arrangements such as the World Trade
Organization and the North Atlantic Treaty Organization (NATO), while
not complete confederations can *also* be regarded as confederal in their
organizing principles.[4] Perhaps reflecting its fluid character, however, the
CIS bears some comparison to all three of these types. A second problem
relates to self-definition: the CIS member states and CIS documents generally

do not use the term "confederation" in describing the organization. Neither of course do comparable bodies (the European Union, the Caribbean Community, etc.) and the point may simply be semantic. However, in the CIS context at least, the terminology does signify an important point. It should be remembered that the CIS was established in December 1991 following two failed efforts on Mikhail Gorbachev's part to save the Soviet Union. The first was a revamped federation based around the aborted treaty on a "Union of Soviet Sovereign Republics"; the second was the far looser "Union of Sovereign States" which Gorbachev tried to cobble together unsuccessfully in the autumn of 1991. Neither was confederal in that Gorbachev would not concede sovereign statehood to the Soviet Union's constituent republics. However, these efforts did result in an increasing disillusionment on the part of some republics (Moldova, Georgia, Azerbaijan, and particularly Ukraine) with any attempt to preserve central coordinating structures, federal, confederal, or otherwise. Upon the foundation of the CIS, some account of this position was seen as vital by Russia, particularly if Ukraine was to be accommodated. This, in turn, resulted in an eschewal of language and organizing principles, which were in any way redolent of the now abandoned Union proposals.[5] It also resulted in a contradiction, which has subsequently haunted the CIS: an awareness of the importance of functional coordination but a marked reluctance to invest the organization with the political mechanisms for effecting it.

In light of the above, one might, therefore, regard the CIS as a "loosely coupled" confederation. In such an arrangement there is no presumption of encroachment by a central authority and no expectation that substantive functional integration is either desirable or likely. The independent constituent members are free to choose the degree of commitment to the limited functions devolved upon common institutions and, where cooperation occurs, it tends to be ad hoc and differentiated (in terms of both the rate of member participation and the intensity of joint efforts in particular issue areas).[6]

State Sovereignty and the Absence of Common Authority

For many of the CIS states, sovereignty has a fictive quality; it exists in a juridical sense but its empirical attributes are often missing.[7] Thus Tajikistan and Georgia have been wracked by prolonged civil wars and a collapse of authority structures; and in Moldova and Azerbaijan separatist regions operate outside the writ of the formally constituted government. Yet it is precisely because statehood is newly acquired and under threat that it is prized so highly. Of all the CIS states, only one—Belarus—has voluntarily set about ceding its formal legal statehood.[8] Even states such as Kazakhstan, Kyrgyzstan, and Tajikistan, reluctant participants in the dissolution of the Soviet Union and supporters of CIS integration thereafter, have rejected any suggestion of an abandonment of their independence or the elevation of the CIS into a post-Soviet state entity. Azerbaijan, Georgia, Moldova, Turkmenistan, Ukraine, and Uzbekistan have opposed such moves even more forcefully. Russia, meanwhile, under both Boris Yeltsin and Vladimir Putin, has done little to promote the organization along these lines.

Essentially then, the CIS has acted as a vehicle for safeguarding the independence of its member states. The organization's founding documents are replete with the language of interstate relations and lack any presumption that the CIS is the precursor to a state union.[9] CIS members have, in fact, gone to some length to uphold formal principles of state sovereignty. Thus, there has been a near total consensus on matters of state succession and territorial integrity[10] and there have been few attempts to utilize the CIS to press issues of domestic political relevance.[11] They have also eschewed the creation of directive political structures that might impinge upon state prerogatives. As its 1993 charter makes clear, the CIS is not an organization possessing supranational powers.[12] Decision making works on strictly intergovernmental lines. The overall development of the organization is steered by councils of heads of state and government (CHS and CHG) with only limited powers over their members. States reserve the right to opt out of any agreement with which they disagree and no enforcement powers exist to ensure that decisions are implemented. The upshot has been uneven rates of participation (according to one estimate, of the 886 documents adopted by the CHS and CHG as of March 1998 only 130 have been signed by all twelve member states)[13] and widespread nonimplementation of agreements. Further down the organizational hierarchy, a similar state of affairs is also in evidence. The CIS possesses an executive committee with no autonomous authority; an economic court that can pass only advisory judgements; an interstate economic committee with the right to pass binding decisions but subject to the nullifying caveat that these require corresponding national legislation to bring them into effect; and an interparliamentary assembly with no cross-national competence.

Limited Functional Abilities

Upon its foundation the CIS acknowledged the necessity of cooperation and policy coordination in several spheres.[14] Such cooperation was seen by Boris

Yeltsin as necessary in order to staunch some of the deleterious effects of the Soviet Union's disintegration.[15] This was also a view shared by Belarus and the Central Asian republics, all of whom were aware of their lack of military and economic self-sufficiency. The initial three members of the CIS (Belarus, Russia, and Ukraine) signed a declaration on 8 December 1991 outlining a comprehensive program of economic cooperation. Article 7 of the "Agreement on the Creation of the Commonwealth of Independent States" meanwhile referred to joint activities in the spheres of foreign policy, the creation of a "common economic space", transport and communications systems, environmental protection, migration policy, and the suppression of organized crime. These provisions were subsequently accepted by the other founding members of the CIS, who in addition signed a series of agreements relating to military and security cooperation.[16] The 1993 CIS charter reiterated these provisions. Subsequent CIS documentation has developed the range of CIS activities still further. On paper, the organization has been the site of a far-reaching set of projects. This has involved defense cooperation (centered on the Collective Security Treaty of 1992 and specific agreements relating to air defense, border protection and peacekeeping), economic integration (based on the Economic Union Treaty of 1993 and related agreements on customs and payments unions, and a free trade regime), and foreign policy coordination. If fully implemented, such efforts would suggest the development of some truly federal elements within the CIS. In reality, however, collaborative undertakings have been scant and a constant source of controversy.

The limits of CIS activities are apparent in numerous ways. First, it should be recognized that in its early guise the CIS was largely concerned with an improvised response to the dissolution of the Soviet Union. This paid some initial dividends in the form of so-called modus vivendi arrangements aimed at the mutually beneficial preservation of Soviet era inter-republican ties.[17] And in certain fields (migration, health care, social security, railway transportation, and aviation and air traffic control) this type of coordination has continued to be relatively effective.[18] However, the more ambitious schemes in this connection proved to be early failures. Attempt to preserve a CIS common currency (the "Ruble zone") and joint armed forces were both abandoned in 1993 owing to the lukewarm participation and at times hostility of several CIS members including, in the case of the latter, Russia.

Thereafter also, CIS cooperative activities have rarely achieved the wholehearted endorsement of its membership. Ukraine, Moldova, Turkmenistan, and Azerbaijan have kept their distance from most military activities, while in the economic field, CIS projects have increasingly settled on a minority core of states (Belarus, Kyrgyzstan, Kazakhstan, Russia, and Tajik-

istan) centered on the CIS Customs Union. Moreover, even where cooperation has occurred, it has been patchy in execution. In the military sphere,
border and air defense and peacekeeping arrangements do exist and are formally overseen by CIS organs. These, however, are far from comprehensive
in geographic scope and still lack the integrity of coverage once provided by
the unified Soviet armed forces. Economically, the weakness of CIS-framed
cooperation is apparent from low levels of mutual trade turnover among its
members, the poor regulatory basis of economic transactions (for instance,
on matters relating to cross-national investment), and the absence of coordinated economic policies and pooled resources.

What is more, even this limited cooperation has been increasingly overlapped by bilateral and other arrangements outside of the CIS framework.
Thus, what passes for CIS military activities has come to rely upon Russian
finances and technical skills, and command structures agreed through bilateral channels. In the economic sphere, meanwhile, Russia has sought (and
often obtained) separate arrangements with regard to the establishment of
trading regimes, the creation and operation of transnational financial industrial groups, energy exploitation, and transportation. At a more general
level, it has signed broad-brush friendship and cooperation treaties (or their
equivalent) with all the other CIS member states and, in the case of Belarus,
has pursued a form of economic, military, and political union through bilateral means.[19] Other states too have shown a clear preference for bilateralism. This has most obviously been the case with Turkmenistan and, to some,
extent also with Azerbaijan, Georgia, Moldova, Ukraine, and Uzbekistan.
These practices are not in spirit incompatible with the CIS (Article 5 of the
CIS Charter, for instance, suggests that bilateralism is an acceptable "legal
basis of interstate relations within the Commonwealth"), but they should
not be regarded as CIS activities in their own right. Indeed, bilateralism
rather than enhancing the authority of the CIS has increasingly acted as a
substitute for it.

The same can also be said of attempted subregional cooperation among
CIS member states. This in some instances meshes with the CIS proper (as in
the case of the "Community of Integrated States" established in 1996 and
coincident in membership, and to some extent purpose, with the CIS Customs Union), but in other instances is in clear juxtaposition to it. The
"GUUAM" group, for instance, initially formed in 1997 is made up of
states—Georgia, Ukraine, Uzbekistan, Azerbaijan, and Moldova—all of
which have been unhappy at Russia's weight within the CIS and who have
consequently participated in the organization in a semi-detached manner.
The Central Asian Economic Community (known prior to July 1998 as the

Central Asian Union),[20] while not inspired by the same objectives does not sit comfortably with the CIS either. It has undertaken projects at cross-purposes with CIS activities (most notably it has sought to develop its own regional customs union) and, in part at least, owes its origins to a perception that the CIS is at the same time ineffective and neglectful of local needs.

Making Sense of the CIS

What is obvious from the foregoing analysis is that the CIS is a body with a rather limited level of development. Intuitively, this state of affairs would appear open to a straightforward set of explanations, which focuses upon the forces set in motion by the collapse of the Soviet Union, the nation-building processes in the former Soviet republics, and the uncertainties of economic and political transformation. The consequent competition between the legacies of interdependence and the disintegrative dynamics of decentralization, this view would argue, has resulted in a shallow form of association in which centrifugal tendencies have tended to trump the development of institutionalization and functional competence.[21] This picture of competing dynamics, drawing partly on principles from comparative politics and partly on the historiography of decolonization, is not one with which I would fundamentally disagree. However, in what follows, I wish to supplement it by an excursion into literature drawn largely from studies in international relations (IR). The utility of this exercise is premised on the assumption that following the dissolution of the Soviet Union, the region covered by the CIS has come to constitute what is, in effect, a system of states.

This part of my study is divided into sections that analyze the level of CIS development in two different ways. First, by subjecting the organization to the voluminous IR literature on interstate cooperation, and second, by a rather old-fashioned consideration of the "background conditions" for integration. Each helps to account for the fact that the CIS encapsulates a process of weak, rather than vigorous, cooperation. Before proceeding, however, one very important preliminary point needs to be made, namely that the limited development of the CIS should not be seen as unusual. It may well have its peculiar sources of explanation, but in comparative terms, the CIS is not radically different from other modern examples of confederation—Senegambia, the United Arab Republic, and post-Tito Yugoslavia were driven by rivalry and were eventually dissolved. And of recent cases of regionally focused confederation, many similarly have collapsed or have developed on the basis of clearly delimited functional and decision-making prerogatives.[22]

The assumption that confederations ought to be stronger than this is largely a function of the influence of the EU, the most advanced example of modern confederation.[23] This is, however, an organization whose development has been the product of specific and fortuitous circumstances not replicated elsewhere. The EU experience, therefore, is sui generis and of limited use as a point of comparison.[24] What relevance it has stems as much from the fact that the EU has given rise to a good deal of theorizing on the nature of integration. As we shall see below, some of this is germane in non-EU contexts.

Explaining the Development of the CIS (1): Cooperation in International Relations

In this section three approaches in international relations (IR) will be considered: neo-realism, neo-liberal institutionalism, and constructivism. These three do not exhaust the richness of commentary in IR, but they are indicative of how the subject has developed—the first two approaches have been dominant in mainstream IR over the last two decades; the third is representative of an alternative and increasingly influential stream of thinking. All three, moreover, have something very explicit to say about cooperation.

Neorealism

A neorealist position can be useful in two senses. First, because its general predisposition against interstate cooperation might be instructive in assessing the shallow bases of the CIS; and second, because, the first point notwithstanding, neorealism, in some formulations, does allow of a particular limited type of cooperation that seems applicable in the CIS context. Cooperation, according to neorealist analysis, is inhibited in at least three ways: first, by virtue of the security dilemma; second, by considerations regarding "relative gains" (the suspicion on the part of one state that collaboration benefits other states more than itself); and third, by anxieties that cooperation will result in ever greater interdependence, and thus exposure and vulnerability.[25] Furthermore, institutions allow of no route to bridge this essentially competitive chasm between states. In fact, to the extent that international institutions do carry out important roles, these have less to do with promoting mutually beneficial cooperation and more with advancing the particular interests of powerful states.[26] In the CIS context these arguments have some applicability. The security dilemma, while not a general phenomenon across the region, does describe the nature of certain localized disputes (e.g., between Armenia and Azerbaijan) and the standoff between Russia and Ukraine (at least until Ukraine relinquished its nuclear weapons in 1994 and agreement was reached on the Black Sea Fleet in 1997). Relative gains considerations might explain the reluctance of, for example, Ukraine to commit itself more fully to cooperative projects out of a fear that the benefits would be reaped disproportionately by Russia. The interdependency argument, meanwhile, has some relevance to energy-rich states such as Azerbaijan, Uzbekistan, and Turkmenistan, which have sought to lessen their dependency (in this case upon Russian control over pipelines) by eschewing CIS economic integration in favor of steps toward external diversification.

Yet as they stand, such arguments are not entirely satisfactory for they fail to capture the essence of what does pass for cooperation within the CIS and are silent on instances where states have willingly succumbed to a dependent position (Belarus, Tajikistan, and, to a lesser degree, Armenia, have become highly reliant—politically, economically, and militarily—upon Russia through the CIS and bilateral channels). In this light, an adapted neo-realist position, more disposed to an interpretation of cooperation is worth considering. Three issues are pertinent here: balancing, hegemony, and regional organization. The first of these, as outlined by Stephen Walt, relates to how states "balance" sources of threat in regional settings through alliance formation.[27] No common source of threat exists for the CIS states however. Furthermore, some members (Ukraine, Azerbaijan, Georgia, Moldova) consider the primary threat to reside not in some external source but in a fellow CIS member (Russia, or in the case of Azerbaijan, Armenia). Both these factors have inhibited military cooperation. Nonetheless, Walt's argument does have some relevance. The Central Asian states of Tajikistan, Kyrgyzstan, and Kazakhstan have sought to balance the threats posed by China and radical Islamic forces in Afghanistan by supporting the putative military dimension of the CIS. Armenia has balanced a perceived Turkish threat in a similar manner. Belarus, meanwhile, has made much of Poland's entry into NATO as a reason for CIS military cooperation and its militarily dependency upon Russia.

The second concerns the relationship between hegemony and cooperation. For realists, a hegemon organizes interstate cooperation largely for reasons of self-interest. Thus, a fading hegemon will want to promote institutions that offer it a favored position as a means of offsetting decline. This is particularly conducive to the creation of regional arrangements. The hegemon remains strong enough to provide regional leadership but, at the same time, weakened to the degree that it views cooperation as necessary to promote its interests, share burdens, and provide international support for its policies.[28] Such a state of affairs has echoes in the CIS given the position of

Russia—a regional hegemon still, but one whose relative position has increasingly been challenged. Moreover, as is noted below, the CIS does offer some opportunities to Russia for the pursuit of its foreign policy goals. As for regional organization, in this regard, some studies, while working within a neorealist frame of reference, have relaxed some of its assumptions in order to address what would otherwise appear theoretically anomalous: cases of well-developed, regionally based cooperation, principally that associated with the EU. The relevance of these studies to the CIS is only indirect, yet it is worth considering two such efforts in that they are suggestive of at least some of the organization's interstate dynamics.

Beginning with the so-called "voice opportunities" thesis of Joseph Grieco, this attempts to account for the resurgence of the EU from the late 1980s, in part, as the outcome of German preferences and the consequent attempts by other EU states to "bandwagon" toward Germany within a context of EU institutions.[29] This type of behavior is somewhat analogous to that within the CIS. Here, the dominant state—Russia—has held the initiative within the organization and other, weaker states have "bandwagoned" towards some of its regional projects as a means of safeguarding their own specific interests. This was apparent at the initial formation of the CIS in 1991 and has been observable in later more specific undertakings such as the CIS Customs Union. The argument, however, fails to translate fully into the CIS experience on at least two counts. First, because "bandwagoning" has become, increasingly, a minority pursuit within the CIS as evidenced by the patterns of participation in its cooperative projects. And second, because "bandwagoning", where it has occurred, has often taken place via a whole range of bilateral links (usually forged with Russia) outside and sometimes at odds with the development of the CIS itself. "Bandwagoning", in other words, has not occurred within, and has not promoted, a multilateral framework of cooperation.

The other adapted neorealist interpretation of the EU relates to intergovernmentalism. This emphasizes interstate bargaining over the terms of cooperation, lowest common denominator decisions and coalition formation involving groups of states traveling at different speeds along cooperative paths.[30] This is, in some senses, redolent of the CIS experience with, however, one very important difference. Bargaining in the EU has resulted in agreements and a ratchetlike movement toward integration. Bargaining in the CIS has resulted in agreements but an absence of meaningful integration. State interests, in other words, are more convergent in the EU than in the CIS. Both organizations are capable of framing agreements, but the former has exhibited a far greater degree of willingness on the part of its members to implement and abide by them.

Neoliberal Institutionalism

Institutionalist analysis seeks to demonstrate that cooperation is easier to achieve than is recognized by the neorealists. This view is derived from a reading of the international system as one of increasing interdependence, something that increases the functional necessity of cooperation between states.[31] Institutions, meanwhile, offer the means to formalize and facilitate such cooperation in world politics.[32] An objective need for institutions is not, however, any guarantee that they will either be formed or that they will persist. The establishment of institutionalized forms of cooperation is seen variously as the outcome of hegemonic action (in a form more benign than the neorealist version outlined above), or, in its absence, of the identification of "zones of agreement" among states in particular issue areas.[33] This picture of the benefits and mechanics of cooperation might, at first sight, seem highly relevant to the CIS area. Here, after all, is a group of states, subject to a still pressing interdependence with seemingly a lot to gain from institutionalized cooperation. The fact that the CIS has survived and in some limited sense has preserved (and built) cooperative links seemingly attests to this logic. However, the development of institutions relies not just on their alleged efficiency in facilitating cooperation but also on their sense of legitimacy.[34] Indeed, an institutionalist account allows for this in that it relies, crucially, on the premise that cooperative outcomes rest on a complementarity of interests among states; when this does not pertain, cooperation would not be expected to appear, nor the institutions that assist it to develop.[35] Adapting this somewhat, it might be suggested that where a minimal convergence of interests occurs, institutionalized cooperation will develop, but in an ad hoc and contested manner. In such circumstances, the legitimacy of the organization will be questioned, its sense of purpose ill defined and its organizational design unsophisticated.[36] This is a description that has a certain ring of familiarity in relation to the CIS. That a minimal convergence of interests has arisen at all, meanwhile, follows, in the institutionalist logic, from unavoidable interdependence accompanied by a sudden sense of crisis that emerged as a consequence of the dislocatory effects of the Soviet dissolution.[37]

Two other implications follow from the institutionalist account. The first concerns Robert Keohane's notion that institutionalized cooperation, and specifically regimes, will survive even with the decline of the hegemon that played a crucial part in its initiation. This follows from the fact that the creation of new regimes is a more exacting process than the maintenance of existing ones and because those that do exist may have proved themselves useful in some (even limited way).[38] Thus, even where the regime generates little enthusiasm it is recognized that to be without it is more of an inconvenience than putting up with its persistence. Again, this has parallels with the CIS situation. Russian decline after the creation of the CIS in 1991 has not meant the termination of the organization.

The second concerns the particular institutional form of cooperation. Here it has been suggested that international institutions reflect the domestic political order of the states that helped create them. Thus, the development of postwar international institutions under American guidance reflected the American domestic institutional context, one which gave precedence to liberal democratic values and associated bureaucratic norms of decision making.[39] Applying this logic to the CIS, its specific development can be seen as the outgrowth of the uncertain institutional environment within the post-Communist states, most importantly within Russia. Bureaucratic and political upheaval, ameliorated only by a general tendency toward neoauthoritarian but often still weak presidentialism, describes well both the domestic polities of the CIS states and the working practices of the CIS itself.

Constructivism

According to institutionalist theories, the initiation of cooperation occurs as a pragmatic response to common problems. The game of cooperation, subsequently, is seen to serve the interests of states and so is prolonged. An alternative approach, derived from constructivism, is to suggest that cooperation is initiated and sustained as a consequence of other variables, two of which are central: norms and identity.[40] Norms can act to socialize states in favor of common goals, while shared identities provide the sense of common purpose necessary for sophisticated forms of multilateral cooperation.[41] Notwithstanding the above, constructivism is, to cite Alexander Wendt, "analytically neutral between conflict and cooperation."[42] Although it has been portrayed as predisposed toward the progressive aspects of world politics,[43] it does not assume that cooperation is a natural state of affairs. It does, therefore, have something to say (albeit by inference) about situations in which cooperative behavior is weak or absent. It is in this respect that the approach can cast some light on the CIS. Emmanuel Adler, for instance, has suggested that the more successful forms of regional cooperation are to be seen in "*liberal* community regions" (specifically the North Atlantic community), where cooperation is bonded by the longterm institutionalization of liberal-democratic norms and values (a "civic culture" of trust).[44] Such norms, by definition, are shallow in nonliberal or post-Communist settings (to wit, the CIS region) and thus of negligible influence in the international politics of those regions. A similar logic can be applied to the matter of identity. If a tight form of regional cooperation is seen as the result of the existence of some form of shared identity, then, by inference, a weak or nonexistent identity of this type, while not ruling out cooperation, can only give rise to it in an arrested form. And among the CIS states, it is precisely a common identity that is lacking. This is not to denigrate the importance of their shared history or the common predicaments of post-Communism. These experiences, however, have had a uncoupling rather than a binding effect. The Soviet (or indeed the imperial) past is hardly seen as a cause for common celebration and is at odds with the nation building strategies and nationalist domestic and foreign policy agendas of both Russia and the other CIS states. Even the Russian-Ukrainian relationship—one seemingly cemented by common ethnic and cultural bonds—has been swept along by these issues of national identity, rendering cooperation problematic and giving rise to competing visions of the CIS and, in the case of Ukraine, an identity orientation focused as much on Europe as on Russia and the CIS region.[45]

The excursion through these three different IR approaches offers no definitive answer to the question of the CIS. The assumptions of all three can be molded to produce an explanatory "fit," but none alone provides a satisfactory account of the circumstances prevailing in the CIS. Each captures important elements: neorealism is relevant to the mistrust and interstate competition that characterizes the organization; institutionalism helps us to understand the impact of interdependence and the mechanics of institutional creation and persistence, while constructivism alerts one to the power of norms and national identity. However, all three, while generating general hypotheses regarding cooperation, seem to work best in the CIS context when loosened or used inferentially. This is perhaps not surprising given the complexity, and in some senses the unique nature, of the processes at work in the post-Soviet region. What is interesting in the current context, however, is that the assumptions of all three are suggestive of a weak CIS.

Explaining the Development of the CIS (2): The Prerequisites of Integration

Here the emphasis shifts somewhat to a consideration of those conditions deemed favorable to promoting integration among states within a given region. This type of analysis (associated closely with neofunctionalism) enjoyed a surge of interest during the 1960s but suffered from charges of automaticity, an underspecification of causation, and a confusion between the causes and the effects of integration.[46] The analysis of this section is aware of these problems, and is intended only to be suggestive. It is also sensitive to the fact that categorizing the conditions favorable to integration can result in an overly lengthy listing process. What follows, therefore, is meant to be indicative rather than exhaustive. Adapting the approach of Andrew Hurrell, it considers the prerequisite approach as one focused on four factors: national elite perceptions, state viability, regime type, and economic convergence.[47]

National Elite Perceptions

One of the standard assumptions of neofunctionalism is that successful integration depends upon a convergence of aspirations toward increased cooperation among national elites and a shift in national loyalties among these actors to supranational authority structures.[48] This assumption retains an intuitive ring of truth. Applying it to the CIS, the attenuated nature of multilateral cooperation is explained by the fact that there is very little consensus among the member states over the way the organization should evolve and a deep division over the desirability of supranationalism. These differences of opinion can be gleaned from the functional and organizational development of the CIS analyzed above. Here, they are outlined more explicitly. In crude terms, the membership of the CIS is divided between enthusiasts and skeptics. Russia belongs to the former category, but is here treated as a special case owing to the peculiarities of its support for the CIS. Among the enthusiasts can be counted Armenia, Belarus, Kyrgyzstan, and Tajikistan. Despite their generally positive participation in its structures, these states, however, can contribute little to CIS development. To varying degrees, all are economically and militarily dependent upon Russia. Their support of the CIS should thus be seen less as a spur to multilateralism and more as a conscious utilization of the organization as a means of consolidating the bilateral link with Moscow. Kazakhstan, too, has appreciated the utility of the CIS in this way, although, under the leadership of Nursultan Nazarbaev, it has seen the utility of the CIS in a broader sense—as a means of promoting economic recovery through a concerted effort at integration (specifically the formation of a free trade zone).[49] To this end, Nazarbaev has also been a rare supporter of supranationalism within the CIS, albeit in a form (the use of qualified majority voting) designed to prevent the dominance of a single member (for which, read Russia).[50]

Juxtaposed to the supporters of the CIS is a group of skeptics that has comprised Azerbaijan, Georgia, Moldova, Turkmenistan, Uzbekistan, and Ukraine. This disparate group of states does view the CIS as providing certain limited benefits: a loose legal guarantee of sovereignty, a convenient setting for bilateral diplomacy, and, in the cases of Azerbaijan, Moldova, and

Georgia, a platform for the articulation of positions on their respective internal conflicts. Yet such benefits are overshadowed by suspicions of Russia's motives within the CIS, and the shared view that the Commonwealth is an impediment to the development of post-Soviet national identities and the pursuit of multifaceted foreign policies. This group has consequently been less than enthusiastic in areas of CIS cooperation and has, as noted above, been adamantly opposed to the creation of supranational structures within the organization. The semi-detached position of these states is a considerable loss to the CIS. Uzbekistan is the geostrategic pivot of Central Asia and, along with Turkmenistan, a source of considerable energy resources. Ukraine, meanwhile, is economically and militarily among the most important of CIS member states (second only to Russia). It also has a considerable political significance, given its European location and status as one of the three original CIS members. For Ukraine to distance itself from the CIS, therefore, is injurious to both its credibility and reach.

Turning to Russia, it has been a consistent supporter of the CIS. Yeltsin was a leading figure in the formation of the organization in 1991 and thereafter, despite all the turbulence in Russian domestic politics and foreign policy, his administration remained publicly committed to its development.[51] Yeltsin's successor, Vladimir Putin, has also displayed a clear commitment to the organization. Russian policy has, admittedly, contained an element of the grandiose and a fair measure of wishful thinking. However, what has mattered for Moscow is not necessarily the actual level of CIS development but the long-term possibilities of the organization. The CIS may well have been characterized by stagnation, but so long as it has survived it has presented at least an avenue of opportunity for Russia to breathe life into post-Soviet interstate cooperation. It should also be noted that even at its current low level of operationalization, the CIS does present Russia with certain benefits. In the first place, the CIS is a convenient mechanism for institutionalizing Russian influence among the successor states in that Russian personnel have since 1991 dominated CIS structures. Second, areas of CIS cooperation have served specific Russian interests. This is particularly obvious in the military sphere where Russia has, under the cover of CIS arrangements (supplemented by bilateral agreements), obtained access to the hardware and facilities (nuclear weapons, air defense infrastructure and border installations) necessary for its own defense needs. In the economic sphere, Russia has been less well served, something that reflects the inability of other CIS states to contribute toward Russia's financial needs and the trend in Russian trade toward international markets. However, there remains a sense in which the CIS has a significance of sorts both as a means of preserving production linkages among the successor states, and (Russia's trade diversification notwithstanding) as a mechanism by which Russia can exploit its position as the leading regional trading state. Third, the CIS is of some note within the broader context of Russian domestic and foreign policies. A commitment to activism among the successor states has been part of the *Zeitgeist* of Russian political discourse since 1991 and both Yeltsin and Putin have felt the need to display a firm rhetorical commitment to the CIS in order to match that of domestic rivals such as the communist leader Gennadi Zyuganov and populist nationalists such as mayor of Moscow Yuri Luzhkov and regional governor Aleksandr Lebed. As for foreign policy, here the CIS has been posited as a counterweight to NATO enlargement,[52] and an institutional barrier against what is viewed as the growing influence of Islamic states (Iran, Afghanistan, and Turkey) in Central Asia and the Transcaucasus.[53] Furthermore, the CIS can be regarded as a form of compensation for the loss of Russia's global standing. Moscow enjoys only a limited influence in international forums generally and the CIS is one of the few bodies in which Russia can realistically play a leadership role consistent with its repeated claims to great power status. Russia does then have clear interests in the CIS. What is less apparent, however, is the *depth* of its commitment to the organization. Moscow has, in fact, displayed a certain caution toward the CIS. One very important consideration here has been the desire to minimize the burdens of CIS-led cooperation upon the failing Russian economy. Russia has been a provider of credits to certain CIS partners, but these have been linked largely to bilateral trade settlements and can hardly be regarded as a subsidization of the CIS as a whole. In fact, since the demise of the Ruble zone in 1993, Moscow has avoided any significant monetary commitments in service of economic integration.

A further point to note is that Russia has not always viewed the CIS as the best means of pursuing policy toward the successor states. This has been plain from the trend toward bilateralism noted above and from an increasingly public disillusionment with the CIS voiced at the highest political levels in Moscow. One barometer of opinion in this regard was Yeltsin's statements at meetings of the CIS. Although these always tended to be frank, during the first five years of the CIS's existence, the Russian president tended to emphasize the organization's ongoing potential and reserved criticisms for its failings to specific areas of activity. This approach effectively ended at the CIS meeting of March 1997. Here Yeltsin's performance amounted, for the first time, to a wholesale cataloguing of the underdevelopment of economic and military cooperation.[54] At the following meeting in October this was supplemented by a speech dedicated to the political and organizational failings of the CIS: its "bureaucratic inertia" and "endless red tape", "the chronic gulf between joint decisions and their subsequent implementation", and the lack of rationality in the "functions and commitments" of CIS bodies.[55] The statements of President Putin, while a little more generous toward the CIS, have also been marked by a similar awareness of the organization's faults.[56]

State Viability

A region inhabited by weak states need not be one characterized by an absence of international organization. In fact, state weakness may actually encourage it. A weak state may be favorably disposed to regional cooperation because it provides legal guarantees of sovereignty, because it holds out the promise of fulfilling certain tasks the state is incapable of (for instance, in the defense field), and because it gives hope of access to otherwise unavailable resources. Such calculations have not been absent in the CIS. State weakness does, however, place limits upon the degree of cooperation. In the absence of fairly sophisticated political and administrative capabilities at the domestic level, successful regional organization is hardly likely to occur, given that it rests upon the requisitioning of organizational and bureaucratic skills and resources from among its member states. Thus, in the CIS case, the shambolic nature of the organization can be read as stemming from the fact that a majority of its members, experiencing often profound processes of state reorganization if not outright destatization (privatization, the breakdown of the rule of law, unregulated decentralization), simply lack the ability to contribute in any meaningful sense to pooled organizational resources. In the more severe cases, for example, Tajikistan and Georgia, where the domestic state has all but collapsed, this is obvious, but even in Russia, the member state which has contributed most to the CIS, it is applicable given how handicapped the country is by its own domestic predicaments. This, moreover, is not just an issue of resources allotted *to* the center. The preoccupation of the CIS states with obtaining the accoutrements of statehood—an army, a national currency, a national economic strategy, the right to pursue a distinct foreign policy, and so on—has contributed to a dispersal of former Soviet infrastructure, and thus a drawing of resources away *from* the center also.

Regime Type

The importance of shared democratic values in promoting regional cooperation has already been noted above. The implication here is obvious, it is not just that similar political systems foster cooperation, but that similar democratic ones do so. Interactions among nondemocracies, even if their political systems are organized in a like manner and are based on a comparable creed or ideology, are unlikely to give rise to anything but temporary and opportunistic forms of cooperation.[57] Similarly, and following the line of argument put forward by Edward Mansfield and Jack Snyder, while democracies may be predisposed toward cooperation, democratizing states are far less so.[58] In assessing the impact of broad domestic political attributes, therefore, two dimensions of comparison are needed: variation in the type of political regime and the extent of democracy. For the CIS area, these are summarized in table 8.1.

Table 8.1 Political Regime Type and Democratization Among the CIS States

State	Regime Type	Level of Democracy		
		Political Rights[1]	Civil Liberties[1]	Freedom Rating
Armenia	president-parliamentary	5	4	partly free
Azerbaijan	Presidential	6	4	partly free
Belarus	Presidential	6	6	not free
Georgia	Presidential	3	4	partly free
Kazakhstan	Presidential	6	5	not free
Kyrgyzstan	Presidential	4	4	partly free
Moldova	premier-presidential	3	4	partly free
Russia	president-parliamentary	3	4	partly free
Tajikistan	Presidential	6	6	not free
Turkmenistan	Presidential	7	7	not free
Ukraine	Presidential	3	4	partly free
Uzbekistan	Presidential	7	6	not free

[1] 1 represents the most free and 7 the least free category.

Sources: Freedom House, *Nations in Transit 1998* (http://www.nff.org/nit98/); M.S. Shugart, "Executive-Legislative Relations in Post-Communist Europe", *Transition* 2, no. 25 (1996): 6–11; G.M. Easter, "Preference for Presidentialism: Postcommunist Change in Russia and the NIS", *World Politics* 49, no. 2 (1997): 184–211.

Two patterns are obvious from this table: some states have experienced democratic change but cannot be considered secure democracies; and amongst a significant number of states there is a tendency toward neoauthoritarian, presidential forms of rule. These patterns are not, in the logic of the argument noted above, conducive to regional cooperation. Conceivably, the situation may alter with a consolidation of democracy. However, such an outcome is far from certain in any of the CIS member states given the profound political, cultural, and economic obstacles it faces in the post-Soviet context. Indeed, in all but one or two cases, the transition to democracy—such that it is—may already have reached its limits. Instead of pluralistic, liberal democracy, the established norm among the CIS states may well come to be hybrid political systems involving quasi-democratic features alongside personalist, presidentialist, and oligarchic forms of rule.

Economic Convergence

Identifying the prospects for integration in economic terms involves a consideration of a range of different indicators. Measuring levels of regional interdependence provides one method, although as we saw in the previous section, while interdependence may create a demand for cooperation or integration this is not an assured outcome. To reiterate in neofunctionalist language, economic linkages need not lead to a "spillover" of policy competencies if these are seen as a source of vulnerability and are politically problematic. The pattern in such circumstances is as likely to be one of "spill around" (organizational stagnation and the creation of rival subgroups) or even "spill back" (the progressive failure of an integrationist scheme).[59] Both phenomena have their relevance in the CIS case. Moreover, the importance of regional linkages can only be judged by reference to the external environment. The trade and investment patterns of the CIS region, for instance, suggest that regional interdependencies have increasingly dissolved owing to trade reorientation and the penetration of the post-Soviet economies by Western sources of finance. All of this, of course, attests to the peculiar circumstances within the CIS area, where high preexisting levels of interdependence have diminished in the wake of the Soviet Union's collapse. Alternatively, one might consider economic complementarities as measured in terms of indices of economic performance. Taking the overall size of the CIS economies for instance, here a fairly wide spread is apparent, measured in both gross and per capita terms (see table 8.2). Such differentiation is not per se an impediment to integration, indeed, arguably the reverse—smaller economies, for instance may favor it as a means of accessing the economic benefits of the richer "core". For such a situation to apply, however, a crucial condition is required, namely that the core economies are growing and are able (and willing) to provide payoffs to the smaller ones.[60] As table 8.2. makes clear, in the CIS context, this is certainly not the case. The larger economies (those of Russia and Ukraine) have been in precipitous decline since 1991, and, as already noted, the Russian (and for that matter the Ukrainian) political elite lacks the will to subsidize the CIS.

A third means of assessing the economic prospects for integration focuses on the compatibility of types of macroeconomic management. If integration depends upon the presence of "common institutional models" of economic management,[61] then the prospects in the CIS are poor. Not only is there an absence of shared approaches (a fact plain to see in wide differences in the rate of marketization across the CIS),[62] but in some instances one might

Table 8.2   Economic Performance of the CIS States

	Total GNP at rate (%) parity in 1997 ($bn)	GNP per capita at purchasing power parity in 1997 ($)	Growth of GDP annual (average) purchasing rate (%)		
			1990-1997	1996	1997
Armenia	8.6	2,280	-21.2	5.8	3.1
Azerbaijan	11.6	1,520	-15.1	1.3	5.8
Belarus	49.7	4,840	-6.5	2.8	10.4
Georgia	10.7	1,980	-2.62	8.6	11.3
Kazakhstan	53.7	3,290	-10.5	0.5	2.0
Kyrgyzstan	9.5	2,040	-12.3	7.1	10.4
Moldova	6.2[1]	1,440[1]	-14.3[2]	-7.8	1.3
Russia	618.4	4,190	-9.0	-3.5	0.8
Tajikistan	5.6	930	-16.4	-16.7	1.7
Turkmenistan	6.6	1,410	-9.6	0.1	-20.0
Ukraine	109.3	2,170	-13.6	-10.0	-3.0
Uzbekistan	58.0	2,450	-3.5	1.7	5.2

[1] figures for 1996.
[2] figures for 1990-95.

Sources: The World Bank, *World Development Report, 1998/99* (Washington D.C., 1998), 190–91, 210–11; Secretariat of the United Nations Economic Commission for Europe, *Economic Survey of Europe 1998*, no. 2 (New York and Geneva, 1998), 12.

conclude that there is no coherent approach at all (a not unreasonable assumption in the Russian case in view of its recurrent financial crises).

This section has demonstrated that the conditions existing within the CIS region suggest a growing diversity and a "logic of disintegration"[63] equally as strong, if not more compelling than those conditions favorable to integration. In essence, the attitudinal, political and economic factors at play here reflect the still transitional nature of post-Soviet life; put another way, they have been part and parcel of efforts toward national assertion. The articulation of specific national priorities and the pursuit of particular forms of national political and economic development have given rise to certain complementarities among the CIS states, but these have tended to be subregional or bilateral in nature (rather than extending throughout the entire CIS region) and have fallen far short of a unifying consensus on the overriding rationale of the CIS. Furthermore, national priorities in some cases have involved a notion of self-reliance, involving a distance from the legacy of Soviet interdependence and a hostility to perceived Russian encroachment. This cannot but stunt the CIS, an organization, after all, which encapsulates projects aimed at preserving such interdependencies and which has been an institutionalized expression of Russian regional weight.

Conclusion

At present the CIS amounts to a loosely coupled confederation. The CIS is confederal in that it is premised upon state sovereignty, functional cooperation, and the limited competencies of common institutions. It is loosely coupled in that its joint structures have tended to be weak and its areas of presumed cooperation characterized by a lack of substance and uneven levels of participation. As such, the CIS is a political form that can hardly be said to amount to a developing or even an emergent form of governance among its member states. It will not, in other words, move from being loosely to tightly coupled. Indeed, what this chapter has tried to show is that any presumption of the progressive evolution of the CIS is misplaced. Expectations to the contrary are based on two assumptions, both of which are of dubious parentage. The first is the notion that the fate of the CIS simply reflects the condition of Russia. It may at present be weak, but this is a state of affairs that should be regarded as temporary not permanent. The revival of Russia will, in turn, revive the CIS, for the former will be accompanied by the historic inevitability of Russian expansion, a process that Moscow might effect through an exploitation of Commonwealth structures. While space precludes a proper treatment of this hoary issue, suffice it to say that there is nothing inevitable about the process. Indeed, divested for the first time in centuries of an imperial burden, many Russians may well come to appreciate indefinitely the benefits of a shrunken territorial base and postimperial role.[64] Moreover, even if such a role is based on a lingering sense of prerogative around its borders, the ability of Russia to integrate the CIS region (either by coercive or more benevolent means) is not likely to follow for several decades, a consequence of its own profound economic, military and political restructuring. Thus, while Yeltsin's successors may well approach the CIS with more activist intentions, they will still have to labor under inescapable constraints.

The second assumption is that, having been unified at one time, the successor states comprise a coherent region out of which cooperative and integrationist impulses naturally follow. As reviewed here, the evidence clearly does not support this either on empirical grounds or in terms of the logical basis of the argument. Furthermore, and something only partially covered in the foregoing analysis, the disintegrative tendencies within the CIS area, have been accelerated by an increasing penetration by extraregional influences. As well as the economic forces already noted above (trade diversification and the impact of foreign sources of finance), other processes are also at work. These are redolent of Karl Kaiser's "postulate of alternative opportunities," which suggests that states within a region will increasingly reorient themselves outside if such action promises reasonable rewards.[65] Space rules out a proper treatment of this pattern, but it is observable in say the pull of attraction of the EU and NATO (pertinent particularly in the case of Ukraine), and the assimilation of Azerbaijan and parts of Central Asia into the energy economies of Western firms and governments. It is a pattern, significantly, which also applies to Russia. Its moorings within the CIS could well be severed should it benefit from the development of proper and equitable relations outside. Membership of the World Trade Organization, for instance, is arguably more important for Russia than the CIS Customs Union, the development of partnership with the EU more of a priority than the CIS Economic Union, and the realization of a security arrangement based upon the Organization for Security and Cooperation in Europe more meaningful to it than the CIS Collective Security Treaty. In short, the CIS may well be a "product of the transition"[66] an organization which, as time passes, will be of less and less concern to its member states. While it may offer certain benefits—the embodiment of the political principles of post-Soviet sovereign statehood and a convenient set of forums for interstate dialogue—its role as a motor for military, economic, and political cooperation is unlikely to be more than negligible.

Notes

1. Earlier versions of this paper were presented to seminars and conferences held at St Anthony's College in Cambridge, the London School of Economics, and the Universities of Birmingham, Loughborough, and Pennsylvania. The author would like to thank all those involved in these meetings and in particular Dave Allen, Jeffrey Hahn, Andreas Heinemann-Grüder, Margot Light, Alex Pravda and Mike Smith.
2. Moldova, Armenia, Azerbaijan, and the five Central Asian states of Kazakhstan, Kyrgyzstan, Tajikistan, Turkmenistan, and Uzbekistan officially joined the CIS on 21 December 1991, some two weeks after the organization's creation. Georgia did not join until December 1993.
3. D. Elazar, *Exploring Federalism* (Tuscaloosa, 1987), 7; D. Elazar, *Constitutionalizing Globalization: The Postmodern Revival of Confederal Arrangements* (Lanham, 1998), 41–42; M. Frenkel, *Federal Theory* (Australian National University, 1986), 62–63, 76–77.
4. D.J. Elazar, comp. and ed., *Federal Systems of the World: A Handbook of Federal, Confederal and Autonomy Arrangements*, 2^d ed. (Harlow, 1991), 311–38; Elazar, *Constitutionalizing Globalization*, 53, 169–70.

5. On the circumstances surrounding the formation of the CIS see J.B. Dunlop, *The Rise of Russia and the Fall of the Soviet Empire* (Princeton, 1993), 265–76.

6. P.C. Schmitter, "Imagining the Future of the Euro-Polity with the Help of New Concepts", in *Governance in the European Union*, ed. G. Marks et al. (London, 1996), 135.

7. This distinction is drawn from R.H. Jackson, *Quasi-States: Sovereignty, International Relations and the Third World* (Cambridge, 1990).

8. Since 1996 Belarus has signed a number of agreements with Russia directed toward political union, the most important being a Union Treaty of December 1999. This is, however, an exceptional case and reflects the peculiarities of Belorussian national identity and the personal political agenda of Aleksandr Lukashenka, the country's president since 1994.

9. The preamble to the "Agreement on the Creation of the Commonwealth of Independent States" refers to a determination to develop "relations on the basis of mutual recognition and respect for state sovereignty, the inalienable right to self-determination, equality (and) non-interference in internal affairs". See *Agreements on the Creation of the Commonwealth of Independent States Signed in December 1991/January 1992* (London, 1992), 1. Such phraseology is also characteristic of another constitutive text, the 1993 CIS Charter.

10. Ukraine has raised some objections with regard to the former issue while Armenia (reflecting its claim to Nagorno-Karabakh, an Armenian populated region in neighboring Azerbaijan) has been the odd state out with regard to the latter.

11. Minority and human rights have been subject to discussions and, in the case of the latter, an agreement within the CIS framework (the 1995 CIS Convention on Human Rights and Freedoms). There is, however, no effective machinery to monitor or enforce such rights (the CIS Human Rights Commission is a body of little consequence) and the CIS has avoided any attempt to prescribe models of good government.

12. Article 1. The Charter is reprinted in *Rossiiskaya gazeta*, 12 February 1993, p.6 as translated in Foreign Broadcast Information Service (FBIS)-SOV-93-028, February 1993, pp.6–12.

13. *Izvestiya*, 18 March 1998.

14. More detailed empirical substantiation of the points developed in this section can be found in R. Sakwa and M. Webber, "The Commonwealth of Independent States, 1991–1998: Stagnation and Survival," *Europe-Asia Studies* 51, no. 3 (1999).

15. B. Yeltsin, *The View from the Kremlin* (London, 1994), 111–12.

16. *Agreements on the Creation of the Commonwealth*, 3, 6 and 11.

17. *The Commonwealth of Independent States: Developments and Prospects*, ed. A. Zagorsky (Moscow, 1992), 7–9, 29–31.

18. *Izvestiya*, 18 March 1998.

19. See note 8.

20. This body was established in December 1994 and comprises Kazakhstan, Kyrgyzstan, Uzbekistan, and (since March 1998) Tajikistan.

21. S. Kux, "From USSR to the Commonwealth of Independent States: Confederation or Civilized Divorce?" in *Federalizing Europe? The Costs, Benefits and Preconditions of Federal Political Systems,* ed. J.J. Hesse and V. Wright (Oxford, 1996), 354.

22. See the discussion of the Nordic Council and the Caribbean Community in Elazar, *Constitutionalizing Globalization*, 97–102, 133–34.

23. Elazar, *Constitutionalizing Globalization*, 111.

24. W. Wallace, "Regionalism in Europe: Model or Exception?" in *Regionalism in World Politics: Regional Organization and International Order,* eds. L. Fawcett and A. Hurrell (Oxford, 1995), 201–27.

25. L. Glaser, "The Security Dilemma Revisited", *World Politics* 50, no.1 (1997), 171–201; J.M. Grieco, "Anarchy and the Limits of Cooperation: A Realist Critique of the Newest Liberal Institutionalism", *International Organization* 42, no.3 (1988), 485–508; K. Waltz, *Theory of International Politics* (Reading, 1979), 105–6, 186–7.

26. J.J. Meirsheimer, "The False Promise of International Institutions", *International Security* 19, no. 3 (1994/95), 13.

27. S.M. Walt, "Alliance Formation and the Balance of of World Power, " International Security 9, no. 4 (1985), 3–43.

28. A. Hurrell, "Explaining the Resurgence of Regionalism in World Politics", *Review of International Studies* 21, no. 4 (1995), 343.

29. J.M. Grieco, "The Maastricht Treaty, Economic and Monetary Union and the Neorealist Research Program", *Review of International Studies* 21, no.1 (1995), 21–40.

30. A. Moravcsik, "Negotiating the Single European Act", *International Organization* 45, no.1 (1991), 25–7.

31. R.O. Keohane, *After Hegemony Cooperation and Discord in the World Political Economy* (Princeton, 1984), chapter 6.

32. "Institutions" encompass not just formal international organizations, but also international law, treaties, and regimes.

33. O.R.Young, "International Regimes: Toward a New Theory of Institutions", *World Politics* 39, no. 1 (1986), 110; W. Mattli, "Explaining Regional Integration Outcomes", *Journal of European Public Policy* 6, no. 1 (1999), 16.

34. F. Kratochwil, "Norms Versus Numbers: Multilateralism and the Rationalist and Reflexivist Approaches to Institutions: A Unilateral Plea for Communicative Rationality", in *Multilateralism Matters: The Theory and Praxis of an Institutional Form,* ed. J.G. Ruggie (New York, 1993), 466.

35. R.O. Keohane and L. Martin, "The Promise of Institutionalist Theory", *International Security* 20, no. 1 (1995), 41–42.

36. Kratochwil, "Norms Versus Numbers", 466–67.

37. On crisis situations as facilitating cooperation see Keohane, *After Hegemony*, 100.

38. Keohane, *After Hegemony*, 102–3.

39. A-M. Burley, "Regulating the World: Multilateralism, International Law, and the Projection of the New Deal Regulatory State", in *Multilateralism Matters,* ed. Ruggie, 125.

40. P.J. Katzenstein, "Introduction: Alternative Perspectives on National Security", in *The Culture of National Security: Norms and Identity in World Politics*, ed. P.J. Katzenstein (New York, 1996), 19–26.

41. A. Wendt, "Anarchy is What States Make of It: The Social Construction of Power Politics", *International Organization* 46, no. 2 (1992), 417; A. Wendt, "Collective Identity Formation and the International State", *American Political Science Review* 88, no. 2 (1994), 386; J. Checkel, "Social Construction and Integration", *Journal of European Public Policy* 6, no. 4 (1999), 545–60.

42. A. Wendt, "Constructing International Politics", *International Security* 20, no. 1 (1995), 76.

43. J. Checkel, "The Constructivist Turn in International Relations Theory", *World Politics* 50, no. 2 (1998), 339.

44. E. Adler, "Imagined (Security) Communities: Cognitive Regions in International Relations", *Millenium: Journal of International Studies* 26, no. 2 (1997), 258–59.

45. I. Prizel, *National Identity and Foreign Policy. Nationalism and Leadership in Poland, Russia and Ukraine* (Cambridge, 1998), chapter 10.

46. R. Hansen, "Regional Integration: Reflections on a Decade of Theoretical Efforts", *World Politics* 21, no. 2 (1969), 242-56.

47. Hurrell, "Explaining the Resurgence of Regionalism", 353–57.

48. E.B. Haas, *The Uniting of Europe. Political, Social and Economic Forces: 1950–1957* (Stanford, 1958), 13–14, 286–87.

49. See Nazarbaev's report to a meeting of the CIS Council of Heads of State reported in *Izvestiya*, 30 April 1998.

50. *Nezavisimaya gazeta*, 8 June 1994.

51. See the following authoritative documents: "Strategicheskii kurs Rossii s gosudarstvami-uchasnikami Sodruzhestva Nezavisimykh Gosudarstv," *Rossiiskaya gazeta*, 23 September 1995; "O natsional'noi bezopasnosti. Poslanie prezidenta Rossiikoi Federatsii Federal'nomy Sobraniyu," supplement to *Nezavisimaya gazeta*, 14 June 1996; "Kontseptsiya natsional'noi bezopasnosti Rossiiskoi Federatsii," *Rossiiskaya gazeta*, 26 December 1997.

52. See the comments of Russian Defense Ministers Andrei Grachev cited in British Broadcasting Corporation, Summary of World Broadcasts (SWB) SU/2055 S1/1, 23 July 1995; of Igor Rodionov in *Nezavisimaya gazeta*, 26 December 1996; and Igor Sergeyev cited in FBIS-UMA-98-026, 26 January 1998 and SWB SU/3541 A/1, 22 May 1999.

53. This was a prominent theme of a report on the CIS presented by Yevgeni Primakov in September 1994 when head of the Russian Foreign Intelligence Service. See *Rossiiskaya gazeta*, 22 September 1994.

54. *Nezavisimaya gazeta*, 5 April 1997.

55. SWB SU/3059 A/1-3, 25 October 1997.

56. Putin cited by Interfax, 22 November 1999.

57. T. Risse-Kappen, "Collective Identity in a Democratic Community: The Case of NATO", in *The Culture of National Security*, ed. Katzenstein, 367, 399.

58. E.D. Mansfield and J. Snyder, "Democratization and the Danger of War", *International Security* 20, no. 1 (1995), 5–38.

59. E.B. Haas, "The Study of Regional Integration: Reflections on the Joy and Anguish of Pretheorizing", *International Organization* 24, no. 4 (1970), 615.

60. Haas, "The Study of Regional Integration", 615.

61. M. Kaser, "How Real are Prospects for Economic Integration in the Commonwealth of Independent States?" Paper presented to a seminar at the British Foreign and Commonwealth Office, 17 May 1996, 5.

62. The IMF has divided the fifteen former Soviet republics into four categories according to the rate of reform. The "advanced reformers" (non-CIS members Estonia, Latvia, and Lithuania); "intermediate reformers" (Armenia, Georgia, Kazakhstan, Kyrgyzstan, Moldova, and Russia); "late reformers" (Azerbaijan, Ukraine, and Uzbekistan); and "others," that is, the slowest reformers (Belarus, Tajikistan, and Turkmenistan). See *IMF Survey*, 8 June 1998, 179.

63. A phrase derived from J. Tranholm-Mikkelsen, "Neo-functionalism: Obstinate or Obsolete? A Reappraisal in the Light of the New Dynamics of the EC", *Review of International Studies* 20, no. 1 (1991), 18.

64. M. Mendras, "Towards a Post-Imperial Identity", in *Russia and Europe: The Emerging Security Agenda*, ed. V. Baranovsky (Oxford, 1997), 90–103.

65. K. Kaiser, "The Interaction of Regional Subsystems. Some Preliminary Notes on Recurrent Patterns and the Role of the Superpowers", *World Politics* 21, no. 1 (1968), 101.

66. A similar phrase was used in the communiqué issued by a summit of the five Central Asian presidents in January 1998. See Radio Free Europe/Radio Liberty, *Newsline*, 7 January 1998.

Section III

---∞∞∞---

NATIONAL APPROACHES
AND FUTURE DIRECTIONS

Chapter 9

EAST MEETS WEST

Cultural Reconfigurations of National Identities in Post-1989 Europe

———⊗⊗⊗———

Willfried Spohn

The decade following the European revolution of 1989–90 has witnessed a progressive reconnection of the divided European civilization.[1] The basic structural pluralism of European civilization, severely damaged by World War II and torn apart by the cold-war system, has been restored.[2] Traditional divergences of center-periphery relations in economic development, state formation and nation building, as well as cultural particularities have reappeared.[3] At the same time, the integration project of the European Union entails a basic reconstruction of European structural pluralism.[4] As a consequence of the European revolution, a fundamental reconfiguration of European civilization is taking place. One crucial cultural component of the reconfiguration of European civilization is the reconstruction of national identities—most visible in the revival of nationalism in the East and the new nationalism in the West.[5] The political and social sciences, however, have been only partially prepared for the analysis of this reemerging phenomenon. Nationalism seemed to be in irreversible decline—in Western Europe through the transnational integration of the European Union and in Eastern

---

Notes for this section begin on page 209.

Europe through the international socialist state system. The transformation research emerging after the breakdown of the Soviet communist order concentrated in similar ways on politicoinstitutional and socioeconomic processes of democratization and marketization. When literature on European integration and transformation research have addressed the issue of nationalism, they have often treated it as a functional effect of economic and political globalization or as a result of the crisis-prone processes of economic and political transformation.[6]

National identities and nationalism, however, will be treated here as essentially cultural phenomena.[7] This is not to deny that national identities and nationalism are embedded in and oriented toward political structures and institutions, presupposing the de-facto or wished-for existence of a nation-state. Nevertheless, the subjective constitution of a national community in the forms of a common political idea, a shared consciousness, and sentiment are of key importance. Following the tradition of Max Weber—and more recently Anthony Smith's approach—the analysis of the structural bases of nation building such as a common history, memory, territory, politicolegal framework and economic system does not suffice; analysis of the cultural components of collective identity formation is crucial as well.[8] From this perspective, analysis of the contemporary revival of nationalism in the decade after 1989 warrants a cultural analysis of the reconfiguration of national identities. I would like to outline some constitutive processes of this cultural reconfiguration of national identities, focusing specifically on the major countries on the (northern) East-West axis in the last decade: Great Britain, France, Sweden, Germany, Poland, and Russia. I will begin with a description of some major trends in the reconfiguration of national identities, proceed to a comparative historical-sociological explanatory approach, and finally offer an interpretation of the consequences of European integration for the reconfiguration of European civilization.

Transformations of National Identities on the East-West Axis

The European project—both as an idea and its realization—originally emerged as a consequence of the near self-destruction of Europe by the nationalistic struggle between the great powers in the two world wars and the hope of regaining a renewed global role through internal pacification, cooperation, and integration.[9] As a consequence of the cold war division of Europe, however, the realization of the European project was restricted to Western Europe. Within these limits, its institutional order was then determined by the formative impact of the major Western European nations, with their respective power potentials, national interests, and conceptions of Europe. The core of the European project was the French-German connection, adding in the second stage Italy and the Benelux countries. For France, the European integration project was a way of keeping up its traditional great power status, compensating for the loss of its colonies, controlling Germany's growing power potential, and shaping Western Europe by administrative means through Brussels. For West Germany, the European integration project meant a form of moral acceptance by the international community, a path to economic reconstruction and development, and an indirect means to regaining a sphere of influence. For Italy, the Netherlands, Belgium, and Luxembourg, integration was an opportunity to participate in West European economic development and an advantageous form of international cooperation.

The other European countries only gradually became oriented towards this transnational European integration project based on the Western European continental core. In essence, it was the growing economic and political power in a globalizing world that made this integration project increasingly more attractive than merely intergovernmental forms of cooperation. Great Britain, with its strong Commonwealth and Atlantic orientations, entered the European Community only reluctantly after its painful experience of imperial and economic decline.[10] The Scandinavian countries, with their own Nordic cooperation framework, also reoriented themselves to European integration only slowly and hesitantly.[11] By contrast, for Southern Europe—Greece, Spain, and Portugal—European integration was a way to move from political authoritarianism and economic backwardness towards democracy and modernization.[12] For East Central Europe, the "return to Europe" became a focus of resistance against the imposition of Soviet rule, without however necessarily identifying "Europe" with the European integration project.[13]

With this backdrop, the collapse of Communism in Eastern Europe signified first and foremost a fulfillment of the European idea by including the whole of Europe. But at the same time it became a turning point for the established Western European integration project. On the one hand, inclusion of the Western European half into the European integration project was almost completed, and "Maastricht" envisioned and required further crucial steps to deepen this process. On the other hand, the geopolitical seachange brought about by the European revolution not only opened the integration process to a field beyond the limited Western European space but also questioned the mere continuation of the same form of transnational integration. With the revolution of 1989–90, each European country was confronted anew with the basic premises of transnational integration, the relationship between European civilization and European integration, the impact of eastward enlargement, the gravitational shift to the east, and, last but not least, the relative growth in the power of united Germany. A redefinition of national identities and European orientations in Eastern and Western Europe was unavoidable.[14]

Let us now take a closer look at these national self-understandings in the main countries on the northern East-West axis in the decade after 1989. The best starting point for description is the core of the integration project: the tandem of France and Germany. France is clearly the nation most disturbed by the sea-change of 1989.[15] France has been the key leader of integration, intending to secure its future role in world politics while both reducing the American-British influence on Europe and controlling Germany as a potential rival. The French strategy of European integration was supposed to guarantee the political dominance of France through economic modernization and administrative control within enlarged European markets and centralized European institutions. Confronted with the change after 1989, France has promoted a deepening of the integration process with the particular aim of monitoring the enhanced power of united Germany. Formally, indeed, the institutional arrangements set out in the Maastricht Treaty seemed to implement this political aim. In practice, however, the gravitational power shift to the east has not only imposed the necessity of the eastern enlargement but also called into question traditional modes of integration. Political integration has shifted towards a more federal multipolar arrangement, and economic integration has moved towards a deregulated model with less state intervention. As a consequence, France's national identity and European orientation have been challenged, fueling the fires of a more particularistic French nationalism.

As a result of the collapse of Communism, divided Germany reunited in the form of an enlarged federal republic. Although "tamed" by internal democratization and external European integration, united Germany's power position as the renewed center of Europe has strengthened considerably.[16] On the one hand, Germany's position of relative dominance, already achieved by West Germany's prior economic development, has become further expanded by the additional demographic, economic, and political weight produced by unification.[17] On the other hand, this relative dominance has also been a consequence of Germany's growing sphere of influence deriving from the opening up of Eastern Europe. As a corollary, Germany's re-centering within Europe is accompanied by considerable changes in Germany's European orientation and strategy. In the transition phase after 1989, Germany still continued to play the role of junior partner vis-à-vis France, further supporting a centralist pattern of Western European integration. Soon, however, the long-term implication of Germany's changed geopolitical position in Europe became more manifest. Germany's political emphasis has shifted towards an enlargement of the European Union to the east, stimulated by geographical proximity, economic potential, and a mission of reconciliation. With Germany's reorientation towards enlargement, the German federal model has become more attractive to prospective Eastern European members as an alternative to the French statist model of integration. At the same time, Germany's enhanced European influence combines stronger national self-centeredness and growing currents of xenophobic nationalism.

In contrast to the approaches of the French-German tandem, Great Britain and Sweden are defensively adjusting to the European integration project. In Great Britain, the European sea-change resulted in an erosion of the traditional skepticism and caution concerning European integration.[18] The weight of the British Commonwealth and of its special connection to the United States diminished, while the advantages of the European framework, specifically with respect to halting British economic decline and solving national questions within the United Kingdom, became more obvious. The opening of the European continent has not only weakened the French statist conception of Europe; it potentially contends with the German federal model as well. Accordingly, the traditional fear of Europe as threatening British sovereignty and freedom has weakened, and the original hope of shaping Europe in more pluralistic and looser modes by strengthening its democratic, constitutional, and decentralized structures has increased. In addition, the gravitational shift of Europe to the east and Germany's growing weight have demonstrated the necessity of breaking from defensive British attitudes. However, as the steps toward deeper European integration, especially in the form of the monetary union, progress, the separate British national identity vis-à-vis continental Europe remains in place, supporting particularistic and sometimes even xenophobic forms of nationalism.

Sweden, like the other Scandinavian countries, presents a case of defensive adjustment to European integration.[19] Here, the sense of a separate Nordic identity materialized in efforts to create a free trade zone and a Nordic cooperation framework as an alternative European regional model. Only when Great Britain began to view the European Community as a superior basis for economic modernization and joined it did an erosion of regionalism begin in the Scandinavian countries, especially in Denmark, Finland and Sweden, and to a lesser degree in Norway. Like Great Britain, Sweden has traditionally preferred a purely intergovernmental Europe, fearing the

French-German centralizing model of European integration as a threat to Swedish values of national independence, individual freedom, and welfare statism. Paralleling the change in British attitudes toward integration, the 1990s witnessed a weakening of the sense of Nordic separateness and related defensive orientations. European integration seemed to present the possibility of shaping a more social-liberal version of Europe, of influencing the eastern enlargement as well as the transformation of the proximate Baltic states with a socially tamed welfare capitalism.

Turning to Poland and Russia on the Eastern European side of the East-West axis, the fall of Communism was accompanied by an image of Europe symbolizing national independence, constitutional democracy, and welfare economy. In "Communist" Poland, which was moved from its central European position into the Soviet Eastern Europe only through the "betrayal" of Yalta, the continuous revolts from 1956 to 1980–81 were motivated by a desire to "return to Europe."[20] At the same time, the cultural bases of anti-Communist resistance were increasingly shaped by Catholicism: the Catholic Church, the Catholic-influenced Solidarnosc movement, and the strengthened influence of Catholicism on national identity formation. In 1989, an independent Polish nation-state with recognized borders and a democratic political system reemerged. The wish to become a member of the Western institutional framework, particularly NATO and the European Union, was clearly strong. At the same time, East Central European forms of intergovernmental cooperation—reinventing of the notion of "Central Europe"—were tried out in order to preserve a more independent regional status. But Poland as well as other East Central European countries soon realized that the reconstruction of the post-Communist societies was best accomplished by associating with and integrating into the powerful European Union. After entering the accession negotiations, however, Poland realized that integration into the European Union goes only through Germany, implies a partial transfer of national sovereignty, and means a confrontation with the Western European secular-materialistic culture—thus strengthening a Catholic nationalistic defensive reaction as well.

In the collapsing Soviet Union, Europe embodied in the eyes of the reform movements an image of an alternative modernization strategy.[21] Gorbachev, like Yeltsin, invoked the image of a "Common House of Europe" as a model of Westernization—clearly in de Gaulle's sense of an intergovernmental cooperation framework rather than a transnational integration process. However, the crises and failures of the transformation process in post-Soviet Russia increasingly weakened the Westernizers and their orientation towards Europe. The dissolution of the Soviet Union not only enabled the establishment of independent nation-states but was also accompanied by a pronounced resurgence of nationalism and ethnonationalistic conflicts. The introduction of religious freedoms enabled a marked revival of religion—dominated by Orthodox Christianity and its imperial-absolutist orientations. Yeltsin's formally liberal-democratic government went hand in hand with the establishment of a presidential absolutism with only minor parliamentary and constitutional control. The economic transformation strategy promoted an oligarchic booty capitalism unable to halt unabated economic decline. As a result, Russia's orientation to the West and particularly to Europe is weakening, and the reorientation to the East, that is to Eurasia—in both the geopolitical and geocultural senses—is regaining strength.[22]

A Comparative Historical-Sociological Approach

The reconnection of Western and Eastern Europe means both a reconstruction of the structural pluralism of European civilization and its reconfiguration.[23] The traditional economic unevenness between Western and Eastern Europe has reappeared; it includes the re-centering of Germany in its relative dominance and the detour of Eastern Europe from periphery to periphery.[24] The multiplicity of nation-states has been restored, and with it the power center has shifted from the Western European Atlantic zone to the Western European continental core.[25] Additionally, the overdetermination of national identities by the cold war has been replaced by a traditional multipolar national-identity matrix.[26] The mentioned reconfiguration of Europe's structural pluralism refers to the institutional framework of integration that generates economic, political, and cultural transformations of nation-states and societies.

Regarding the cultural reconfiguration of national identities (including their respective European orientations), the comparative situation of the major countries on the East-West axis can be summarized as follows. First, the core tandem of the European integration project has undergone a substantial power shift towards united Germany; the French state-centered functional integration model is challenged by the German federal subsidiarity model. French national identity with regard to its European role is confronted with a new German assertiveness and reconciliatory policy in Eastern Europe. Second, the defensive adjusters to the European integration project, Great Britain and Sweden, have become more proactive in their European orientations. While still strongly embedded in their separate British and Nordic identities, both envision greater pluralism of the European project and opportunities for greater influence—Great Britain in strengthening the democratic and constitutional structures of European integration, Sweden in developing stronger social-liberal welfare institutions. Third, the Eastern European returnees to Europe—Poland and Russia—are clearly different and ambiguous in their European attitudes. Poland is eager to join the EU but at the same time fears the loss of national independence (particularly vis-à-vis Germany) and Catholic integrity. Russia, disappointed by its failing reforms, turns instead increasingly towards a separate Eastern Eurasian identity.

In order to explain these different national reactions, I start from the premise—following Shmuel Eisenstadt[27]—that the reconstitution of European structural pluralism is characterized by institutionally and culturally varying paths to modernization. These trajectories include different types of state formation and nation building, divergent paths to economic development, as well as differing cultures, religions, and secularization patterns. From this perspective, it is crucial to analyze the historical-structural determinants of each national identity within the European matrix. I propose an historical-sociological approach to the reconstitution and reconfiguration of European structural pluralism in the decade after the European revolution.[28] For the six major countries on the East-West axis, I will characterize three main dimensions of modernization that I consider crucial for the formation of national identities.

First, regarding the political bases of national identity formation, the different nation-states on the East-West axis are not simply the historical product of similar though nonsimultaneous processes of state formation and nation-building—as evolutionist modernization theories have often assumed—but instead follow varying developmental paths with differing institutional and cultural outcomes. As Stein Rokkan and Ernest Gellner have observed,[29] the six countries on the East-West axis have traveled on different trajectories of state formation and nation-building as a result of the different "time zones" in which these processes of modernization have been taking place. Great Britain, France, and Sweden belong to the Atlantic state formation zone, where centralizing states formed early on, and nations and national identities were formed within established state frameworks. These countries' relationships to Europe include a strong emphasis on national independence within a European integration model. In contrast, Germany belongs to the city-belt zone, which experienced a protracted history of fragmentation and a belated form of nation-state building. In Germany, there emerged not only a decentralized type of federalism but also a cultural rather than a political form of national identity. As a consequence, neither a statist nor a liberal, but a federal, concept of European integration is favored. Further East, Poland belongs to the zone of peripheral nation state formation.

Here, nation-building came first, since state formation was for a long time part of foreign imperial domination, and a secure, independent nation-state emerged only after 1989. Hence, integration into a Western European transnational framework also revives the fear of peripheral dependency. Finally, Russia belongs to the continental zone of empire building, and a modern nation-state never emerged even after the demise of the Soviet Union. It remains therefore to be seen whether or not a nation state will emerge in Russia in the near future. Here, any form of European integration other than intergovernmental cooperation seems to be neither possible nor desirable.

Second, regarding the economic bases of national identity formation, the different dynamics and speeds of economic development and the differing forms of economic unevenness separating the more developed core countries from the more backward semi-peripheral and peripheral countries have been crucial in establishing the balances of political power between the different nation-states and the embedded interrelationships between national identities. As a result of the rise of the Atlantic economy in the modern era, a secular economic disparity between Western and Eastern Europe emerged, but at the same time the six countries on the East-West axis experienced considerable changes in their geoeconomic positions, with different impacts on economic cultures and related collective identities. Great Britain, as the dynamic core of the Atlantic economy, the first industrial nation and the most powerful builder of colonial empire, developed a long tradition of liberal capitalism until the first half of the twentieth century. Even after the marked decline of Britain's industrial leadership and colonial empire after World War II, the country continued to be dominated by a rather cosmopolitan, liberal, and anti-state economic culture and therefore critical of any continental European statist or corporatist regulations. Confronted with Britain's economic hegemony, by contrast, France, Germany, and, to a certain degree, Sweden suffered from moderately backward and belatedly developing economies receiving substantial support from the state and, on this basis, developing a strong tradition of mercantilism and corporatism. Even with these countries' success in catching up with modernization and the growing challenge to Britain's European hegemony from the late nineteenth century onward, the state-interventionist and corporatist components of their national economies remain strong to date. Correspondingly, a more state-regulated and neocorporatist European integration model is still influential in those countries. By contrast, Poland's economic development remained peripheral during the modern era—dependent initially on the partitioning powers in the nineteenth and first half of the twentieth centuries and later on the Soviet economy in the era after World War II. Both depen-

dencies prepared the ground for Poland's post-Communist, neoliberal transformation strategy and her reorientation towards the Western European
economy. Russia's economy never escaped its peripheral status within the
European and world economies. Endowed with a strong autocratic and
imperial state tradition, modernization went hand in hand with highly centralized state control—in Tsarist as well as Communist times. Features of
centralism are once again at the core of Russia's recent attempts to find a
way out of the crisis-ridden reform experiment.

Third, regarding the cultural bases of national identity formation, of
special importance are the types of religion and secularization patterns
embedded in each trajectory of nation-state formation. Again, modernization does not imply a general evolutionist movement towards secularism
and secular forms of national identity formation. Rather, different forms of
religion generate different secularization patterns, and these cultural figurations have an impact on modernization patterns and the cultural components of national identity. As noted by Stein Rokkan and the British
sociologist of religion David Martin,[30] the six countries on the East-West
axis belong to different religious-cultural zones within European Christian
civilization. Great Britain and Sweden are predominantly Protestant countries with limited forms of religious pluralism and weak secularization. In
Great Britain, Protestantism has been characterized by a mixture of Angli-
canism and Calvinist forms of dissent, stressing a community-centered,
active individualism. In Sweden, Protestantism has been shaped by Luther-
anism and Lutheran pietist revival movements, emphasizing a more passive,
state-centered form of individualism. Hence, while British identity is centered on a civic social-liberal individualism, Swedish national identity is
oriented towards a welfare-state form of individualism. In contrast, France
and Poland are Catholic countries with religious monopolism and disparate
secularization tendencies. In France, due to early independent state formation and the French revolution, secularization succeeded, but in a reversed
form of state-oriented republican secularism, whereas in Poland, due to
peripheral nation building, secularization remained rather weak in the face
of a nation-centered Catholicism, resulting in diverging forms of secularist
versus Catholic nationalism. Germany represents a Protestant-Catholic
mixed pattern with duopolistic state churches. Germany is marked by an
asymmetrical secularization process resulting in an overarching secular
national identity with interconfessional undertones. Finally, Russia was
originally an Orthodox Christian country with a caesaropapist monopoly
and radical secularization tendencies. In Soviet Russia, a reversed form of
secularist ideocracy became institutionalized, provoking inversely a reli-

gious revival with strong religious components in contemporary post-Soviet imperial nationalism.

The contemporary reconstitution of the structural pluralism of European civilization means the reconnection of these different nation-states with their interrelated but differing political, economic, and cultural trajectories of modernization and collective identity formation. To summarize the political, economic, and cultural components of nation-states, six configurations of national identity and European orientation are brought together on the East-West axis: (1) In France, a long established state-centered, mercantilist and secularist-enlightened national identity combines with the vision of a centralizing European integration project; (2) Great Britain, on the basis of a long established liberal economy, civil society and pluralistic collective identity, is most favorably inclined toward a pluralistic, liberal form of Europe; (3) similarly, Sweden favors a more democratic Europe, supplemented by a welfare-state orientation; (4) in contrast to these northwestern, politically stable national formations, German identity, on the background of a culturally diversified, conflicting, and traumatized history of national unification, is oriented towards a federal, culturally pluralistic, and economically regulated form of European integration; (5) Poland, with its strongly Catholic national identity, is ambivalent to a European integration that, albeit economically attractive, imposes anew political semi-sovereignty, economic dependency, and Western European secularism; and (6) Russia, on an imperial-Orthodox track, is even more ambivalent about Europe. Pushed to a minor role within Europe, it reinvigorates the eastern imperial-missionary traditions.

European Structural Pluralism and European Integration

The reconstitution of the structural pluralism of European civilization resulting from the collapse of the Soviet order entails the reconnection of Western European with Eastern European national figurations on the East-West axis. At the same time, the traditional structural pluralism of European civilization as a plurality of independent and conflicting nation-states has been fundamentally transformed by European integration. Western European integration reacts to both the past forces of nationalistic self-destruction and the present forces of accelerating globalization; it is intended to overcome the separate and independent European nation-states with a transnational framework that combines the power of European regions and nation-states and limits their sovereignty. Contrary to some versions of globalization theory, this transnational framework is not identical with the dissolution of the nation-state, but it increasingly imposes a transnational political regime that limits national policy making.[31] Furthermore, the structural pluralism of European civilization places obstacles to legitimizing a homogeneous form of integration.[32]

In hindsight, it is more obvious than before that European integration, culminating in the formation of the European Union in 1992, had been initially bound to the specific framing conditions of the cold war division of the European continent. The territorial boundaries of integration were more or less clearly defined, and the inclusion of all Western European states into European integration was almost completed with the three major enlargement steps to the northwest, the south, and the north. Along with this Western European territorial consolidation, the integration process also deepened incrementally. It left behind the first intergovernmental associational stage and moved increasingly towards a sort of federation. Although the possibility of a united European federal state appeared at the horizon, the degree of integration reached with the Single European Act, the Treaty of Maastricht, and the introduction of the Euro currency still falls short of a fully developed European federal union. The European Union at its present stage is thus best defined as a mixture between an interstate and a federal union.[33] Any further movement in the direction of a fully developed federal union has to reckon with substantial national resistance in crucial member states, and further steps aimed at deepening integration seem to require parallel steps toward democratizing the EU's political institutions.

The collapse of Soviet communism in Eastern Europe decisively changed the framing conditions of Western European integration. On the one hand it pushed integration considerably in the direction of a federal union in order to control Germany and to guarantee a minimal unity in face of the opening Eastern European space. At the same time, integration had reached a crucial turning point. The opening of the Eastern European space raised anew the fundamental question of Europe's territorial boundaries—a question that, regarding the European civilizational identity and the number of potential future EU members, could not easily be answered. The definition of the boundaries of European civilization has now emerged more urgently than before and has led to a more explicit exclusion of Russia and Turkey. In addition, the new geopolitical situation has brought more visibly to the surface the diverging interests of the European Union members. As noted above, in the cases of Great Britain, France, Sweden, and Germany, a pronounced diversification regarding the aims of European integration has emerged. State-centered, federal, and intergovernmental concepts of European integration compete more openly with each other than ever before. Different social structures and levels of economic development, dissimilar conceptions of capitalism and social equality, opposing political interests and public opinions, as well as cultural and religious variances are articulated more openly. The result is a concept of "variable geometry union" that, while holding to the unity of integration, allows for different economic, political, and cultural speeds in integration.[34] However, the "variable geometry union" also recognizes that further development of the European Union into a federal union is considerably farther away than before.

The turning point of European integration is especially well crystallized in the question of eastern enlargement. In contrast to former rounds of enlargement, which could be viewed as sequential steps in a defined evolutionary direction, the eastern enlargement newly revives critical issues such as European territory, identity, and modes of integration.[35] The eastern enlargement is a focus of diverging economic and political interests as well as cultural and political orientations. The most outspoken supporter of the eastern enlargement is united Germany. The primary reasons for this are not only its territorial proximity and the economic opportunities of new export and investment markets but also the historical feeling of guilt and the resulting quest for reconciliation. Under the missionary invocation of the common European identity, Germany's economic, political, and security interests favor a concentration of the eastern enlargement on its closest East Central European neighbors.[36] Great Britain and Sweden also belong to the group of countries sympathetic to the eastern enlargement. In the Swedish case, here similar to that of Germany, economic and political interests in the stabilization of the adjacent Baltic regions combine with shared historical legacies.[37] In the British case, unlike Germany and Sweden, economic and political interests in Eastern Europe combine with an underlying concern to halt a too speedy centralization of Europe.[38] By contrast, France is more ambivalent about the eastern enlargement of the European Union. On the one hand, there is a political interest in controlling Germany and its eastern commitment; on the other hand, direct economic gains in Eastern Europe weigh less against the expected economic losses, particularly in the agrarian sector.[39] Furthermore, the peripheral countries of the European Union fear direct economic competition in both their agrarian and industrial sectors, which are supported by the European structural funds.[40] As a combined result, the overall interest of the European Union in expanding to the east is limited. This is strongly reflected in the planned two phases of the enlargement process, first negotiating with the economically more developed and geopolitically closer countries, and only later considering the less promising and more distant ones.

From the Eastern European perspective, however, the enlargement of the EU looks quite different. The identities of the East Central European countries are not only based on the claim of a common European heritage but also connected with liberation from Soviet rule. The post-Communist transformation processes have been intimately connected with a Western European orientation.[41] Democratic transition, capitalist transformation, and the welfare state are supposedly bringing Western and Eastern Europe together. Related expectations have crystallized with particular force in the desire for quick integration into the EU. However, confronted with the prerequisites of European integration, high hopes and expectations were moderated. Certainly, the European Union and individual Western European countries support Eastern European transformation with special programs of economic, financial, and cultural aid. But the first association negotiations and treaties also revealed the predominant interest of the European Union to protect its own economies from Eastern European competition. The stiffening of immigration policies is similarly intended to protect the Western European labor markets from Eastern European labor migrants and wage competition.[42] Furthermore, the accession negotiations made clear that the EU is now imposing a transnational framework, originally designed only for Western Europe, on Eastern European accession candidates. This experience is particularly disturbing for countries that have just regained their national sovereignty and are now supposed to limit it again within a preexisting framework whose shape they have no possibility of determining. Last but not least, those Eastern European applicants left out in the first round are potentially losing any hope for integration, increasing their ambivalence over following the proposed Western European modernization path. In the case of Poland as a candidate for accession in the first round, high hopes for successful completion of the economic transformation phase combine with increasing uneasiness about the imposed political and legal framework, resulting in defensive-nationalistic currents.[43] Russia, due to its territorial size and unconsolidated state structures, is not an eligible candidate for the European Union in the foreseeable future, remaining at best a potential partner in special trade agreements. The Russian case reveals at the same time how disappointment about Western reform strategies stimulates anti-Western sentiments.[44] Poland is typical of the first accession candidates, Russia of those left out; in the end, European civilization might be divided between a widened European Union and Russian-reoriented parts of Eastern and South Eastern Europe.

The relationship between the structural pluralism of European civilization and European integration is not a simple matter of harmonious congruence but represents a dynamic and contentious field of reconnection. European civilization, with its Roman-Hellenistic and Judeo-Christian foundations, is defined not only by the physical boundaries separating it from other civilizations, especially the Islamic one, but also by crucial internal cultural and structural divergences. In terms of its cultural pluralism, the most important distinctions pertain to different religious regions, linguistic cultures, and ethnonational groups. In terms of its structural pluralism, the most important feature is the plurality of nation-states and the interpenetration of centers and peripheries. European integration is both a form of ecumenical interconnection among pieces of a culturally pluralistic Europe and a form of transnational centralization. In political terms, the peoples of individual EU member states will use their democratic authority to limit the degree of centralization within the union. In cultural terms, the degree of inclusion reflects the internal and external boundaries of European civilization. The external and internal cultural boundaries of European civilization can be either softened or hardened by the political forms of integration. Regarding the present expansion of the European Union to the east, the potential danger rests in an integration limited to the Western Roman sphere of European civilization, thereby hardening the borders with Christian Orthodox and Islamic Europe. Instead, the European integration project must accommodate the full diversity of Europe's structural pluralism.[45]

Notes

1. See, among others, K. von Beyme, *Systemwechsel in Osteuropa* (Frankfurt/M., 1994); R. Dahrendorf, *Reflections on the Revolution in Europe* (London, 1990); S. Garcia, ed., *European Identity and the Search for Legitimacy* (London: Pinter Publishers, 1993); S. Hanson and W. Spohn, ed., *Can Europe Work. The New Germany and the Reconstruction of Postcommunist Societies* (Seattle, 1995); W. Merkel, E. Sandschneider, and D. Segert, eds., *Systemwechsel. Die Institutionalisierung der Demokratie* (Opladen, 1996); H. Miall, ed., *Redefining Europe: New Patterns of Conflict and Cooperation* (London, 1994); H. Wollmann, H. Wiesental, and F. Bönker, eds., "Transformation sozialistischer Gesellschaften. Am Ende des Anfangs, " *Leviathan*, Sonderheft 15 (1995).
2. The concept "structural pluralism" is specified, particularly in comparison to India, by S.N. Eisenstadt, *The European Civilization in Comparative Perspective* (Oslo, 1987).
3. See particularly D. Chirot, ed., *The Origins of Backwardness in Eastern Europe* (Berkeley, 1989); N. Davies, *Europe: A History* (Oxford, 1996); M. Haller, ed., *Class Structure in Europe: New Findings for East-West Comparisons of Social Structure and Mobility*

(Armonk, 1990); E. Gellner, *Conditions of Liberty* (London, 1994); Brian Jenkins and S.A. Sofos, eds., *Nation and Identity in Contemporary Europe* (London, 1996); T. Jordan, *The European Culture Area: A Systematic Geography* (New York, 1988); M. Mann, "European Development: Approaching a Historical Explanation," in *Europe and the Rise of Capitalism*, ed. Jean Baechler, John Hall, and Michael Mann (Oxford, 1988); J. Szücs, *Die drei historischen Regionen Europas* (Frankfurt/M., 1990); G. Therborn, *European Modernity and Beyond: The Trajectory of European Societies 1945–2000* (London, 1996).

4. See, among others, J. Caporaso, G. Cowles, T. Risse, eds., *Europeanization and Domestic Change* (Ithaca, 2000); E. Haas, *Nationalism, Liberalism, and Progress: The Rise and the Decline of the Nation-State* (Ithaca, 1997); J. Hayward and E. Page, eds., *Governing Europe* (Durham, 1995); M. Jachtenfuchs and B. Kohler-Koch, eds., *Europäische Integration* (Opladen, 1996); P. Katzenstein, eds., *Mitteleuropa: Between Europe and Germany* (Providence, 1997); P. Katzenstein, ed., *Tamed Power: Germany in Europe* (Ithaca, 1997); A. Markovits and S. Reich, *The German Predicament: Memory and Power in the New Europe* (Ithaca, 1997); Richard Münch, *Das Projekt Europa* (Frankfurt/M., 1994); A. Smith, *Nations and Nationalism in a Global Era* (Oxford, 1995); W. Weidenfeld and J. Janning, eds., *Europe in a Global Change* (Gütersloh, 1997); H.A. Winkler and H. Kaelble, eds., *Nationalismus, Nationalitäten, Supranationalität* (Stuttgart, 1993).

5. See particularly H. Berding, ed., *Nationales Bewußtsein und kollektive Identität* (Frankfurt/M., 1993); B. Giesen, ed., *Nationale und kulturelle Identitäten* (Frankfurt/M., 1991); R. Caplan and J. Feffer, ed., *Europe's New Nationalism* (New York:, 1996); C. Kupchan, ed. *Nationalism and Nationalities in the New Europe* (Ithaca, 1995); Y. Kreijci and V. Velimsky, *Ethnic and Political Nations in Europe* (London, 1981); M. Mommsen, ed., *Nationalismus in Osteuropa* (Munich, 1992); P. Sugar, ed., *Nationalism in Eastern Europe in the Twentieth Century* (Seattle, 1995); M. Teich and R. Porter, eds., *The National Question in Europe* (Cambridge, 1993); E. Tiryakian and R. Ragowski, eds., *New Nationalism in the Developed West* (Boston, 1985).

6. For explanatory approaches to the revival of nationalism in Europe see K. Barkey and M. von Hagen, eds., *After Empire. Multiethnic Empires and Nation-building* (Boulder, 1997); Klaus von Beyme, *Systemwechsel in Osteuropa*; R. Brubaker, *Nationalism Reframed. Nationhood and the National Question in the New Europe* (Cambridge, 1996); G.-J. Glaeßner, *Demokratie nach dem Ende des Kommunismus* (Opladen, 1994); A. Motyl, ed., *Thinking Theoretically About Soviet Nationalities: History and Comparison in the Study of the USSR* (New York, 1995); C. Offe, *Der Tunnel am Ende des Lichts* (Frankfurt/M., 1994); R. Rudolph and D. Good, eds., *Nationalism and Empire. The Habsburg Empire and the Soviet Union* (Minnesota, 1992); H. Seton Watson, *Nations and States* (Boulder, 1977).

7. For new theoretical approaches to nationalism see P. Alter, *Nationalismus* (Frankfurt/M., 1985); B. Anderson, *Imagined Communities* (London, 1983); J. Armstrong, *Nations before Nationalism* (Chapel Hill, 1982); G. Balakrishnan, ed., *Mapping the Nation* (London, 1996); C. Calhoun, *Nationalism* (Minneapolis, 1997); E. Gellner, *Nations and Nationalism* (Oxford, 1983); L. Greenfeld, *Nationalism: Five Roads to Modernity* (Cambridge, 1993); A. Smith, *The Ethnic Origins of Nations* (Cambridge, 1986); A. Smith, *Nationalism and Modernism* (London, 1998); and as an overview, J. Hutchinson and A. Smith, eds., *Nationalism* (Oxford, 1996).

8. Max Weber, *Wirtschaft und Gesellschaft* (Tübingen: Siebeck and Mohr, 1964); A. Smith, *National Identity* (Reno, 1992).

9. E. Haas, *Beyond the Nation-State* (Stanford, 1964); J. Galtung, *The European Community: A Super-Power in the Making* (London, 1973); D. Urwin, *The Community of Europe:*

A *History of European Integration since 1945* (London, 1991); W. Wallace, *The Transformation of Western Europe* (London, 1990).

10. S. George, ed., *Britain and the European Community: The Politics of Semi-Detachment* (Oxford, 1992); J. Northcott, *The Future of Britain and Europe* (London, 1995).

11. C. Ingebritsen, *The Nordic States and the European Union* (Ithaca, 1998).

12. A. William, ed., *Southern Europe Transformed* (London, 1984); J. Linz and A. Stepan, *Problems of Transition and Consolidation of Democracy: Southern Europe, Latin America and Post-Communist Europe* (Baltimore, 1996).

13. Katzenstein, *"Mitteleuropa"*; Linz and Stepan, *Problems of Transition.*

14. Garcia, ed., *European Identity*; Hugh Miall, *Redefining Europe.*

15. G. Flinn, ed., *Making the Hexagon: The New France in the New Europe* (Boulder, 1995); B. Jenkins and N. Copsey, "Nation, Nationalism and National Identity in France," in *Nation and Identity*, ed. B. Jenkins and S. Sofos, 101–124; G. Ziebura, "Nationalstaat, Nationalismus, supranationale Integration," in *Nationalismus, Nationalitäten, Supranationalität*, ed. Winkler and Kaelble, 34–56.

16. Katzenstein, *The Tamed Power*; Katzenstein, *Mitteleuropa*; and Markovits and Reich, *The German Predicament.*

17. W. Spohn, "United Germany as the Renewed Center in Europe. Continuity and Discontinuity of the German Question," in *Can Europe Work*, ed. Hanson and Spohn, 79–128.

18. George, ed., *Britain and the European Community*; Northcott, *The Future of Britain and Europe*; C. Wurm, "Die Integrations- uind Europapolitik Frankreichs und Großbritanniens seit 1945 im Vergleich," in *Nationalismus, Nationalitäten, Supranationalität*, ed. Winkler and Kaelble, 334–357.

19. Ingebritsen, *The Nordic States and the European Union*; O. Soerensen and B. Strath, eds., *The Cultural Construction of Norden* (Oslo, 1997).

20. A. Wlodek, T. Byrne, and E. Iankova, "Poland: Return to Europe," in *Mitteleuropa*, ed. Katzenstein, 39–100; C. Bryant and E. Mokrzycki, eds., *Democracy, Civil Society, and Pluralism in Comparative Perspective: Poland, Great Britain and the Netherlands* (Warsaw, 1995); M. Belka, et al., eds., *The Polish Transformation from the Perspective of European Integration* (Warsaw, 1996); J. Hauser, et.al., eds., *Accession or Integration? Poland's Road to the European Union* (Warsaw, 1998).

21. I. Neumann, *Russia and the Idea of Europe* (London, 1996); R. Sakwa, *Russian Politics and Society* (London, 1996).

22. T. McDaniel, *The Agony of the Russian Idea* (Princeton, 1996).

23. See particularly Eisenstadt, *The European Civilization*; S. Eisenstadt, "Center-Periphery Relations in the Soviet Empire," in *Thinking Theoretically About Soviet Nationalities*, ed. Motyl, 205–224; S. Eisenstadt, "The Break-Down of Communism and the Vicissitudes of Modernity," in *The Exit From Communism*, ed. Stephen Graubard *Daedalus* 121, (1992): 21–42.

24. I. Berend, *Central and Eastern Europe. Detour from Periphery to Periphery* (Cambridge, 1996).

25. J. Iivonen, ed., *The Future of the Nation-State in Europe* (Hants, 1993); E. Page, "Patterns and Diversity in European State Development," in *Governing the New Europe*, ed. Hayward and Page, 9–43.

26. Garcia, ed., *European Identity*; A. Smith, "The Nations in Europe after the Cold War," in *Governing the New Europe*, ed. Hayward and Page, 44–66.

27. Eisenstadt, *The European Civilization*; Shmuel Eisenstadt, *Antinomien der Moderne* (Frankfurt/M., 1998).

28. I have outlined my historical-sociological approach in W. Spohn, "Social Transformation and Historical Modernization Patterns: Germany, Poland, and Russia in Comparison," in

East Meets West, ed. Raimo Blom (Helsinki 2001, forthcoming); W. Spohn, "Zur Programmatik und Entwicklungsperspektive der neuen historischen Soziologie," *Berliner Journal für Soziologie* 3 (1996): 75–91; and W. Spohn, "Historische Soziologie zwischen Theorien sozialen Wandels und Sozialgeschichte," in *Soziologische Theorie und Geschichte,* ed. Frank Weltz, (Opladen, 1998).

29. S. Rokkan, "Dimensions of State Formation and Nation-Building: A Possible Paradigm for Research on Variations in Europe," in *The Formation of National States in Western Europe,* ed. C. Tilly, (Princeton, 1975), 541–600; S. Rokkan, "Eine Familie von Modellen für die vergleichende Geschichte Europas," *Zeitschrift für Soziologie* 9, no. 2 (1980); for an extension of this model to Eastern Europe, see P. Bakka, "Imperial Break-Down, Political Fragmentation and State-Building. An Attempt at Extending Stein Rokkan's Conceptual Map to All of Europe" (unpublished manuscript, Bielefeld, 1994); Gellner, *Nations and Nationalism*; Gellner, *Conditions of Liberty*; and Gellner, *Nationalism and the Development of European Societies,* 19–30.

30. Rokkan, *Dimensions of State Formation and Nation-Building*; David Martin, *A General Theory of Secularization* (Oxford, 1978); see also J. Casanova, *Public Religions in the Modern World* (Chicago, 1994); and W. Spohn, "Religion und Nationalismus. Osteuropa im westeuropäischen Vergleich," in *Religiöser Wandel in den postkommunistischen Ländern Ost- und Mitteleuropas,* ed. Detlef Pollack, Irena Borowik and Wolfgang Jagodzinski, (Würzburg, 1998), 87–120.

31. M. Mann, "Nation-States in Europe and Other Continents: Diversifying, Developing, Not Dying," in *Mapping the Nation,* ed. Balakrishnan, 295–316.

32. Garcia, *European Identity and the Search for Legitimacy.*

33. P. Graf Kielmannsegg, "Integration und Demokratie," in *Europäische Integration,* ed. Jachtenfuchs and Kohler-Koch, 47–42; R. Keohane and S. Hoffmann, eds., *The New European Community. Decision-Making and Institutional Change* (Boulder, 1991); M. Kreile, ed., *Die Integration Europas* (PVS Sonderheft 23, Opladen, 1992); R.M. Lepsius, "Nationalstaat oder Nationalitätenstaat als Modell fur die Weiterentwicklung der Europäischen Gemeinschaft," in *Staatswerdung Europas? Optionen für eine Europäische Union,* ed. R. Wildenmann (Baden-Baden 1991), 19–40; A. Sbragia, ed., *Euro-Politics. Insitutions and Policy-Making in the "New" European Community* (Washington, 1992).

34. Northcott, *The Future of Britain and Europe,* 312.

35. S. Baier, *Osterweiterung. Europas größte Herausforderung* (Stuttgart, 1998); J. Pinder, *The European Community and Eastern Europe* (London, 1991); C. Preston, *Enlargement and Integration in the European Union* (London, 1997), chapter10. For observations on the relationship between Turkey and the European Union see C. Bakir and A. Williams, eds., *Turkey and Europe* (London, 1993).

36. Katzenstein, *Mitteleuropa.*

37. Ingebritsen, *The Nordic States and the European Union.*

38. Northcott, *The Future of Britain and Europe.*

39. Flinn, *Making the Hexagon.*

40. Preston, *Enlargement and Integration in the European Union,* 195–209.

41. N. Ganaris, *The European Community, Eastern Europe, and Russia* (London, 1994).

42. Preston, *Enlargement and Integration in the European Union,* 195–209.

43. A. Wlodek, "Return to Europe."

44. T. McDaniel, *The Agony of the Russian Idea*; I. Neumann, *Russia and the Idea of Europe.*

45. See the critical reflections by R. Dahrendorf, *After 1989: Morals, Revolution, and Civil Society* (New York, 1997).

Chapter 10

NEW AND OLD REGIONS IN EUROPEAN AND GLOBAL POLITICAL ECONOMIES

Henry Teune

The forces determining the future of the political systems of Europe are radically different than those that drove their economic and political integration since the 1950s. Those that led to the European Union were targeted on the twin questions of how to make the nation-states of Western Europe "bigger" to assure their prosperity in order to offset the appeals of communism and enhance their military capacities against the Soviet Union. The means to meet those objectives were the European Community and NATO. Western Europe countries acquired semblances of a federation because of a common enemy. They long before had a common political culture. Today, neither the rewards of economic integration nor the fear of conquest prevail in any compelling way. The European Union and NATO can be declared successes for their times as the world moves on. The generals and bureaucrats in Brussels whose rationale was the cold war will continue to fuss with defining their missions but will be unable to persuade with arguments buttressed by fears about the risks of domination by foreign troops and ideologies.

When big threats that force unity fade, then more established proclivities come to the fore along with more willingness to take risks pursing new opportunities. That is the point of departure of this analysis and presentation of data which demonstrate local revitalization and regional political reconfigurations in Europe. The main political cultures of Europe were formed over several centuries and then were reinforced by the industrial and trade patterns in the first decades of the twentieth century. Whatever happened after that made much less of a difference than whatever happened before. Comparisons will be made throughout Europe extending into Asia to show the persistence of political cultures. The data to be presented support relationships among affirmations of local autonomy, commitment to democratic values, and a global orientation. The picture will be of the new sitting on the old. After the great European wars of this century, episodes with fascism and communism, and the collapse of the last European empire, ethnic identities have been renewed; old territorial affiliations reaffirmed; and the projections of international movements in capital, labor, and goods that were made earlier in this century have been redefined by transnational activities and institutions. Other than in the least developed European peripheries of the Balkans and Baltics, with long suppressed ethnic identities, the pathologies of nationalism elsewhere are for the moment contained, even as their histories have regained legitimate political voice.

The states of modern Europe reflect four centuries of political consolidation with various empires agglomerating parts of it usually for short periods of time. Europe moved from several thousand little local political entities about five centuries ago to a little over twenty-five states, and a few trivial ones, by 1990. Since then, more states have emerged, and more are to come. At the same time, regions, a few bigger than states and many smaller ones, both old and new, are taking shape, also with more to come. In the following pages, I present a sketch of theoretical arguments for the re-structuring of the territorial world order of states and then turn to some data from the Democracy and Local Governance research program.[1] These data, cast in terms of localities and regions, are consistent with a more complex mosaic of localities and regions made up of traditional patterns than a Europe of cities and states.

The Globalization of Development

The main macro dynamics of change today are the globalization of development and the push for democratic governance compatible with local cultures and political values. Absent any ascendant territorial empires, one of the consequences of those dynamics in Europe are multiple tier, overlapping, informal local and regional arrangements, open even to little countries, cities, and regions. Insofar as political and legal conditions help to promote the prosperity of localities and secure their cultures, they will be pursued as fluid and adaptable intergovernmental and interregional agreements. The "bond until death" of strong states, including that of federations, is neither compelling nor advantageous in an environment of competing regional and global political economies of opportunity. In Europe, current world conditions as well as the European Union support the relative weakening of central governments, a spread of localism, a refashioning and strengthening of old regions, and an emerging definition of five macro regions—Northern-Baltic, Southern-Mediterranean, Western, Central, and Eastern. The result will be messy, changing systems of political arrangements. Development, conceived as the integration of diversity, is a general process that became the social foundation not only for the modernization of societies and the economic wealth of nations during the past three centuries or so but also the basis of the modern bureaucratic state. Development is variety driven, changing not only the nature of components of societies but also the relationships among them.[2] Not only did national development provide the preconditions for the state, but it also is now coming together globally as the dynamics of localization and regionalization.

The central question is why development has shifted to the global, weakening intermediary hierarchies while strengthening local ones. The answers can be found in the logic of development as the increasing scale of social systems. Developmental processes are inclusive, absorbing variety and bringing it together to produce more variety in something new or better. At some level of development, social systems seek out variety from more encompassing systems with more variety. As a system develops, the variety available and accessible to it expands initially from neighbors and then to other areas and, finally, to the world as a total system.[3] The world did not develop as a single system. It was enveloped by a few expanding ones over the centuries through empires, whose stretch eventually weakened as internal diversity exceeded central hierarchical capacities. But the economic benefits of empire today are available without the costs of control in a stable, decentralized world system. The anomalies of small and resource-poor countries being more developed than large and resource-rich ones, the contrasts between the Netherlands and Switzerland with China and India, speak to radically different levels of integration of diversity, as well as access to the global system without empire.

The macro relationship between the emergence of strong intermediate hierarchies and development is curvilinear. Rapid increases in diversity are conditions inviting control through coordination and centralization. As diversity becomes integrated at some point those same hierarchies slow

down the rate of development. Hierarchies, represented in the political institutions of nation-states during the past two centuries, commanded integration through information-gathering (censuses), transportation networks,
and standardization of transactions through law and institutions to adjudi-
cate conflicts. Several states forced consolidation of production and markets,
which may have jump-started economic growth in some countries in a short-
term time frame. There are many stories of national economic development,
and the contributions to it by necessary forced standardization in communication, production, schooling, contracts, and finances, and, in many countries, regulation of labor. At some point, hierarchical control interferes with
access to variety and must be restrained lest it impede development and collapse. The salient example was the Soviet Union in the 1970s. That was the
dilemma of Gorbachev in the middle of the 1980s. He sought a middle
ground between openness and control and dropped in the chasm.

We roughly mark the strengthening of states in modernizing societies as
beginning in the first half of the nineteenth century and peaking sometime in
the 1970s, when highly developed countries began decentralizing government,
"disestablishing" state economic organizations, and globalizing production
and distribution.[4] The expansion of state power during the nineteenth century was massive, easily understood in the difference between the 600,000
of Napoleon's troops invading Russia and the millions mobilized for war by
the Great Powers a century later. The potential global reach of state military
power was demonstrated during the Second World War and the hot engage-
ments of the cold war of the 1960s and 70s. Soon thereafter, state control
began to be seen, not as the stimulant of economic growth and prosperity,
but as its enemy. Nearly every wealthy country for the past thirty or more
years has been taking about 40 percent or more of their annual production
and provision of services, officially accounted as monetized wealth, for a
variety of national purposes, the main ones being security and social justice.
That percentage steadily increased faster than growth in their national
economies, since the middle of the nineteenth century.[5] That meant that
from about 1850 until the 1970s there were no clear political trade-offs
between public appropriation for welfare and private accumulation. On the
issue of economic distribution versus investment, the political parties of both
the left and right could exercise their passions for justice with credibility. As
these governmental expenditures began to exceed half of the GNP, including
indirect taxes of regulation, a trade-off between higher taxes for welfare and
restraints on government for growth became apparent, initially identified in
the first half of the 1970s as stagflation and later personally with the names
of Prime Minister Thatcher and President Reagan.

Also in the 1970s, with the first significant global financial crises since 1945, the idea of a global political economy became credible and national governments of wealthy countries strengthened international standards in trade, monetary transactions, and transportation in various incipient governmental institutions, including the G-7, the IMF, and several GATT agreements. In the 1980s they adopted similar taxation policies on personal incomes with reductions in high marginal tax rates and fewer tax categories.[6] In addition to responding to the oil shocks of the previous decade, international trade intensified, production dispersed, and markets expanded. Exchanges moved beyond the control of states, reflected in the recognition of governmental failures to moderate prices of commodities and currencies and the existence of large "underground" economies. Cross-national shipments among dispersed centers of production and assembly began to dominate those directly from producer in one country to consumers in others.

The imperatives of development are variety and its integration. Setting aside access to "natural resources, " development is the putting together of existing variety into something new, innovation, or moving things and ideas about more efficiently. That requires skills and high priced-labor, and yields wealth. Integrating variety is a significantly slower process than generating variety or importing it. When developing societies achieve a level where their capacities to absorb new variety are greater than those to produce it on their own, they must "open" to variety to sustain development necessary for economic growth, or they will stagnate. Importing variety has more developmental "payoff" in highly developed societies where variety can be easily used to produce more variety than in less developed ones, where what is foreign threatens to destabilize. If that happens, a backlash of closure becomes politically attractive.

The early response of Western European national governments to openness and growth after 1945 was to use it for welfare policies. The more "open" countries took more of their GNP for welfare than less open ones, perhaps to offset the impact of economic change.[7] Openness to variety is disruptive, whether in automobiles, airplanes, or computers. As a society develops, it must retire the old in agriculture, industry, and public services. In democracies this is difficult. But the lessons are that "open economies" tend to have higher, sustained levels of economic growth than closed ones. What is also the case is that poorly developed countries are easily destabilized by rapid increases in variety and growth, either from domestic sources or imports. That lesson has yet to be translated into policies that respond to the fact that variety may be more quickly introduced into a locality than it can be integrated in ways that contribute to both growth and stability. The result has been ideologies and programs to resist globalization locally. Openness was at the core of the "crises" of the closed bureaucratic systems of Communist states, where efficiencies after a certain point no longer yielded either development or accumulation for investment. That point was reached sometime in the late 1970s when moving labor from agriculture to industry began to have diminishing returns in productivity and almost nothing new was produced. A departure from convergence to divergence between the open and closed national economies became obvious by the 1980s and merged into political forces for loosening national political barriers to global exchanges. With the end of the cold war around 1990, it was empirically persuasive to speak of a global political economy, even with its weak political institutions. The run-down systems of Burma, Cuba, and North Korea decisively demonstrated the passing of the old order of national development to global innovation and exchange. The recent openness of countries provides new choices for localities to link their fortunes to relationships other than with their national capitals while at the same time organizations and groups within them have also become globalized and their alternatives increased. The world city movement, the internationalization of cities, special arrangements among regions blossomed, especially in Europe.[8] Indeed, regional political institutions, the European Union being the prime example, were potential by-passes around the state, even for regions that were not formally affiliated with them. But these regional governing bodies as an alternative for the local to the state are also available to other, new regional arrangements, both formal and informal.

The Local-Regional Advantage

The developmental forces that weaken the intermediate, exclusive hierarchies of the state in favor of the local and complex relationships among them and with other political entities, both weak and strong, have been presented. The logic of hierarchies biases internal capacities to respond to changes. First, as hierarchies encompass more complexity, the proportion of their effort to control it increases at a faster rate than the rate of increase in their complexity. This is part of the explanation for the increase, until recently, of government expenditures relative to the growth of the economies of wealthy countries. There are limits to ratios of expansion of hierarchy and the growth of subsystems of all developing systems. The devolution of central governmental functions and deregulation continued in 1980s across a number of wealthy countries with different kinds of governing political coalitions. That is one response to complexity. An immediate consequence is a loss in control of the center relative to others in the system. The center still controls more than it did previously, but loses out relative to competing control centers. The longer term consequence is a change in the nature of central government, becoming a useful switching node but with reduced capacities to induce and coerce. An alternative response to complexity and openness is to increase governmental efforts to control. That will lead to a run-down system, where the government accelerates its control activity in response to deviation inducing activities that it generates itself. That process was well underway in the 1970s in most Communist countries. They intensified bureaucratic control as the underground economy expanded, public services deteriorated, and criminal activity and smuggling increased. Both of these responses—devolution or control—in the 1970s occurred during a period when computers radically reduced the information costs for central control, indeed, providing access to every individual and organization. The governmental control technologies of the 1950s would never have sustained the growth of governmental programs of the 1960s.

Second, a corollary of the first, is that in hierarchical territorial organizations, which all nation-states primarily are, increasing complexity at a certain point tips the advantage in favor of the local. With increased complexity or any relaxation of central control for whatever reason, horizontal relationships become more dense relative to the vertical ones. The nodes in a hierarchy increase geometrically with any new activity that is added to its structure of vertical integration, but the possible horizontal relationships increase even more. The noise in the vertical communications within the hierarchy compounds as it expands. To this must be added that the greater the choices for horizontal linkages, the more important subjective information becomes—whom you know and trust, and, especially, yours and their intentions. Local, regional, and national have always been conflictive and competitive and understood as such by those involved in zero-sum game theoretic terms. One source of "power" in those situations is that the local will always know more about itself than the national; whereas the national will know more about other locals than the locals about other locals.[9] This is an incentive to form alliances or regions, among usually better known near neighbors, to resist initiatives from higher levels of authority or to take better advantage of them.

The European Union and its future involves an intensification of central control and at the same time an increase of its diversity by new members, under whatever rules. This will be done without the coercive powers of a unified police force, a single military command, or loyal tax collectors with jails. The Union has a bank and a court and thousands of lawyers and translators. While attempting jurisprudential consolidation, new political economies are forming in the Baltic, the Mediterranean, South Central Europe, the Alpine countries, and elsewhere. Neither a single European political economy nor a global one is likely to be much more than an umbrella of an increasing number of these units.

Why Federations are Obsolete

Federalism has always been in the package of political options for those promoting the political integration of Europe. The two strong conditions for federalism are fear and gain. The former is an immediate and compelling enemy; the latter, rewarding political experiences that can be generalized, once called the "spillover" effect. Among contributing conditions are compatibility of values and open circulation of "elites."[10] More complex factors are interests of strong neighbors, especially those that may become a stronger friend or foe. These conditions were present in Western Europe at the end of the 1940s and, of course, processes of political integration took hold and worked, including in the end, the friend being stronger than the foe. What is also known is that in so far as federation is voluntary, there must be some parity among the federating units. That condition hardly prevails in an expanding Europe today, where the poor and small see security and economic benefits in the EU, or any other prosperous region, and the rich and large see obligations and costs, as well as the irritations of supplicants. With the lack of immediate security imperatives and the expansion of options among a growing number of global economies, the weight of the conditions favoring federation in the traditional sense of government have almost certainly fallen below any positive threshold.

Federations were a response to the multiplication of political units after empire and were designed to respond to expanding empires or to take advantage of their legacies. The implosions of the Soviet Union, Yugoslavia, and the weakening federations of Canada and India are not attractive models. The United States is moving toward informal regionalism and has more or less liberated its states and major cities to seek economic and other ties outside of the constitutionally licensed monopoly on foreign relations of the federal government. That too is a response to global political economies that pull different regions within the United States toward the Caribbean, the Atlantic, the Pacific, Mexico, and Canada. The relative ease of political adjustments of federal systems to transnational regional developments remains one of their strengths.

Democratization and Globalization

Related to localization is democratization. Globalization came before the "Second Democratic Revolution" of 1989, which stimulated not only independence movements but also pressures for decentralization. It made possible the viability of local political economies as an alternative to large nation-states. Democracy also made a separable contribution to both globalization and localization. It was a global phenomenon with promises to free the pursuit of political aspirations of groups. Not only had political forces based on economic interests been suppressed by authoritarian and totalitarian states, but also expressions of local political culture. The theoretical arguments for the relationship between globalization and democratic values and processes can be stated in summary fashion. Globalization depends on openness as does democracy; both are inclusive in disposition; both must be "tolerant" of diversity and conflicts; and both must have instrumental views of authority.

What happened after the collapse of the Russian empire were a number of "new" countries in Europe and elsewhere, which by the standards of the great consolidations of nation-states in the nineteenth century were very small countries, believed to lack the size and scale necessary for economic survival, autonomy in the international system, and sustained development of democratic institutions. The fear of "small" and "poor" prompted the leadership of the republics of the Soviet Union to tie their independence to a political and economic confederation. In fact, two of the very smallest of the "new" countries, Estonia with a population of less that 1.5 million and Slovenia, less than two million, are doing just fine with open economies, difficult neighbors, and new democratic institutions. The regions of Russia have been going it alone for a few years now, some prospering and some failing, regardless of their relationships with Moscow. Ideas about globalization, market economies, and democracy and decentralization had penetrated most of the world's regions by the 1980s. There was also improved understanding about democracy and openness from experiences with the totalitarian and authoritarian governments and their efforts to incorporate the local. Whereas the new European democracies of the 1920s focused on political parties, the voting franchise, and free elections, as well as civilian command of the military; the new and restored democracies of the 1990s attempted to add independent judiciaries and local self-government. One of the results has been the absence of success of nationalist political movements in open elections, even in circumstances where nationalism was presented as a solution to economic failures.

Research Findings from the Democracy and Local Governance Project

The globalization-democratization hypothesis is the guiding theme of the Democracy and Local Governance Research program started in June 1990.[11] It looks at one stratum in a mosaic of political developments, local governments and their leaders. The hypothesis asserts a positive association between the openness of localities to the global and the enhancement of the local as a point of responsibility in support of democratic values, process, and institutions. The findings from this research are that those local political leaders with democratic values are both more globally and locally oriented than those with leaders who do not support or reject democratic values. This relationships holds true for individual leaders without regard to locality, region, or country. Further, value differences on democracy and a market economy are politicized everywhere. Endorsement of democratic values, however, diminishes as one moves from West to East in Eurasia. In Western European countries, more democratically inclined leaders are less supportive of the values of a market economy whereas in Central and Eastern Europe, democratic leaders affirm its values.

The research has been completed in twenty-six countries (twenty-four are reported on here, with the exclusion of Iceland and the merging of "two" Germanies), including nine former communist countries at two points in time (the most recent data are used here). The research was conducted between 1992 and 1997. Random national samples of cities and communes were taken, ranging in population from 25,000 to 250,000 (adjusted upward in cases of highly urbanized countries, like Japan, and downward in those with a large number of small towns and a few big cities, like Hungary). Fifteen leaders were targeted for interviews in each political unit, starting with the mayor and continuing to the deputy mayor, council representatives, and political party leaders, and where appropriate, leading administrators, often financial officials. In all but four countries, the interviews were face-to-face. The basic point of observation was an individual leader with a legally defined political position in a constituted local government and an identifiable public presence with an address and access to one or more telephones. The samples of localities ranged from a low of nineteen in Slovenia and Slovakia to as high as seventy-three in Russia in order to anchor the sample across the major regions there. Eight local political leaders in each locality is the minimum for it to enter into the analysis as a community. Each country is broken down into a few major regions, ranging from a high of seven in Russia to a low of two in Switzerland, the German and French speaking cantons. The regions are constructed from known, identifiable areas within each country with slight adjustments, always a bit controversial, and hopelessly so in Spain. The German sample is two independent samples, East and West, and four regions; but the community file is not included in this analysis. The Taiwan sample is six districts or counties outside of Taipei. Over four hundred variables were constructed from the questionnaire, many used to create composite variables. The most important of these are derived from the value scales of about forty-five, of an "agree" and "disagree" nature. These items were designed to assess the values of economic equality, political participation, political equality, pluralism (acceptance of conflict), economic development, capitalism, honesty (transparency in public affairs), and political responsibility (political leaders should do what is right).

Global Patterns

From the value scale items two cross-national dimensions stand out: democratic values (pluralism-conflict, political equality, and minority versus majority rights) and the value of a market economy. One version of the democratic values variable is DemScore, constructed by simple scoring of nine value items from three value scales: political participation, political equality, and pluralism. The second is a five item scale on a market economy. Both are reproduced in more sophisticated ways in "confirmatory" factor analyses, adding items and weighing them. Another composite measure of democracy is "civic" society, the support groups sought out by local leaders when making decisions. A list of sixteen groups, adjusted specifically to national circumstances, was presented to the leaders for affirmation as important to obtaining political support and the total number mentioned entered as a general variable. A third measure of democracy was institutional participation, the leaders' perception of the ways in which people can influence decisions in the locality, ranging from elections to political parties to participation in meetings. The number of such channels of participation selected is the variable. The three main democracy variables, DemScore, Support Groups, and Ways of Influencing Decisions are taken from thirty-one different responses of the selected local political leaders in twenty-four national samples.[12] The global pattern of the democratic values of local political leaders is presented in Table 10.1. The conclusion is that democratic politics is politicized locally nearly everywhere. That means that local political leaders are divided on the issue of democracy. A second order of local politicization on values concerns a market economy. The focus here is democratic values.

Table 10.1 DemScore Correlations with Democratic Practices Across
Levels (0.000 level of significance)

	Leaders	Communities	Regions	Countries
Number of support groups sought	.21	.40	42	.53
Ways of influencing decisions	.24	.36	.40	.43[1]
N =	11,202	628	120	24

[1] significant at .04 level

What Table 10.1 shows is that regardless of countries, locality, or region,
local political leaders who are committed to democratic values also seek out
support from a larger number of groups accessible locally and believe that the
people have a wider range of means of influencing decisions. These strong
correlations generally hold, but they disguise regional differences, which in
cross-national terms means that somewhere about 90 percent of local leaders
in Sweden can be put into a democratic value camp; about 12–15 percent of
those in Russia, and less than 10 percent in Central Asia. Although democratic values have taken root locally, they thrive poorly in most political soils.

A pattern of local and global relationships can be seen in whether or not
local political leaders believe that they have sufficient powers and autonomy
to solve problems (across ten issue areas, including education, finance,
employment); whether or not political differences divide their communities
(another measure of politicization), and the extent to which they identify
with regional entities outside of their localities and countries, global identification. These relationships can be interpreted as local political leaders who
are more democratic in their values would like to have more powers to
address local problems, believe that people in their locality have different
political views, and identify with a more global political-economic entity,
usually Europe, Central Europe, Asia, or East Asia. Again these correlations
are robust for leaders without regard to community or region. The relationship, however, does not hold in cross-national analysis of the twenty-four
countries but the pattern of the relationships across individuals, communities, and regions does.

Table 10.2 DemScore Correlations: Local Autonomy, Political Conflicts,
and International Identity (significant at 0.000 level)

	Leaders	Communities	Regions
Sufficient local autonomy	-.09	-.20	-.27
Political differences in locality	.10	.27	.40
International identity	.20	.32	.37
N =	11,202	628	120

The most contested value component of local politics globally is over a market economy. The general relationship between the values of democracy and those of a market economy, however, differs across the Western, Central, and Eastern European regions. In Western Europe, local political leaders who see a lot of impact of foreign trade, labor, media are more democratic; whereas those in Eastern Europe are negative. Local leaders committed to democratic values in Central Europe, Eastern Europe, and Central Asia are also accepting market economy values, but not so in Western Europe, reflecting social democratic political party policies. Also, the impact of "foreign" differs across these regions. Although localities and regions that are more involved in exports and other things "foreign" have leaders that are more strongly committed to a market economy and democratic values for all the twenty-four countries in this study, there are marked differences across the regions of Europe. These relationships are presented in Table 10.3.[13]

Table 10.3   Demscore Correlations by Regions of Europe: Individual Leaders (significant at 0.000 level)

	Western	**Central Europe**	**Eastern Europe**
Value of Market			
Economy	-.12	.23	.10
Impact of Foreign			
Total	.10	–	-.06[1]
N =	3,593	2,695	1,349

[1] significant at .05 level

The Regions

Theoretical interpretations of the regions of Europe have used two ecological models: invasion and dominance and diffusion and adaptation, both mixed with great European historical events. The former asks who settled and dominated what areas; the later, who are your neighbors and what are they like. The defining historical events include the reach of the Roman Empire, the spread of Church, the Church schism in the eleventh century, the Reformation, the occupation of Napoleon, and urbanization following the First World War. Such an approach is a maddening theoretical-interpretative exercise that has long been favored by a select number of European scholars. One of the most persistent of these was the late Stein Rokkan of Bergen, whose hundreds of papers and notes have been reconstructed into an interpretation of Europe, its diversity and development.[14] Recasting the data from the Democracy and Local Governance research

project into ecological and event histories—something that was unplanned—
yielded surprising results.

The simplest, single piece of information that predicts the most about the
responses of these thousands of local political leaders is where they are from.
It would be better to know in what region within a country rather than simply the country, although country alone would do very well in the case of
Sweden and a few others. Once one knew the region of the leader, then the
next best thing to know would be what locality in that region that leader
comes from, although in Western European countries, knowing the political
party affiliation of the leader would give even better information. Rokkan's
analysis of Europe, as interpreted by his followers, is easily vindicated by this
research without any intention or interest to do so, other than to please the
disciples. Europe shaped its political cultures over several centuries and its
local political cultures would have been established, according to Rokkan's
interpretations, sometime in the 1920s. The distribution of democratic values by local community, represented by the Demscore, is given in map 10.1.
The most important of the main regions of Europe are defined by three political cultures.[15] The lines divide Western, Central, and Eastern Europe.
Within those broad regions, it is possible to argue about specific little regions
and where they fit. Although subject to a number of historical interpretations
of particular interest in publications circulating now in Europe, probably the
easiest to use is that of the Hungarian Jeno Szucs.[16] The historical forces of
the political developments of the West moved East while those of Asia moved
West. They clashed and mixed in Middle Europe. That is a long story, and
only the regional details would satisfy the contenders in the battle for interpretations of Europe. But these old regions are likely in their main outlines
to persist for another generation or more. The second main fault line, one
that can only be given scant credibility with the data from the Democracy
and Local Governance project, is on a North-South axis, going somewhere
across the middle of Europe, but going north to include most of France. This
involves Rome, Latin and all of that history. Data forthcoming from Greece
and Italy will be necessary to make a plausible case, especially since data
from France are unlikely to be forthcoming. In addition to this, there are
clear indications that the Baltic Sea is a "Phoenix" on the Sea, and despite
denials and because of regionalzation in Russia, it will pull in St. Petersburg
and parts of European Russia. The axis of the North might well be pinned
to Berlin. But those assertions await data from the Baltic countries. These
developments are likely to form new regional configurations, however they
are constrained by the older ones. This leaves the Balkans out of the picture,
but the fault lines of the past are present in the turmoil there today.[17] Except

Map 10.1

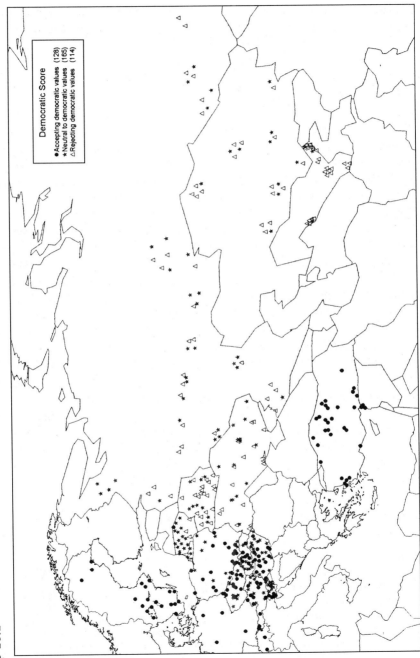

Democratic Score
● Accepting democratic values (128)
★ Neutral to democratic values (165)
△ Rejecting democratic values (114)

for the Catholic regions that encompass Slovenia and Croatia and their integration into Central Europe, most of it may remain as it was for several centuries, not a periphery of European developments, but outside of them.

Concluding Comments

What globalization has wrought is a complex pattern of world political organization. What created the modern political world of the twentieth century were urbanization and state formation. The former produced the giant cities that today constitute a tier of world cities, but a few hundred other places became concentrations of a million or more people, especially in the second half of the twentieth century. The latter ended up in the enclosure of the world's land mass into about 200 states, with a few of those of great size, all of which are being relatively weakened or threatened with dissolution by both the push to the global and the pull to the local. The great achievements of political, economic, and military unification in Europe in the second half of the twentieth century in the European Union and NATO at their high points remained weak. They were, nonetheless, stimulants for globalization and localization, that have begun to undermine the rationale for both the Union and NATO becoming stronger or consolidating as political entities.

What we see now are localities of all kinds, little regions, mesoregions, regions, and incipient institutions of a global system emerging under and over the cities and countries spawned by the industrialization and nationalisms of the nineteenth century. It is a "messy arrangement" but one that allows for both stability and development, even if with pockets of episodic violent conflicts and residues of inequality among regions and localities.

Notes

1. The Democracy and Local Governance research program began in the summer of 1990 initially targeted three countries, Poland, Slovenia, and Sweden. It is now approaching completion in thirty countries and nine former communist countries were studied at least at two points in time. It has been funded by the United States Institute of Peace and the U.S. National Science Foundation (SBR-9423801), the Polish Committee for Academic Research, and other private foundations and governmental agencies.

2. The discussion on development is taken from H. Teune and Z. Mlinar, *The Developmental Logic of Social Systems* (Beverly Hills, 1978) and its application to hierarchies and the state from H. Teune, "Development, Modernization, Democracy, and Conflicts," in *Of Fears and Foes: Security and Insecurity in an Evolving Global Political Economy*, ed. Jose Ciprut (Westport, 2000).

3. See Z. Mlinar and H. Teune, "Development and the Openness of Systems," in *Boundaries and Regions*, ed. R. Strassoldo (Trieste, 1973).

4. See L. Sharpe, "The Growth of Sub National Expenditures in the Democratic State," in *Local Finances in the Contemporary State*, ed. Institute of Political Science (Oslo, 1988), as well as other, earlier articles by the same author.

5. H. Vatter and J. Walker, *The Inevitability of Government Growth* (New York, 1990).

6. F. Kjellberg and H. Teune, "The Interventionist State and Taxation Reforms: How Are the Re-distribution Issues Handled?" Paper Presented at the Fifteenth World Congress of the International Political Science Association, Buenos Aires, 1991.

7. D. Cameron, "The Expansion of the Public Economy: A Comparative Analysis," *American Political Science Review* 72 (1978): 1243–61.

8. U. Bullman, "The Politics of the Third Level, " in *The Regional Dimension of the European Union: Toward a Third Level in Europe*, ed. C. Jeffery (London, 1997).

9. These arguments are taken from H. Teune, "Information, Control, and Territorial Political Systems, " *Studies in Comparative International Development* 14 (1979): 77–89.

10. See A. Hurrell, "Regionalism in Theoretical Perspective," in *Regionalism in World Politics*, ed. L. Fawcett and A. Hurrell (New York, 1995), and P. Jacob and H. Teune, "The Integrative Process," in *The Integration of Political Communities*, ed. P. Jacob and J. Toscano (Philadelphia, 1964).

11. The basic information can be found on www.ssc.upenn.edu/dlg/. Also see B. Jacob et al., *Democracy and Local Governance* (Honolulu, 1993).

12. Some of this analysis is taken from K. Ostrowski and H. Teune, "Globalization: Regions, Meso Regions, and the World System," Paper Presented at the Fourteenth World Congress of the International Sociological Association, Montreal, 1998.

13. Western European countries in the research are: Austria, Germany (independent samples from the East and West), the Netherlands, Spain, Sweden, and Switzerland; Central Europe, Czech Republic, Hungary, Lithuania, Poland, Slovakia, and Slovenia; Eastern Europe, Belarus, Russia, and Ukraine.

14. P. Flora et al., *State Formation, Nation-Building and Mass Politics in Europe: The Theory of Stein Rokkan*, New York, 1999.

15. See K. Ostrowski and H. Teune, "Three Political Cultures of Europe: Interpretations, Evidence, and Theories," Paper Presented at the Theory Confrontation Symposium, Moscow, 1996 and various versions, including, K. Ostrowski and H. Teune, "Local Democracy in Russia, Central and Western Europe", in *Democracy, Economy, and Civil Society in Transition*, ed. The Finnish Institute of International Affairs (Helsinki, 1997).

16. J. Szucs, "The Three Historical Regions of Europe: An Outline," *Acta Historica Hungariae* 29 (1983): 131–184.

17. For one historical interpretation, see G. Stokes, *Three Eras of Political Change in Europe* (New York, 1997).

Chapter 11

FEDERALISM DOOMED?

Institutional Implications
of European Union Enlargement

———— ✜ ————

Michael Kreile

When the Maastricht Treaty on European Union had been signed and ratified, the building of a European federal state seemed to have been definitely
relegated to Utopia. Not only had the British government managed to ban
the infamous f-word from the preamble of the treaty—the phrase, "process
leading gradually to a Union with a federal goal" being replaced by "an ever
closer union among the peoples of Europe"[1]—but member countries that
had always been staunch supporters of the federalist cause had developed
second thoughts about it. In Germany, for instance, relevant sectors of elite
opinion came to realize that progress towards a European federal state
might involve the surrender of highly valued German institutions. Many
commentators had rediscovered that the nation-state is not obsolete, that
sovereignty matters, and that there is not a European people on which a federal state could rest its legitimacy. The debate over the ratification of the
Maastricht Treaty indicated that the zeitgeist of the nineties would not be
propitious for the United States of Europe. It revealed that the integration
philosophies of leading member countries continued to diverge widely. The

entry of Austria, Finland, and Sweden added to the heterogeneity of the EU and thus to the diversity of views regarding the finalité politique of the integration process. In fact, for a number of member countries federalism represents a threat to what is left of national sovereignty and identity.

No wonder that many academic observers tended to agree with the assessment that the future of the European Union is best summed up as "Maastricht forever."[2] The "Amsterdam patchwork"[3] that emerged from the 1996 intergovernmental conference clearly confirms this scenario. The member states had balked at far-reaching institutional innovations, and Amsterdam thus failed conspicuously in its objective to make the EU fit for enlargement. To put it bluntly, the constitutionalist vision of a federal Europe has evaporated on the road to Maastricht and Amsterdam in the sense that it refers less than ever to a viable political project; nor does it inspire the integration policy of leading member countries. Does this mean that federalism is doomed as an organizing principle explaining European integration and as a strategy for promoting it? Not at all, if we consider its academic career. As Alberta Sbragia shrewdly observed, "the political debate about federalism does not reflect the elasticity of federalism as an organizing concept."[4] If the European Union, as eminent scholars have argued, already shows the marks of a federal system, federalism holds out some promise for the analysis of the EU and may well provide a conceptual framework for strategies of institutional reform.

According to Forsyth, the "classical political theory of federalism" conceives federalism as "the ensemble of structures and processes whereby a union of states or a union of polities is created and sustained, whether such a union results from a unitary system disaggregating itself, or from a number of political units coming together, or from a simultaneous movement in both directions."[5] Given the "federal elements" in the European Union, such as the common market, supranational law, and common citizenship, the EU in Forsyth's view satisfies the criteria of the theory of federalism. "It may be true that the Community is not a 'state' or a 'federal state', but this does not prevent it from being a federal union, that is to say a permanent linking together of states to form a corporate entity with a distinct boundary *vis-à-vis* the outside world, and possessed of two coexistent structures of government, one at the centre, and one at the level of the member states."[6]

In dealing with the "European Community as a Confederal System, " William Wallace emphasizes three federal elements in the Community model: the system of Community law with the European Court of Justice establishing and securing its supremacy; the European Parliament with gradually strenghtened powers; and the Community budget, which amounts to a "rudimentary system of fiscal federalism."[7] If we allow for some concept-stretching and treating the question of federalism in European integration as a matter of degree, and not as an all-or-nothing proposition, we find that the comparative analysis of federalism may still serve as a useful intellectual tool for understanding the institutional logic of the specific system of multilevel governance into which the EU has developed.[8] We may then hypothesize that the ideological rejection of federalism on the part of member governments does not exclude a sort of "creeping federalism" driven by the innate instability of the Amsterdam treaty institutions, the political dynamism of Economic and Monetary Union, the collective ambition to establish the EU as a great power capable of policing its environment, and the urgent need to secure efficient governance in a Union enlarged to twenty or thirty members. Indeed, the prospect of a new intergovernmental conference had already given rise to calls for a "new and radical reform of the Treaty."[9] In addition, at least in Germany, think tanks and government officials have expressed the conviction that "the time is ripe for a new constitutional initiative."[10]

The following section will therefore explore the question of to what extent the elements of federalism present in the EU system are being strengthened by the Amsterdam treaty and how the dynamism of Economic and Monetary Union will affect patterns of policy-making in the future. Eastern enlargement will undoubtedly strengthen the camp of the antifederalist forces, as the new member countries have no, or no positive, experience with federalism and remain attached to their regained sovereignty. On the other hand, as will be demonstrated in the third section, institutional deepening is a precondition for the admission of new member countries and will require a new institutional compromise between the EU-15. In its final section, the paper will discuss the far-reaching institutional implications of the preaccession strategy which requires the adoption of the bulk of the *acquis communautaire* on the part of the associated countries even ahead of membership. Whether the institutional convergence taking place at the level of regulatory systems and administrative structures represents another instance of creeping federalism matters less than its contribution to the uniting of the New Europe.

The Potential for Creeping Federalism

In their comparative study of U.S. federalism and European integration published in 1986, Elazar and Greilsammer discussed factors working in favor of a "federal progression of the Community" and those going counter to such an evolution. A movement toward federalism, they expected, might be fostered by developments like the economic crisis that affected the member states during the first half of the eighties, the enlargement of the Community beyond the then ten member states, and the increase in regional imbalances which would result from the entry of the Iberian countries. The dynamics of integration would also be promoted, as the two authors saw it, by the growth of the Community budget and the "judicial activism" of the Court of Justice. As factors working against the transformation of the EC into a federal regime they cited the democracy deficit, the weakness of the Community budget, and "lack of 'federalist' feelings" among most Europeans.[11]

As the EU moved into the next millennium, the negative factors remained by and large unchanged. Since the signing of the Maastricht Treaty, federalist feelings have been on the decline where they existed. Instead of a European citizenry, citizens-against-Europe movements have emerged. The democratic deficit has become the stock-in-trade of an academic growth industry that is also turning out proposals for constitutional reform. Although the Community budget has grown substantially over the last fifteen years, it is bound not to exceed the ceiling of 1.27 percent of EU GDP, a modest proportion compared to the relative size of national budgets.[12]

When we look at the factors that were expected to promote federalism at the Community level, the picture is somewhat ambiguous. The ambition to offer a way out of "Eurosclerosis," as the economic crisis was labeled, was certainly an important motive behind the single market project which, together with Southern enlargement, contributed to the expansion of the budget. But neither the economic crisis nor the enlargement to EC-12 or EU-15 led to innovations in policy-making and institutional capabilities which would have qualified as "a federal progression." Of course, completing the single market with the introduction of a common currency managed by a European Central Bank very much looks like a great leap forward toward a federal system of economic governance or at least provides an illustration of "segmented federalism."[13] As for the Court of Justice, it felt obliged to temper its "judicial activism" in the nineties after member state governments had strongly criticized a number of decisions which implied heavy burdens on national budgets. As the Court moves toward judicial self-restraint, it will be less able to function as an engine of European integration.[14]

Having examined—with the benefit of hindsight—the prospects for federalism in the EC as they presented themselves in the mid-eighties, we may now ask how the federal elements that characterize the EU system are being affected by the Amsterdam treaty. The purpose of the intergovernmental

conference leading to Amsterdam was to revise the Maastricht Treaty "'with
the aim of ensuring the effectiveness of the mechanisms and the institutions
of the Community.'"[15] The agenda of the conference was rather broad and
included three main objectives: First, in order to achieve "a Union closer to
its citizens," cooperation with regard to visa, asylum and immigration policies was to be improved, and employment policy was to become a major
concern of the EU. Second, with the prospect of enlargement, institutional
reforms were required providing for efficient decision making and democratic control in the framework of a larger Union. Third, the Union's capacity
to conduct a coherent common foreign and security policy had to be
strengthened.[16] Not surprisingly, the outcome of the conference did not live
up to the more ambitious goals individual national governments had set
themselves.[17] Although the Amsterdam treaty is not a masterpiece of institutional architecture and failed to prepare the EU for Eastern enlargement,
it nonetheless introduced a number of institutional innovations which do
strengthen the federal elements of the system. The scope of supranational
policy making expands as the third pillar of the Maastricht treaty, cooperation in the fields of justice and home affairs, is partly transferred from the
domain of intergovernmental cooperation into the Community pillar. However, the provisions regarding the transitional period of five years and the
opt-out clauses for the United Kingdom and Ireland as well as Denmark
clearly limit the advance of supranational policy making in the framework
of the EC treaty.[18]

The role of the European Parliament in the legislative process is significantly enhanced by the extension of the codecision procedure. However, the
Parliament remains deprived of the right of legislative initiative. Its elective
function is enhanced by the new requirement that the nominee for president
of the Commission has to be approved by the Parliament before being
appointed by the Council. Union citizenship, as introduced by the Maastricht treaty, has not been bolstered by the granting of additional rights. It
thus remains basically limited, first, to freedom of movement, and second, to
voting in and standing for municipal elections and elections to the European
Parliament, even if one is not a national of the country in which one resides.
In order to reassure the Danes, who worried particularly about the implications of union citizenship, the treaty explicitly states that "citizenship of the
Union shall complement and not replace national citizenship."[19] Reform of
the budget was not on the Amsterdam agenda but became the most contentious issue in negotiations about Agenda 2000 under the German presidency in 1999. From a federalist point of view Amsterdam was clearly
a disappointment: "Certainly, much still remains to be done in order to

achieve the federal constitutional settlement of the Union we seek, so that people will know how they are governed, by whom and from where."[20]

According to many observers, it is monetary union that will trigger a spillover process, moving the EU beyond the Maastricht and the Amsterdam treaties. The dynamism of the common currency is expected to lead to a supranational economic policy and, finally, to the establishment of a political union. It should be recalled, in this respect, that critics of the Maastricht scheme for monetary union had argued that monetary and political union must come together. A currency union, it was said, creates financial transfer needs (to compensate member countries for the effects of asymmetric shocks), which presuppose a high degree of political solidarity. Therefore political union, which would have to take the form of state-building institutions, was advocated as a precondition for monetary union.[21] Whereas this position amounted to a rejection of the Maastricht treaty, those who stress the dynamism of monetary union reverse the logic of the argument and assume that the Euro will act to accelerate political integration. This process would not necessarily result in a neatly designed federal state, but it might follow a logic of federalization.

At any rate, dissatisfaction with the institutions and rules governing monetary union is reflected in the French proposal of a *gouvernement économique* to be established at the European level. It could act as a counterpart to the technocracy of the European Central Bank, thus strengthening the democratic legitimacy of the Economic and Monetary Union. The Red-Green government in Germany advocates an active European employment policy and progress toward a social union without, however, envisaging a substantial increase in the Community budget.[22] The Euro is also held to be the answer to globalization, and the EU is called upon to save the "European model of society" and to negotiate as a monetary power on equal terms with the United States. Moreover, the Euro, as some academics and policy-makers believe, will force the transformation of the EU into a global power.[23] The international responsibility thrust upon the EU would finally enable it to overcome a situation where "the only policy areas in which a clear European identity fails to emerge and in which going beyond strict intergovernmentalism seems a hardly attainable goal are precisely those that CFSP and WEU address."[24] Whether the management of EMU or the elusive "communitarization" of foreign and security policy will evolve as a process of "creeping federalism" will depend to a large degree on the way the member states react to the challenges just mentioned. Creeping federalism will possibly represent a middle course between institutional stagnation and the framing of a European constitution.

The Challenge of Enlargement

The Eastern enlargement of the European Union is a political project designed to promote peace and prosperity on a pan-European scale by stabilizing democracy and the market economy in the countries of Central and Eastern Europe. It aims not only at facilitating the modernization of post-Communist societies but also at extending to the East the "security community" that emerged in Western Europe after World War II. It is obvious that the accession of ten new member countries will profoundly affect the structure of the EU. The heterogeneity of the Union will increase sharply, as the prospective members have levels of economic development below those of the poorest EU-15 countries. The decision of the Helsinki summit (December 1999) to accept Turkey as a legitimate candidate for membership aggravates the problem of sustainable heterogeneity. The structure of the EU will also be transformed by the emergence of new interests and coalitions. For countries like Ireland, Greece, Portugal, and Spain, the EU has functioned in large part as a "development assistance community,"[25] and this will also apply to the new member countries from Central and Eastern Europe. The struggle for budgetary resources will thereby intensify, pitting the new periphery against the old one. The new member states will have an interest in watering down Community standards in areas like environmental protection and the NATO members from Central Europe may be less than enthusiastic in promoting the new European Security and Defense Policy.

Enlargement is also a major challenge for the institutions of the EU. The accession of up to thirteen new member countries is widely perceived as an external shock which carries the risk of institutional paralysis. Without changes in the composition and working methods of the Commission, the Council, the committees, and the Parliament, the increase in membership threatens to undermine the decision-making capacity of the main EU bodies. As many areas of activity are still governed by the unanimity rule, the presence of more veto-holders and the proliferation of competing interests are likely to result in frequent stalls in decision making. Furthermore, it can be expected that the veto will be used more frequently for blackmail in a system of generalized horse trading. From the perspective of the big member states, enlargement will also increase the imbalance between them and the small member states, which characterizes the voting weights in the Council when qualified majority voting applies. Poor member states will be able to form "transfer coalitions" exploiting blocking minorities in order to maximize financial transfers.[26]

Although there is no dearth of proposals for institutional reform, the framers of the Amsterdam Treaty chose to postpone the adaptation of the institutions to the requirements of an enlarged Union. In a "Protocol on the institutions with the prospect of enlargement of the European Union," they agreed upon the following, rather modest and vague provisions:

Article 1

At the date of entry into force of the first enlargement of the Union, notwithstanding Article 157 (1) of the Treaty establishing the European Community, ... the Commission shall comprise one national of each of the Member States, provided that, by that date, the weighting of the votes in the Council has been modified, whether by re-weighting of the votes or by dual majority, in a manner acceptable to all Member States, taking into account all relevant elements, notably compensating those Member States which give up the possibility of nominating a second member of the Commission.

Article 2

At least one year before the membership of the European Union exceeds twenty, a conference of representatives of the governments of the Member states shall be convened in order to carry out a comprehensive review of the provisions of the Treaties on the composition and functioning of the institutions.[27]

In a declaration on this protocol, Belgium, France, and Italy observed that "the Treaty of Amsterdam does not meet the need ... for substantial progress towards reinforcing the institutions." These countries considered "that such reinforcement is an indispensable condition for the conclusion of the first round of accession negotiations" and favored "a significant extension of recourse to qualified majority voting."[28] In Germany, the Schröder government upon entering office soon came to advocate the extension of decision making by qualified majority voting and restriction of the unanimity requirement in the long run to issues of fundamental importance such as amendments to the treaty.[29]

The linkage established by the protocol between the reduction of the number of commissioners and the voting system in the Council is, of course, questionable to the extent that the former is supposed to enhance the efficiency of the Commission and therefore does not necessarily require compensation for the big member states that lose their second commissioner. It is also worth noting that "a strict interpretation of the protocol allows for a scenario in which reducing the size of the Commission is blocked by non-decision on the issue of weighted Council votes."[30] In this case, up to five new member states could be admitted to the EU with a mere adjustment of numbers in an institutional setup that had originally been created for six member countries. But this is a rather hypothetical scenario. The member countries are determined to proceed with enlargement only after the successful conclusion of Amsterdam II, the intergovernmental conference (IGC) programmed to lead to the Treaty of Nice at the end of the year 2000. Irrespective of the need for an efficient system of governance for a larger Union, institutional reform has tactical value for some member countries in a situation where the diversity of interests with regard to the conditions and consequences of Eastern enlargement shows through a facade of consensus.

On matters of substance the politics of institutional reform is likely to be marked by the defense of vested interests on the part of those member states that are bound to incur losses of status and power. The most controversial issues are those which affect the distribution of power (or better, of institutional capabilities) between big and small member states and the protection of vital national interests, which are also linked to the notion of democratic legitimacy. In relation to population size, the smaller member countries are definitely overrepresented in the Council when it comes to qualified majority voting.[31] To a lesser degree this is also true for the European Parliament. A reweighting of votes in the Council had earlier been resisted by the smaller member states, on the grounds that the imbalance in voting rights pays tribute to the principle of sovereign equality among states. On the other hand, the overrepresentation of smaller subnational entities is a familiar feature of federations. However, the discussion of voting weights should also take into account what we know about Council practice, namely that there is "no systematic cleavage between smaller and larger members; on the contrary both winning and blocking coalitions are typically constructed of a range, not primarily to attain a specific voting threshold, but based on affinities of interests and/or ideas."[32] As to the European Parliament, a redistribution of seats in the course of enlargement is inevitable, as the Amsterdam treaty limits the maximum number of seats to 700. The transition to generalized majority voting with few exceptions might improve the efficiency of Council decision making by eliminating opportunities for obstruction and blackmail, yet the radical solutions advocated by think tanks are unlikely to be adopted by the member states. Eliminating unanimity requirements altogether,[33] for instance, is not a workable proposition. In most of the member countries, amendments to the treaty on European Union taken by qualified majority vot-ing (QMV) would be patently unconstitutional. In a number of member countries, unanimity is still valued as a device for guaranteeing democratic accountability of the national government on issues involving vital national interests. Certainly, it can be argued that the EU after enlargement can no longer afford the "symbolism of the national veto."[34] But risk aversion will probably remain a strong motive in the protracted process of institutional reform. The proponents of majority voting have also been reminded that the Council "is deeply consensual in its habits," that "votes can be taken and are taken, but not all that often, and great efforts are made to accomodate the individual dissenter."[35] If a significant extension of QMV materializes, it will raise the question whether all matters governed by majority voting should be subject to approval by the European Parliament under the codecision procedure. On the one hand, this would enhance the democratic accountability of decisions that otherwise would largely be reached through the workings of an impenetrable technocratic committee system, but on the other hand it would just strengthen another authority capable of blocking decisions after the veto power flowing from unanimity requirements has been eliminated. An alternative remedy for the democratic deficit, the greater involvement of national parliaments in EU decision making (which is almost necessarily limited to the national level), is unlikely to improve the capacity for collective action of a larger Union.

The prospect of enlargement also raises the question whether the practice of rotating the Council presidency every six months needs to be reformed. Here again the problem is how to reconcile considerations of efficiency with the recognition of equality among member states. Excluding the smaller member states from the presidency would obviously be incompatible with the second criterion. Maintaining the present system while extending it to new member countries would increase the risks of poor Council management. These risks have primarily arisen when countries holding the presidency have been absorbed with domestic crises or election campaigns. Moreover, new and inexperienced member states with weak administrative structures may have difficulties coping with the burden the presidency entails. An elegant solution satisfying both criteria might be an elective presidency for a one-year or two-year term.[36] A solution more palatable to those afraid of either being passed over all the time or holding the office only once in a century would be to give up the principle of a single presidency and introduce different presidencies for the various technical councils in addition to that of the General Affairs Council.[37] However, this might aggravate the GAC's "inability to coordinate the Technical Councils" and "its almost complete lack of control over the Committees and Working Groups."[38] Given the coordination problems created by the existence of almost two dozen technical councils, the proposal to reduce the number of councils to eight or nine, each being responsible for a broad area of policy (e.g., human resources, infrastructure), deserves closer scrutiny.[39] As for the composition of the Commission, the solution envisioned by the Amsterdam protocol, one commissioner per member state, will still yield an oversized Commission with a number of excessively small portfolios when all the applicants will have joined the Union. Reducing the number of commissioners to a range of ten to fifteen would certainly enhance the efficiency, independence, and esprit de corps of the institution, as the principle of national representation would have to be abandoned. The president of the Commission would be empowered to choose his colleagues according to their qualifications for the job and with due consideration for balanced geographical representation.[40] However, as long as the EU remains a joint venture of nation-states, renouncing national representation on the Commission requires an act of self-denial on the part of smaller member states, for it is hardly conceivable that France, Germany, or Britain would gracefully accept being excluded from the Commission. But the smaller member states are already being asked to live with fewer votes in the Council and to forgo the protection provided by unanimity requirements.

Another topic that ranks high on the agenda of institutional reform is the organization of the Commission. It became a matter of urgency when the Santer Commission was forced to resign in March 1999 after it was implicated in cases of fraud, mismanagement, and nepotism. This provoked widespread indignation and an assault on the Commission by the European Parliament. The report submitted by a panel of independent experts confirmed the existence of structural distortions. In spite of an enormous task expansion and a shift in functions from policy initiation to policy implementation and, in particular, the administration of spending programs, the organization and the modus operandi of the Commission had been left largely unchanged while the bureaucracy had grown in size.[41] The Prodi Commission has embarked on a large-scale reorganization of the Commission bureaucracy and its working methods in order to achieve both efficiency and accountability. With the implementation of these measures, the subsidiarity principle could profitably be applied where spending programs do not yield a "European surplus value," being determined rather by policy entrepreneurship of the Commission or exercises in image politics and clientelism on the part of the European Parliament.

This brief discussion indicates that institutional reform is a task of remarkable complexity, but it also highlights the fact that measures designed to improve the coordination function of the Council or the performance of the Commission bureaucracy do not require amendments to the treaties. As soon as a new IGC approaches, blueprints for institutional reform tend to flourish again, and the idea of a European constitution gains momentum in the political and academic debate. What are the attractions of a European constitution? It would, as its proponents emphasize, create more transparency in the institutional setup and the decision making processes of the EU and "maintain the federal balance" between the Union and the member states. It would thereby strengthen the legitimacy of the European institutions. The key elements of this constitution would be:"a clear division of powers" between the Union and the member states, a bicameral legislature formed by the European Parliament and the Council, and a European bill of "fundamental civil and human rights."[42]

The project of a European constitution would have the advantage of moving the institutional debate beyond the logic of incrementalism that has dominated previous revisions of the treaties, but its possibly fatal weakness consists in the fact that a European constitution with an unmistakably federal imprint is far from being welcomed by all the member states. In some countries it might lead instead to divisive political debate and referendum campaigns with outcomes that may bury the project for good. In any case, it is unlikely to speed up institutional reform in the run-up to Eastern enlargement.

The Transfer of Institutions in the Enlargement Process

For the associated countries of Central and Eastern Europe, preparing for membership is a very demanding but also highly structured process. It requires nothing less than the adoption of political, economic, judicial, and administrative institutions that are compatible with those of the EU. As the road to accession is fraught with obstacles, the EU has provided a route plan spelling them out in considerable detail and obliging the candidate countries to remove them, for the most part before joining the Union. The enlargement process is governed by the criteria laid down by the European Council of Copenhagen (1993), other landmark decisions taken by this body, and by the Commission acting as supervisor of the applicants and as manager of the preaccession strategy.

The Copenhagen criteria specify in general terms the conditions for membership:

- stability of institutions guaranteeing democracy, the rule of law, human rights, and respect for and protection of minorities;

- the existence of a functioning market economy, as well as the capacity to cope with competitive pressure and market forces within the Union;
- the ability to take on the obligations of membership, including adherence to the aims of political, economic, and monetary union.[43]

These criteria became the basis for the opinions on the applications for membership which the Commission submitted in Agenda 2000 in 1997. Acting upon the Commission's recommendation, the European Council held in Luxembourg in December 1997 decided to open negotiations for accession with five CEE countries (Czech Republic, Estonia, Hungary, Poland, and Slovenia) and with Cyprus. Partly in reaction to the crisis in the Balkans in the wake of the Kosovo War, it was decided at the European Council held in December 1999 in Helsinki to invite five more CEE countries (Rumania, Bulgaria, Slovakia, Latvia, and Lithuania) and Malta to the negotiation table. As operationalized and interpreted by the Commission, the Copenhagen criteria also provide the standards by which country performance has been assessed in the "Reports on progress towards accession by each of the candidate countries."[44]

Although the Council is not bound by the Commission opinions or progress reports, these documents carry political weight given the expertise acquired by the Commission and the divergence of views on enlargement among the member states.[45] Moreover, the power of the Commission in the enlargement process is not only based on its ability to act as gatekeeper by defining the conditions for opening accession negotiations with applicants. It is also linked to the fact that the Commission is mainly responsible for the implementation of the preaccession strategy. When assessing the ability of candidate countries to take on the obligations of membership, the Commission based its judgement on the performance of a country in implementing the "Europe Agreement" (i.e., the association agreement concluded with the EU) and its record in adopting the *acquis communautaire*. The *acquis* has become the quintessential criterion for membership, as it consists of the mountain of Community law and the stock of Community policies which the prospective member countries must largely take over before acceding to the Union. The core of the *acquis* is embodied in the internal market legislation, the phased adoption of which is the essential element of the preaccession strategy launched by the Essen European Council in December 1994.[46] What the adoption of the internal market *acquis* means and requires has been listed with painstaking care in the Commission's white paper on the preparation of the associated countries for integration into the internal market.[47]

The adoption of the internal market *acquis* not only requires, as the Commission insisted, that the associated countries adapt their relevant legislation. Legal approximation must also be complemented by adequate institutional measures which ensure the effective implementation of Community laws and regulations. "Implementation requires both an institutional infrastructure for implementation and an effective means of enforcement."[48] In other words, regulatory authorities have to be set up in order to implement competition policy or environmental policy. And the courts must provide legal remedy against administrative decisions.[49] Applying the *acquis* therefore requires efforts in institution building and administrative and judicial reform that often strain the human and financial resources of the candidate countries. However, it is also worth pointing out that "around 30 percent of the *acquis communautaire* has already been incorporated into the Europe Agreements," which are a key element of the preaccession strategy.[50] These agreements have aided the transition to the market economy in the associated countries by promoting legal and institutional convergence with the EU. Financial and technical assistance are also ingredients of the preaccession strategy. The enhanced preaccession strategy adopted by the Luxembourg European Council in December 1997 provides for "accession partnerships", that is, for bilateral agreements with the applicant countries, which include a National Programme for the Adoption of the *acquis,* and financial assistance made conditional upon progress in implementing the Europe Agreement as well as the National Programme. This "carrot-and-stick" approach smacks of paternalism; so does, almost unavoidably, the whole preaccession strategy. For it is bound to reflect the gap in economic and institutional development between the EU and the candidates for accession as well as the asymmetry in bargaining power between the parties to the enlargement process.

Ambition to join the EU has clearly determined the path of political and economic transformation chosen by the elites of several CEE countries.[51] Having entered a patron-client relationship with the EU, they had to commit themselves to invest heavily in an economic constitution and regulatory regimes of remarkable legal and institutional complexity. The EU, for its part, has been extremely reluctant to accept any binding commitments as far as the timing of enlargement and its own preparations for it are concerned. This complicates the task of adjustment for the applicant countries, as the EU presents itself as a moving target.[52]

Nevertheless, the impact of the European Union's policy toward the associated countries on the political and economic transformation has certainly been positive so far. Progress toward the consolidation of democracy has mostly been achieved through the dynamics of domestic politics, but the political requirements of EU membership and the monitoring process organized by the EU provide safeguards against the temptations of authoritarianism and the mistreatment of ethnic minorities. Appropriately enough, Article 7 of the Amsterdam treaty introduces the possibility of suspending membership rights of a state if "a serious and persistent breach" of the principles on which the Union is founded (liberty, democracy, respect for human rights, etc.) has been verified. The association agreements have provided for far-reaching trade liberalization on the part of the EU which benefits the CEE countries in their efforts to integrate themselves into a pan-European division of labor. The prospect of membership has stimulated foreign investment in the frontrunner countries. The transfer of institutions, which is taking place as the adoption of the *acquis* progresses, contributes to the modernization of the applicant countries and creates an economic constitution on a pan-European scale. Still, the institutional convergence which the EU tries to promote at the level of regulatory authorities, administrative structures, and judicial systems, while taking Western Europe as a model, will coexist with and be limited by the diversity of institutional cultures and differences in institutional performance that the West European experience amply illustrates.

Conclusion

What does this discussion of Eastern enlargement tell us about the prospects for federalism at the level of the European Union? To some extent, the answer depends on the concept of federalism one prefers. As a political vision inspiring the supporters of the United States of Europe, federalism, for better or worse, now belongs to the history of political ideas. The new member states from Eastern Europe will not line up to promote the federalist cause, and the Fifteen will not feel sufficiently threatened by the growing heterogeneity of the Union to adopt a federal constitution. The answer is different when we follow the scholarly usage of the term. Assuming that the EU is already a federal system or at least one marked by federal elements, we are bound to find that federalism has a brighter future. The comparative analysis of federalism continues to serve as a tool for understanding the interplay between the tiers of government in the European Union and the dynamism of its institutional system, and it can be used as a source for proposals in the debate on institutional reform. From the perspective of Eastern enlargement, it is useful to recall that the Amsterdam treaty has introduced institutional innovations that strengthen the federal elements of the system. Whether the practice of economic and monetary union or the development of a truly common foreign and security policy will promote a sort of "creeping federalism" is a matter of speculation.

Enlargement has imposed another round of institutional reform. Strengthening the federal elements in the EU system might be the adequate means to ensure the efficient and legitimate government of a larger Union. However, the more radical innovations advocated by think tanks and academics from individual member countries are unlikely to meet the consensus of the member states during the 2000 intergovernmental conference. An alternative strategy for moving a larger and more heterogeneous Union forward is flexible (or differentiated) integration. To what extent flexible integration is compatible with a restructuring of European institutions along federal lines is a question that deserves further scrutiny.

Notes

1. Quoted from M. Forsyth, "The Political Theory of Federalism: The Relevance of Classical Approaches," in *Federalizing Europe? The Costs, Benefits, and Preconditions of Federal Political Systems*, ed. J.J. Hesse and V. Wright (Oxford, 1996), 27.
2. M. Jachtenfuchs and B. Kohler-Koch, "Einleitung: Regieren im dynamischen Mehrebenensystem," in *Europäische Integration*, ed. M. Jachtenfuchs and B. Kohler-Koch (Opladen, 1996), 21.
3. J.J. Hesse and M. Schaad, "Amsterdam and the European Union: Leap-frogging, Side-stepping or Paradise Lost?" *The European Yearbook of Comparative Government and Public Administration* 3 (1996): 59.
4. A.M. Sbragia, "Thinking about the European Future: The Uses of Comparison," in *Euro-Politics: Institutions and Policymaking in the "New" European Community*, ed. A.M. Sbragia (Washington, D.C., 1992), 261.
5. Forsyth, "The Political Theory," 35.
6. Ibid., 40.
7. W. Wallace, *Regional Integration: The West European Experience* (Washington, D.C., 1994), 38–41.
8. W. Wallace, "Government without Statehood: The Unstable Equilibrium," in *Policy-Making in the European Union,*" ed. H. Wallace and W. Wallace (Oxford, 1996), 445f.
9. G. Bonvicini, "Key Issues for the German Presidency," TEPSA-Report, Conference on "Germany and the European Union," Bonn, 26–27 November 1998, 9.
10. W. Weidenfeld and C. Giering, "Die Europäische Union nach Amsterdam—Bilanz und Perspektive," in *Amsterdam in der Analyse*, ed. W. Weidenfeld (Gütersloh, 1998), 87; see

also the speech by Foreign Minister J. Fischer "Die Schwerpunkte der deutschen Rat-
spräsidentschaft," *Bulletin* 2 (1999): 11f.

11. Daniel J. Elazar and Ilan Greilsammer, "Federal Democracy: The U.S.A. and Europe Compared: A Political Science Perspective," in *Integration Through Law*, vol. 1, book 1, ed.
M. Cappelletti, M. Seccombe, and J. Weiler (Berlin, New York, 1986), 113–121.

12. This was the position taken by the member states with the conclusion of the negotiations
on Agenda 2000.

13. Sbragia, "Thinking about the European Future," 262.

14. E. Schultz, "Die relative Autonomie des Europäischen Gerichtshofes: Rechtsprechung vor
und nach Maastricht. Eine neo-institutionalistische Analyse" (Doctoral thesis, Humboldt-
Universität Berlin, 1998), 285.

15. *The Treaty of Amsterdam: Text and Commentary*, ed. A. Duff (London, 1997), xxx.

16. Ibid., xxxi–xxxii.

17. See the Foreword by Lamberto Dini, ibid., xxvii–xxix.

18. Hesse and Schaad, "Amsterdam," 60ff.

19. Treaty of Amsterdam, Article 8 (1).

20. *The Treaty of Amsterdam*, ed. A. Duff, xxxvi.

21. O. Issing, "Geld stiftet noch keine Staatlichkeit," *Frankfurter Allgemeine Zeitung*, 15 July
1995, p.13.

22. Fischer, "Die Schwerpunkte"; speeches by Schröder, "Prioritäten des deutschen EU-Vor-
sitzes," and Fischer, "Zukunftsfähigkeit und Legitimität der Europäischen Union," *Bulletin* 4 (1999): 33–39.

23. See W. Weidenfeld and J. Janning, "Europa vor der Vollendung," *Frankfurter Allgemeine
Zeitung*, 3 July 1998, p.8.

24. A. Missiroli, "Background," in *Flexibility and Enhanced Cooperation in European Security Matters: Assets or Liabilities?* ed. A. Missiroli, Occasional Papers 6 (The Institute for
Security Studies, Western European Union, January 1999), i.

25. Ch. Deubner, *Deutsche Europapolitik: Von Maastricht nach Kerneuropa?* (Baden-Baden,
1995), 124.

26. On the institutional problems that arise from Eastern enlargement see Günter F. Schäfer,
"Die institutionellen Herausforderungen einer EU-Osterweiterung," in *Europa öffnen*,
ed. W. Weidenfeld (Gütersloh, 1997), 25–100; R. Bieber and F. Bieber, "Institutionelle
Voraussetzungen der Osterweiterung der Europäischen Union," ibid., 101–155.

27. Quoted from European Union, Treaty of Amsterdam (Luxembourg, 1997), 111.

28. Ibid., 144.

29. Fischer, "Die Schwerpunkte," 11.

30. Hesse and Schaad, "Amsterdam," 69.

31. See A. Mayhew, *Recreating Europe. The European Union's Policy towards Central and
Eastern Europe* (Cambridge, 1998), 323.

32. F. Hayes-Renshaw and H. Wallace, *The Council of Ministers* (Houndmills, London,
1997), 295.

33. As advocated by Friedrich-Ebert-Stiftung, Arbeitsgruppe "Europäische Integration,"
"Eine erweiterte EU braucht größere Entscheidungsfähigkeit und mehr Demokratie,"
mimeo (Bonn, January 1999).

34. Hayes-Renshaw and Wallace, "The Council of Ministers," 57.

35. Ibid., 275.

36. C. Giering, "Institutionelle Reformchancen," in *Kosten, Nutzen und Chancen der Osterweiterung für die Europäische Union*, ed. Bertelsmann Stiftung, Forschungsgruppe Europa
(Gütersloh, 1998), 65.

37. Bieber and Bieber, "Institutionelle Voraussetzungen," 150.
38. Bonvicini, "Key Issues," 9.
39. Schäfer, "Die institutionellen Herausforderungen," 89.
40. Ibid., 67.
41. Ibid., 57ff.; Ausschuß Unabhängiger Sachverständiger, "Erster Bericht über Anschuldigungen betreffend Betrug, Mißmanagement und Nepotismus in der Europäischen Kommission," 15 March 1999, Chapter 9.4.
42. *Europe '96: Reforming the European Union*, ed. W. Weidenfeld (Gütersloh, 1994), 11–18, 32, 39.
43. Quoted from Agenda 2000, Commission Opinion on Poland's Application for Membership of the European Union, A.a), http://europa.eu.int/comm/dg1a/agenda 2000/en/opinions/poland/a.htm.
44. The purpose of the reports is to encourage the applicant countries to persist in their efforts to meet the requirements for membership. They also provide a basis for a possible Council decision to open accession negotiations with countries seen as catching up with the frontrunners.
45. See also Mayhew, "Recreating Europe," 175.
46. Ibid., 165.
47. Ibid., 208ff.
48. Ibid., 221.
49. Ibid.
50. B. Lippert, "From Pre-accession to EU-Membership—Implementing Transformation and Integration," in *Towards EU Membership: Transformation and Integration in Poland and the Czech Republic*, ed. B. Lippert and P. Becker (Bonn, 1998), 28.
51. Ibid., 58.
52. See also Mayhew, "Recreating Europe," 224f.

SELECTED BIBLIOGRAPHY

Adler, E. "Imagined (Security) Communities: Cognitive Regions in
   International Relations." *Millenium: Journal of International Studies*
   26, no.2 (1997): 258–59.
Agreements on the Creation of the Commonwealth of Independent States
   Signed in December 1991/January 1992. London, 1992.
Ahrens, J. "Systemtransformation von unten—Über die Bedeutung der
   national-staatlichen Ordnung für den russischen Systemwandel."
   Osteuropa. Wirtschaft 1 (1995).
Almond, G.A. "Foreword." In *Can Democracy Take Root in Post-Soviet
   Russia?* ed. H. Eckstein, F.K. Fleron, E.P. Hoffmann, and W.M.
   Reisinger. Lanham, Boulder, New York, Oxford, 1998.
Alter, P. *Nationalismus.* Frankfurt/M., 1985.
Anderson, B. *Imagined Communities.* London, 1983.
Andeweg, R. "The Reshaping of National Party Systems." In *The Crisis of
   Representation in Europe*, ed. J. Hayward. London, 1995, 58–78.
Armstrong, J. *Nations before Nationalism.* Chapel Hill, 1982.
Aslund, A. *How Russia Became A Market Economy.* Washington, D.C.,
   1995.
Baier, S. *Osterweiterung. Europas größte Herausforderung.* Stuttgart, 1998.
Bakir, C., and A. Williams, eds. *Turkey and Europe.* London, 1993.
Bakka, P. *Imperial Break-Down, Political Fragmentation and State-
   Building: An Attempt at Extending Stein Rokkan's Conceptual Map to
   All of Europe.* Unpublished Manuscript, Bielefeld, 1994.
Balakrishnan, G., ed. *Mapping the Nation.* London, 1996.
Banting, K. "The Past Speaks to the Future: Lessons from the Postwar
   Social Union." In *Canada: The State of the* Federation, *1997, Non-
   Constitutional Renewal*, ed. H. Lazar. Kingston, 1998.
Barkey, K., and M. von Hagen, eds. *After Empire: Multiethnic Empires
   and Nation-building.* Boulder, 1997.

Bebler, A. "Yugoslavia's Variety of Communist Federalism and Her Demise." *Communist and Post-Communist Studies* 26, no. 1 (1993): 72–86.

Belka, M., ed. *The Polish Transformation from the Perspective of European Integration.* Warsaw, 1996.

Berding, H., ed. *Nationales Bewußtsein und kollektive Identität.* Frankfurt/M., 1993.

Berend, I. *Central and Eastern Europe: Detour from Periphery to Periphery.* Cambridge, 1996.

Beyme, K. von *Systemwechsel in Osteuropa.* Frankfurt/M., 1994.

Bieber, R., and F. Bieber. "Institutionelle Voraussetzungen der Osterweiterung der Europäischen Union." In *Europa öffnen*, ed. W. Weidenfeld. Gütersloh 1997.

Bird, R.M. *Federal Finance in Comparative Perspective.* Toronto, 1986.

Bonvincini, G. *Key Issues for the German Presidency.* TEPSA-Report, Conference on "Germany and the European Union. Bonn, 26–27 November 1998.

Bremmer, I. "Reassessing Soviet Nationalities Theory." In *Nations and Politics in the Soviet Successor States*, ed. I. Bremmer and R. Taras. New York, 1994.

Broek, Hans van, High-Level Group of Experts on the CFSP. *First Report. European Security Policy Towards 2000: Ways and Means to Establish Genuine Credibility.* " Brussels, 19 December 1994.

Brubaker, R. *Nationalism Reframed: Nationhood and the National Question in the New Europe.* New York, 1996.

Bryant, C., and E. Mokrzycki, eds. *Democracy, Civil Society, and Pluralism: In Comparative Perspective: Poland, Great Britain and the Netherlands.* Warsaw, 1995.

Brzezinski, Z., and P. Sullivan, eds. *Russia and the Commonwealth of Independent States. Documents, Data and Analysis.* New York and London, 1997.

Bull, H. *The Logic of Anarchy.* Oxford, 1977.

Bullman, U. "The Politics of the Third Level." In *The Regional Dimension of the European Union: Toward a Third Level in Europe*, ed. C. Jeffery. London, 1997.

Bulmer, S. "Domestic Politics and European Community Policy Making." *Journal of Common Market Studies* 21 (1982–1983): 349–363.

_____. "The Governance of the European Union: A New Institutionalist Approach," *Journal of Public Policy* 13, no. 4 (1994): 351-380.

Bulmer, S., and W. Wessels, *The European Council.* London, 1987.

Bundesminister der Justiz, ed. *Bundesgesetzblatt*, part 2 (BGBl II). Bonn, 1986.

Bundesrat, ed. *Vierzig Jahre Bundesrat*, Baden-Baden, 1989.

Burgess, M. "Introduction: Federalism and Building the European Union." *Publius. The Journal of Federalism* 26, no. 4 (1996), 1–15.

Buzan, B., C. Jones, and R. Little, *The Logic of Anarchy: Neorealism to Structural Realism*. New York, 1993.

Calhoun, C. *Nationalism*. Minneapolis, 1997.

Cameron, D. "The Expansion of the Public Economy: A Comparative Analysis." *American Political Science Review* 72 (1978): 1243–61.

Cameron, D., and R. Simeon. "The Expansion of the Public Economy: A Comparative Analysis". *American Political Science Review* 72 (1978): 1243–61.

_____."Intergovernmental Relations and Multilevel Governance: A Citizens' Perspective." Paper Presented at a Joint Session of the Canadian Political Science Association and the European Community Studies Association. University of Ottawa, June, 1998.

Campara, A. *"Washington Agreements": The Modern Concept of Confederation*. Strasbourg, 1994.

Caplan, R., and J. Feffer, eds., *Europe's New Nationalism*. New York, 1996.

Caporaso, J. "The European Union and Forms of State: Westphalian, Regulatory or Post-Modern?" *Journal of Common Market Studies* 34 (1996): 29–52.

_____. *Across the Great Divide: Integrating Comparative and International Politics*. European University Institute Working Papers 97/58, Robert Schuman Centre, San Domenico di Fiesole, Florence, Italy, 1997, 1–38.

Caporaso, J., M.G. Cowles, and T. Risse, eds. *Europeanization and Domestic Change*. Ithaca, 2000.

Casanova, J. *Public Religions in the Modern World*. Chicago, 1994.

Checkel, J. "The Constructivist Turn in International Relations Theory." *World Politics* 50, no. 2 (1998).

Chirot, D., ed. *The Origins of Backwardness in Eastern Europe*. Berkeley, 1989.

Constitution Watch, *Eastern European Constitutional Review* 32 (1998).

Dahrendorf, R. *Reflections on the Revolution in Europe*. London, 1990.

_____. *After 1989. Morals, Revolution, and Civil Society*. New York, 1997.

Davies, N. *Europe: A History*. Oxford, 1996.

Delors, J. *Das neue Europa*. Munich, 1993.

Deubner, C. *Deutsche Europapolitik: Von Maastricht nach Kerneuropa?* Baden-Baden 1995.

Deudney, D. "Nuclear Weapons and the Waning of the Real-State," *Daedalus* 124, no. 2 (1995): 209–231.

_____. "The Philadelphia System: Sovereignty, Arms Control, and the Balance of Power in the American States-Union, 1787-1861," *International Organization* 29, no. 2 (1995).

_____. *Binding Sovereigns: Authority, Structure, and Geopolitics in Philadelphia Systems*, in *State Sovereignty as Social Construct*, ed. T. Biersteiker and C Weber. New York, 1996.

Deudney, D., and G. J. Ikenberry "Structural Liberalism: The Nature and Sources of Postwar Western Political Order." Paper Presented at a Conference on "Realism and International Relations Theory after the Cold War," Harvard University, December 1995.

Deutsch, K.W., ed. *Political Community and the North Atlantic Area.* Princeton, 1957.

Deutscher Bundesrat, ed. *Handbuch des Bundesrates 1994–95.* Baden-Baden, 1995.

Deutscher Bundestag and Bundesrat, ed. *Verhandlungen des deutschen Bundestages. Stenographische Berichte und Drucksachen.* 12. Wahlperiode.Bundesdrucksache 12/3540. Bonn.

Diner, D. *Ever Closer Union? An Introduction to the European Community.* Boulder, 1994.

Donahue, J.D. *Disunited States.* New York, 1997.

Döpfner, A. *Keine Angst vor Europa. Umbrüche, alte Ideen und neue Formen des Föderalismus*, in *Keine Angst vor Europa. Föderalismus als Chance*, ed. A. Döpfner. Zürich, 1992.

Dorff, R.H. "Federalism in Eastern Europe: Part of the Solution or Part of the Problem?" *Publius. The Journal of Federalism* 24, no. 2 (1994): 99–114.

Duffield, J.S. "International Regimes and Alliance Behavior: Explaining NATO Conventional Force Levels." *International Organization* 46, (1992), 819–55.

Dunleavy, D., and B. O'Leary *Theories of the State.* London, 1987.

Dunlop, J.B. *The Rise of Russia and the Fall of the Soviet Empire.* Princeton, 1993.

Easter, G. M. "Preference for Presidentialism: Postcommunist Change in Russia and the NIS," *World Politics* 49, no. 2 (1997): 184-211.

_____. "Redefining Centre-Regional Relations in the Russian Federation: Sverdlovsk Oblast." *Europe-Asia Studies*, 49, no. 4 (1997): 617–635.

Eichengreen, B. "European Monetary Unification," *Journal of Economic Literature* 31 (September 1993): 1321–57.

Eisenstadt, S. *The European Civilization in Comparative Perspective.* Oslo, 1987.

_____. "The Break-Down of Communism and the Vicissitudes of Modernity." In *The Exit From Communism*, ed. S. Graubard. *Daedalus* 121, (1992): 21–42.

_____. *Antinomien der Moderne.* Frankfurt/M., 1998.

Elazar, D. *Exploring Federalism.* Tuscaloosa, 1987.

_____. *Constitutionalizing Globalization: The Postmodern Revival of Confederal Arrangements.* Boulder, 1998.

_____. ed. *Federal Systems of the World. A Handbook of Federal, Confederal and Autonomy Arrangements*, 2d ed. Harlow, 1991.

Elazar, D., and I. Greilsammer, "Federal Democracy: The U.S.A. and Europe Compared. A Political Science Perspective. " In *Integration Through Law*, vol.1, book 1, ed. M. Cappelletti, M. Seccombe, and J. Weiler. Berlin and New York, 1986.

Elster, J. "Consenting Adults or the Sorcerer's Apprentice?" *East European Constitutional Review* 4, no. 1 (1995): 36–41.

Fafard, P. "Green Harmonization: The Success and Failure of Recent Environmental Intergovernmental Relations." In *Canada: The State of the Federation. Non-Constitutional Renewal,* ed. H. Lazar. Kingston, 1998.

Fawcett, L., and A. Hurrell, eds. *Regionalism in World Politics.* New York, 1995.

Federalno Ministarstvo Pravde, ed. *Ustavi Bosne i Hercegovine,* Sarajevo, 1997.

The Finnish Institute of International Affairs, ed. *Democracy, Economy, and Civil Society in Transition.* Helsinki, 1997.

Fish, S.M. *Democracy from Scratch: Opposition and Regime in the New Russian Revolution.* Princeton, 1995.

Flinn, G., ed. *Making the Hexagon: The New France in the New Europe.* Boulder, 1995.

Flora, P., ed. *State Formation, Nation-Building and Mass Politics in Europe: The Theory of Stein Rokkan, Based on his Collected Works.* New York, 1999.

Forsyth, M. *Unions of States: The Theory and Practice of Confederation.* New York, 1981.

Frenkel, M. *Federal Theory.* Australian National University. Canberra, 1986.

Friedrich, C. J. *Trends of Federalism in Theory and Practice.* New York, 1968.

Frowein, J. "Bundesrat, Länder und Europäische Einigung." In *Vierzig Jahre Bundesrat.* ed., Bundesrat. Baden-Baden, 1989.

Galtung, J. *The European Community: A Super-Power in the Making.* London, 1973.

Ganaris, N. *The European Community, Eastern Europe, and Russia.* London, 1994.

Garcia, S., ed. *European Identity and the Search for Legitimacy.* London, 1993

Gellner, E. *Nations and Nationalism.* Oxford, 1983.

_____. *Conditions of Liberty.* London, 1994.

George, S., ed. *Britain and the European Community: The Politics of Semi-Detachment.* Oxford, 1992.

Gibbins, R. *Conflict and Unity.* Toronto, 1982.

_____. "Alberta's Intergovernmental Relations Experience." In *Canada: The State of the Federation. Non-Constitutional Renewal,* ed. H. Lazar. Kingston, 1998.

Giering, C. "Institutionelle Reformchancen". In *Kosten, Nutzen und Chancen der Osterweiterung für die Europäische Union,* ed. Bertelsmann Stiftung. Forschungsgruppe Europa. Gütersloh 1998.

Giesen, B., ed. *Nationale und kulturelle Identitäten.* Frankfurt/M., 1991.

Glaeßner, G.-J. *Demokratie nach dem Ende des Kommunismus.* Opladen, 1994.

Glaser, E. "The Security Dilemma Revisited." *World Politics* 50, no. 1 (1997): 171–201.

Goldman, M.F. *Revolution and Change in Central and Eastern Europe: Political, Economic, and Social Challenges.* Armonk, 1997.

Gordon, P.H. "The Limits of Europe's Common Foreign and Security Policy." In *Centralization or Fragmentation? Europe Facing the Challenges of Deepening, Diversity, and Democracy,* ed. A. Moravcsik. New York, 1998.

Greenfeld, L. *Nationalism: Five Roads to Modernity.* Cambridge, 1993.

Grieco, J.M. "Anarchy and the Limits of Cooperation: A Realist Critique of the Newest Liberal Institutionalism." *International Organization* 42, no. 3 (1988): 485–508.

_____. "The Maastricht Treaty, Economic and Monetary Union and the Neo-realist Research Program." *Review of International Studies* 21, no. 1 (1995): 21–40.

Haas, E.B. *The Uniting of Europe: Political, Social and Economic Forces,*
  1950–1957. Stanford, 1958.

———. *Beyond the Nation-State.* Stanford, 1964.

———. "The Study of Regional Integration: Reflections on the Joy and
  Anguish of Pre-theorizing." *International Organization* 24, no. 4
  (1970): 615.

———. *Nationalism, Liberalism, and Progress: The Rise and the Decline of*
  the Nation-State. Ithaca, 1997.

Haller M., ed. *Class Structure in Europe: New Findings for East-West*
  Comparisons of Social Structure and Mobility. Armonk, 1990.

Hallstein, W. *Europe in the Making.* London, 1972.

Hansen, R. "Regional Integration: Reflections on a Decade of Theoretical
  Efforts." *World Politics* 21, no. 2 (1969): 242–56.

Hanson, S., and W. Spohn, eds. *Can Europe Work? The New Germany*
  and the Reconstruction of Postcommunist Societies. Seattle, 1995.

Hardin, R. *One for All: The Logic of Group Conflict.* Princeton, 1995.

Harries, O. "The Collapse of the West." *Foreign Affairs* 72, no. 4 (1993):
  41–53.

Hauser, J., ed. *Accession or Integration? Poland's Road to the European*
  Union. Warsaw, 1998.

Hayes-Renshaw, F., and H. Wallace, *The Council of Ministers.* London,
  1997.

Hayward J., and E. Page, eds., *Governing Europe.* Durham, 1995.

Held, D. *Political Theory and the Modern State.* Cambridge, 1984.

Herz, J.H. "Rise and Demise of the Territorial State." *World Politics* 9, no.
  4 (1957): 473–493.

Hesse, J.J., and M. Schad. "Amsterdam and the European Union: Leap-
  Frogging, Side-Stepping, or Paradise Lost?" *The European Yearbook of*
  Comparative Government and Public Administration 3 (1996).

Hesse, J.J., and V. Wright, "Federalizing Europe: The Path to
  Adjustment." In *Federalizing Europe? The Costs, Benefits, and*
  Preconditions of Federal Political Systems, ed. J.J. Hesse, and V. Wright.
  Oxford, 1996.

Hesse, K. *Grundzüge des Verfassungsrechts der Bundesrepublik*
  Deutschland. Karlsruhe, 1994.

Hoffman, S. "Reflections on the Nation State in Western Europe Today."
  Journal of Common Market Studies 21 (1982–1983): 21–37.

Holbrooke, R. *To End A War.* New York, 1998.

Hrbek, R. "Bundesländer und Regionalismus in der EG." in *Bundesländer und Europäische Gemeinschaft*, ed. S. Magiera and D. Merten. Berlin, 1988.

Hrbek, R., and U. Thaysen, eds. *Die deutschen Länder und die Europäischen Gemeinschaften*. Baden-Baden, 1986.

Hrbek, R. Die Auswirkungen der EU-Integration auf den Föderalismus in Deutschland. *Aus Politik und Zeitgeschichte* B 24 (1997).

Hughes, C. "Confederation." In *The Blackwell Encyclopaedia of Political Institutions*, ed. V. Bogdanor. Oxford, 1987.

Hurrell, A. "Explaining the Resurgence of Regionalism in World Politics." *Review of International Studies* 21, no. 4 (1995).

Hutchinson, J., and A. Smith, eds., *Nationalism*. Oxford, 1996.

Iivonen, J., ed. *The Future of the Nation-State in Europe*. Hants, 1993.

Ikenberry, John G. "Creating Yesterday's New World Order: Keynesian 'New Thinking' and the Anglo-American Postwar Settlement." In *Ideas and Foreign Policy: Beliefs, Institutions, and Political Change*, ed. J Goldstein and R.O. Keohane. Ithaca, 1993.

Ingebritsen, C. *The Nordic States and the European Union*. Ithaca, 1998.

Innes, A. "The Breakup of Czechoslovakia: The Impact of Party Development on the Separation of the State," *East European Politics and Societies* 11, no. 3 (1997): 393–435.

International Crisis Group, ed. *Doing Democracy a Disservice: 1998 Elections in Bosnia and Herzegovina*. Washington, D.C., September 9, 1998.

Jachtenfuchs, M., and B. Kohler-Koch, eds. *Europäische Integration*. Opladen, 1996.

Jackson, R.H. *Quasi-States: Sovereignty, International Relations and the Third World*. Cambridge, 1990.

Jacob, B., ed. *Democracy and Local Governance*. Honolulu, 1993.

Jacob, P., and J. Toscano, eds. *The Integration of Political Communities*. Philadelphia, 1964.

Jeffery, C., ed. *The Regional Dimension of the European Union: Toward a Third Level in Europe*. London, 1997.

Jenkins, B., and N. Copsey, "Nation, Nationalism and National Identity in France." In *Nation and Identity*, ed. B. Jenkins and S. Sofos, London, 1996, 101–124.

Jenkins, B., and S.A. Sofos, eds. *Nation and Identity in Contemporary Europe*. London, 1996.

Jensen, D.N. "How Russia is Ruled—1998." *Radio Free Europe/Radio Liberty Report, section IV. Institutions of government,* *http://www.rferl.org.*

Jepperson, R.L., A. Wendt, and P.J. Katzenstein, "Norms, Identity, and Culture in National Security." In *The Culture of National Security: Norms and Identity in World Politics,* ed. P. Katzenstein. New York, 1996.

Jordan, T. *The European Culture Area: A Systematic Geography.* New York, 1988.

Kaiser, K. "The Interaction of Regional Subsystems: Some Preliminary Notes on Recurrent Patterns and the Role of the Superpowers." *World Politics* 21, no. 1 (1968).

Kaser, M. "How Real are Prospects for Economic Integration in the Commonwealth of Independent States?" Paper presented to a seminar at the British Foreign and Commonwealth Office, 17 May 1996.

Katzenstein, P. *The Culture of National Security: Norms and Identity in World Politics.* New York, 1996.

_____. ed. *Tamed Power: Germany in Europe.* Ithaca, 1997.

_____. *Mitteleuropa: Between Europe and Germany.* Providence, 1997.

Kennedy, P. *The Rise and Fall of the Great Powers.* New York, 1987.

Kennett, S.A. *Securing the Social Union: A Commentary on the Decentralized Approach.* Kingston, 1998.

Kenney, S.J. *For Whose Protection?* Ann Arbor, 1992.

Keohane, R.O. *After Hegemony: Cooperation and Discord in the World Political Economy.* Princeton, 1984.

_____. ed. *Neorealism and its Critics.* New York, 1986.

Keohane, R.O., and S. Hoffmann, eds. *The New European Community: Decision-Making and Institutional Change.* Boulder, 1991.

Keohane, R.O., and L. Martin, "The Promise of Institutionalist Theory." *International Security* 20, no. 1 (1995): 41–42.

Kielmansegg, P. Graf, "Integration und Demokratie." In *Europäische Integration,* ed. Markus Jachtenfuchs and Beate Kohler-Koch. Opladen, 1996.

Kirchner, E., *Decision-Making in the European Community: The Council Presidency and European Integration.* Manchester, 1992.

Kjellberg, F., and H. Teune, "The Interventionist State and Taxation Reforms: How Are the Re-distribution Issues Handled?" Paper Presented at the Fifteenth World Congress of the International Political Science Association, Buenos Aires, 1991.

Knipping, F., ed. *Federal Conceptions in EU Member States: Traditions and Perspectives*. Baden-Baden, 1993.

Knox, R.H. "Economic Integration in Canada through the Agreement on Internal Trade." In *Canada: The State of the Federation, 1997, Non-Constitutional Renewal*, ed. H. Lazar. Kingston, 1998.

Krasner, S.D. "Westphalia and All That." In *Ideas and Foreign Policy*, ed. J. Goldstein and R.O. Keohane. Ithaca, 1993, 235–264.

Kratochwil, F. "Norms Versus Numbers: Multilateralism and the Rationalist and Reflexivist Approaches to Institutions—A Unilateral Plea for Communicative Rationality." In *Multilateralism Matters. The Theory and Praxis of an Institutional Form*, ed. J.G. Ruggie. New York, 1993.

Kreijci, Y., and V. Velimsky, *Ethnic and Political Nations in Europe*. London, 1981.

Kreile, M., ed. *Die Integration Europas*, PVS Sonderheft 23, Opladen, 1992.

Kupchan, C., ed. *Nationalism and Nationalities in the New Europe*. Ithaca, 1995.

Kux, S. "From USSR to the Commonwealth of Independent States: Confederation or Civilized Divorce?" In *Federalizing Europe? The Costs, Benefits and Preconditions of Federal Political Systems*, ed. J.J. Hesse and V. Wright. Oxford, 1996.

Kymlicka, W. "Ethnic Relations and Western Political Theory," in *Managing Diversity in Plural Societies*, ed. M. Opalski. Nepean, Ontario, 1998, 278-283.

Kymlicka, W., and J.R. Raviot, "Living Together: International Aspects of Federal Systems." *Canadian Foreign Policy 5*, no. 1 (1997): 1–51.

Laffan, B. "The Politics of Identity and Political Order in Europe." *Journal of Common Market Studies 34*, no. 1, (1996): 81–102.

Laitin, D. *Identity in Formation: The Russian-Speaking Minority in the Near Abroad*. Ithaca, 1998.

Lake, D.A. "Anarchy, Hierarchy, and the Variety of International Relations," *International Organizations 50*, no. 1 (1996): 1–33.

Laufer, H., and Th. Fischer *Föderalismus als Strukturprinzip für die Europäische Union*. Gütersloh, 1996.

Leonardy, U. "Costs and Benefits of Federalization: The Political Dimension." Discussion Paper No.10. Centre for European Studies. Nuffield College, Oxford, Nov. 1991.

Lepsius, M.R. *Interessen, Ideen und Institutionen*. Opladen, 1990.

_____. "Nationalstaat oder Nationalitätenstaat als Modell für die Weiterentwicklung der Europäischen Gemeinschaft." In *Staatswerdung*

Europas? Optionen für eine Europäische Union, ed. R. Wildenmann. Baden-Baden, 1991, 19–40.

Lijphart, A. *The Politics of Accommodation: Pluralism and Democracy in the Netherlands.* Berkeley, 1976.

Lindberg, L., and S.A. Scheingold *Regional Integration: Theory and Research.* Cambridge, 1971.

Linz, J. "Transitions to Democracy." In *Transitions to Democracy,* ed. Geoffrey Pridham. Dartmouth, 1995.

Linz, J., and A. Stepan *Problems of Transition and Consolidation of Democracy: Southern Europe, Latin America and Post-Communist Europe.* Baltimore, 1996.

Lippert, B., and P.Becker, eds. *Towards EU Membership: Transformation and Integration in Poland and the Czech Republic.* Bonn 1998.

Lodge, J. "European Political Cooperation towards the 1990s." In *The European Community and the Challenge of the Future,* ed. J. Lodge. London, 1989.

Loughlin, J. "'Europe of the Regions' and the Federalization of Europe." In *Publius. The Journal of Federalism* 26, no. 4 (Fall 1996): 141–162.

Lukic, R., and A. Lynch *Europe from the Balkans to the Urals: The Disintegration of Yugoslavia and the Soviet Union.* Oxford and New York, 1996.

MacMillan, G.M. "Summitry, Legitimacy and Integration: Canada and the European Community Compared." Paper Prepared for Workshop on European Union, European Consortium for Political Research, University of Limerick, 31 March–4 April, 1992.

_____. *State, Society and Authority in Ireland: The Foundations of the Modern State.* Dublin, 1993.

_____. "Canadian Executive Federalism and European Community Summitry." In *The European Community, Canada and 1992,* ed. G.M. MacMillan. Calgary, 1994.

_____. "The European Community: Is it a Supranational State in the Making?" In *Federalism and the New World Order,* ed. S. Randall and R. Gibbins. Calgary, 1994.

_____. "Intergovernmentalism and Multi-Level Governance in the European Union." Paper Presented at the First Annual Meeting of the European Community Studies Association, Canada, Brock University, June 1996.

Magiera, S., and D. Merten, eds. *Bundesländer und Europäische Gemeinschaft* Berlin, 1988.

Magomedov, A.R. "Politiceskie elity rossiiskoi provintsii." *Mirovaya ekonomika i mezhdunarodnye otnosheniya* 4 (1994): 72–80.

Majone, G. "The European Community Between Social Policy and Social Regulation." *Journal of Common Market Studies* 31, no. 2 (1993): 153–170.

_____. "The European Community: An 'Independent Fourth Branch of Government'?" In *Verfassungen für ein ziviles Europa*, ed. G. Bruggemeier. Baden-Baden, 1994, 23–43.

Mancini, G.F., and D.T. Keeling. "Democracy and the European Court of Justice." *The Modern Law Review* 57, no. 2 (1994): 175–190.

Mann, M. "European Development: Approaching a Historical Explanation." In *Europe and the Rise of Capitalism,* ed. Jean Baechler, John Hall, and Michael Mann. Oxford, 1988.

Mansfield, E.D., and J. Snyder. "Democratization and the Danger of War." *International Security* 20, no.1 (1995): 5–38.

Markovits, A., and S. Reich. *The German Predicament: Memory and Power in the New Europe.* Ithaca, 1997.

Marks, G. "Comparing European Integration and Nation-Building." Paper Prepared for a Conference on "Markets, States, and Social Citizenship." New York, 1994.

Martin, D. *A General Theory of Secularization.* Oxford, 1978.

Massucelli, C. *France and Germany at Maastricht: Politics and Negotiations to Create the European Union.* New York, 1997.

Mayhew, A. *Recreating Europe: The European Union's Policy Towards Central and Eastern Europe.* Cambridge 1998.

McDaniel, T. *The Agony of the Russian Idea.* Princeton, 1996.

Mearsheimer, J.J. "Back to the Future: Instability of Europe after the Cold War." *International Security* 15 (1990): 5–57.

_____. "The False Promise of International Institutions." *International Security* 19, no. 3 (1994/95).

Mendras, M. "Towards a Post-Imperial Identity." In *Russia and Europe: The Emerging Security Agenda*, ed. V. Baranovsky. Oxford, 1997.

Merkel, W., E. Sandschneider, and D. Segert, eds. *Systemwechsel. Die Institutionalisierung der Demokratie.* Opladen, 1996

Miall, H., ed. *Redefining Europe: New Patterns of Conflict and Cooperation.* London, 1994.

Mietzsch, O. "Institutionalisierte Interessenvertretung der Regionen und Kommunen in der EU." *Aus Politik und Zeitgeschichte* B 25-26 (1998), 34–39.

Millward, A. *The European Rescue of the Nation State.* Berkeley, 1992.

Missiroli, A. "Background." In *Flexibility and Enhanced Cooperation in European Security Matters: Assets or Liabilities?* ed. A. Missiroli. Occasional Papers 6. The Institute for Security Studies, Western European Union, January 1999.

Mitrany, D.A. *A Working Peace System.* Chicago, 1970.

Mlinar, Z., and H. Teune. "Development and the Openness of Systems." In *Boundaries and Regions,* ed. R. Strassoldo. Trieste, 1973.

Mommsen, M., ed. *Nationalismus in Osteuropa.* Munich, 1992.

Moravcsik, A. "Negotiating the Single European Act: National Interests and Conventional Statecraft in the European Community," *International Organization* 45, no. 1 (1991): 19–56.

_____. "Liberalism and International Relations Theory." Working Paper, Center of International Affairs, Harvard University, 1992.

_____. "Preferences and Power in the European Community: A Liberal Inter-governmentalist Approach." *Journal of Common Market Studies* 31, no. 4 (1993): 473–524.

_____. *Does International Cooperation Strengthen National Executives? The Case of Monetary Policy in the European Union.* Center for European Studies, Harvard University. Boston, 1998.

Motyl, A., ed. *Thinking Theoretically About Soviet Nationalities: History and Comparison in the Study of the USSR.* New York, 1995.

Münch, R. *Das Projekt Europa.* Frankfurt/M., 1994.

Neumann, I. *Russia and the Idea of Europe.* London, 1996.

Northcott, J. *The Future of Britain and Europe.* London, 1995.

Nugent, N. *The Government and Politics of the European Union,* 3d ed. Durham, 1994.

Nye, J. S. *Bound to Lead: The Changing Nature of American Power.* New York, 1990.

O'Brien, C.C. "The Future of the West," *The National Interest* 30 (1992/93): 3–10.

O'Connell, J. "The Making of Europe: Strengths, Constraints and Resolutions." In *A Constitution for Europe,* ed. P. King. London, 1991, 23–61.

O'Keefe, D. "Judicial Protection of the Individual by the European Court of Justice." *Fordham International Law Journal* 19, no. 3 (1996): 901–914.

Oates, W.E. *Fiscal Federalism.* New York, 1972.

Offe, C. *Der Tunnel am Ende des Lichts.* Frankfurt/M., 1994.

Office for Official Publications of the European Communities. *TEU: Treaty on European Union.* Luxembourg, 1992.

Ostrowski, K., and H. Teune. *Three Political Cultures of Europe: Interpretations, Evidence, and Theories.* Paper Presented at the Theory Confrontation Symposium, Moscow, 1996.

_____. *Local Democracy in Russia, Central and Western Europe,* in *Democracy, Economy, and Civil Society in Transition,* ed. The Finnish Institute of International Affairs. Helsinki, 1997.

_____. *Globalization: Regions, Meso Regions, and the World System.* Paper Presented at the Fourteenth World Congress of the International Sociological Association. Montreal, 1998.

Petro, N. *The Rebirth of Russian Democracy: An Interpretation of Political Culture.* Cambridge and London, 1995.

Pierson, P. "The Path to European Union: An Historical Institutionalist Approach." *Comparative Political Studies* 29, no. 2 (1996): 123–163.

Pinder, J. *The European Community and Eastern Europe.* London, 1991.

Pithart, P. "The Division of Czechoslovakia: A Preliminary Balance Sheet for the End of a Respectable Country." *Canadian Slavonic Papers* 38, nos. 3–4 (1995): 321–338.

Pöhle, K. *Das Demokratiedefizit der Europäischen Union und die nationalen Parlamente. Bietet COSAC einen Ausweg?* Zeitschrift für Parlamentsfragen 1 (1998), 77–99

Preston, C. *Enlargement and Integration in the European Union.* London, 1997.

Prizel, I. *National Identity and Foreign Policy: Nationalism and Leadership in Poland, Russia and Ukraine.* Cambridge, 1998.

Puchala, D.J. "International Transactions and Regional Integration." *International Organization* 24, no 4 (1970): 732–63.

_____. "Integration Theory and the Study of International Relations." In *From National Development to Global Community: Essays in Honor of Karl W. Deutsch,* ed. R.L. Merritt and B.M. Russett. London, 1981.

Puchala, D.J., and R.F. Hopkins, "International Regimes: Lessons from Deductive Analysis." In *International Regimes,* ed. S. Krasner. New York, 1983, 61–92.

Renzsch, W. "Deutsche Länder und Europäische Integration. Kompetenzverlust und neue Handlungschancen in einem "Europa der Regionen." Aus Politik und Zeitgeschichte B 28 (1990): 28–39.

Reuter, J. "Die politische Entwicklung in Bosnien-Herzegowina. Zusammenwachsen der Entitaten oder nationale Abkapselung." *Südosteuropa,* nos. 3–4 (1998): 97–116.

Riker, W.H. *Federalism: Origin, Operation, Significance.* Boston, 1964.

_____. "European Federalism: The Lessons of Past Experience." In *Federalizing Europe? The Costs, Benefits, and Preconditions of Federal Political Systems*, ed. J.J. Hesse and V. Wright. Oxford, 1996.

Risse-Kappen, T. "Exploring the Nature of the Beast: International Relations Theory and Comparative Policy Analysis Meet the European Union," *Journal of Common Market Studies* 34, no. 1, (1996): 54–80.

_____. ed. *Bringing Transnational Relations Back In: Non-State Actors, Domestic Structures and International Institutions*. New York, 1995.

Roeder, P.G. "Soviet Federalism and Ethnic Mobilization." *World Politics* 43, no. 2 (1991): 196–232.

Rokkan, S. "Eine Familie von Modellen für die vergleichende Geschichte Europas," *Zeitschrift für Soziologie* 9, no. 2.

_____. "Dimensions of State Formation and Nation-Building: A Possible Paradigm for Research on Variations in Europe." In *The Formation of National States in Western Europe*, ed. C. Tilly. Princeton, 1975, 541–600.

Rudolph, R., and D. Good, eds. *Nationalism and Empire: The Habsburg Empire and the Soviet Union*. Minnesota, 1992.

Ruggie, J.G. "Continuity and Transformation in the World Polity: Toward a Neorealist Synthesis." In *Neorealism and its Critics*, ed. R. O. Keohane. New York, 1986, 131–157.

_____. "Territoriality and Beyond: Problematizing Modernity in International Relations." *International Organization* 47, no. 1 (1993): 139–174.

Sakwa, R. *Russian Politics and Society.* London and New York, 1996.

Sakwa, R., and M. Webber. "The Commonwealth of Independent States, 1991–1998: Stagnation and Survival." *Europe-Asia Studies* 51, no. 3 (1999).

Sbragia, A. *Debt Wish: Entrepreneurial Cities: U.S. Federalism and Economic Development*. Pittsburgh, 1996.

_____. ed. *Euro-Politics: Institutions and Policy-Making in the "New" European Community.* Washington, 1992.

Schäfer, G.F. "Die institutionellen Herausforderungen einer EU-Osterweiterung." In *Europa öffnen*, ed. W. Weidenfeld. Gütersloh 1997.

Schlötzer-Scotland, C. "Viel reisen in Europa, wenig entscheiden für Europa." *Süddeutsche Zeitung*, 8 July 1992.

Scharpf, F. *Regieren in Europa. Effektiv und demokratisch.* Frankfurt, New York, 1998.

Schmitter, P.C. "Imagining the Future of the Euro-Polity with the Help of New Concepts." In *Governance in the European Union*, ed. G. Marks. London, 1996.

Scholz, R. "Grundgesetz und europäische Einigung: Zu den reformpolitischen Empfehlungen der Gemeinsamen Verfassungskommission." *Neue Juristische Wochenschrift* 41 (1992): 83–102.

_____."Die Gemeinsame Verfassungskommission. Auftrag, Verfahren und Ergebnisse." Aus Politik und Zeitgeschichte B 52/53 (1994): 3–5.

_____. "Grundgesetz und Europäische Einigung." *Neue Juristische Wochenschrift* 45 (1994).

Schultz, E. "Die relative Autonomie des Europäischen Gerichtshofes: Rechtssprechung vor und nach Maastricht. Eine neo-institutionalistische Analyse." P.D. thesis, Humboldt University, 1998.

Secretariat of the United Nations Economic Commission for Europe. *Economic Survey of Europe 1998*, no. 2. New York and Geneva, 1998.

Sekretariat des Bundesrates, ed. *Bundesrat und Europäische Gemeinschaften*. Bonn, 1988.

Sen, S.R. "Centre-State Relations in India." *Economic and Political Weekly* [Bombay] 6 August 1988, pp.1637–1641.

Seroka, J. "Jugoslovenski federalizam danas: nuznost stvaranja i jacanja medurepublickih komunikacija." In *Federacija i Federalizam*, ed. J. Dordevic and M. Jovicic. Nis, 1987, 321–327.

_____. "The Dissolution of Federalism in East and Central Europe." In *Evaluating Federal Systems*, ed. B. de Villiers. Dordrecht, 1994, 208–224.

Seton Watson, H. *Nations and States*. Boulder, 1977.

Sharlet, R. "The Prospects for Federalism in Russian Constitutional Politics." *Publius. The Journal of Federalism* 24 (1994): 115–27.

Sharpe, L. "The Growth of Sub National Expenditures in the Democratic State." In *Local Finances in the Contemporary State*, ed. Institute of Political Science. Oslo, 1988.

Shugart, M.S. "Executive-Legislative Relations in Post-Communist Europe." *Transition* 2, no. 25 (1996): 6–11.

Simeon, R. *Federal-Provincial Diplomacy: The Making of Recent Policy in Canada*. Toronto, 1970.

Simeon, R., and I. Robinson, *State, Society and the Development of Canadian Federalism*. Toronto, 1990.

Smiley, D. *The Federal Condition in Canada*. Toronto, 1987.

Smith, A. *The Ethnic Origins of Nations*. Cambridge, 1986.

_____. *National Identity.* Reno, 1992.

_____. *Nations and Nationalism in a Global Era.* Oxford, 1995.

_____. *Nationalism and Modernism.* London, 1998.

Smith, J.E. *John Marshall: Definer of a Nation.* New York, 1996.

Snyder, T., and M. Vachundova, "Are Transitions Transitory? Two Types of Political Change in Eastern Europe Since 1989." *East European Politics and Societies* 11, no. 1 (1997): 1–35.

Spohn, W. "Zur Programmatik und Entwicklungsperspektive der neuen historischen Soziologie." *Berliner Journal für Soziologie* 3 (1996): 75–91.

_____. "Historische Soziologie zwischen Theorien sozialen Wandels und Sozialgeschichte." In *Soziologische Theorie und Geschichte*, ed. Frank Weltz,. Opladen, 1998.

_____. "Religion und Nationalismus. Osteuropa im westeuropäischen Vergleich." In *Religiöser Wandel in den postkummunistischen Ländern Ost- und Mitteleuropas,* ed. D. Pollack, I. Borowik, and W. Jagodzinski. Würzburg, 1998, 87–120.

_____. "Social Transformation and Historical Modernization Patterns. Germany, Poland and Russia in Comparison." In *East Meets West*, ed. Raimo Blom. Helsinki 1999.

Spruyt, H. *The Sovereign State and its Competitors.* Princeton, 1994.

Stanger, A. "Czechoslovakia's Dissolution as an Unintended Consequence of the Velvet Constitutional Revolution." *East European Constitutional Review 5*, no. 4 (1996): 40–46.

Steffani, W., and U. Thaysen, ed. *Demokratie in Europa: Zur Rolle der Parlamente.* Opladen, 1995.

Steinberg, J. *Why Switzerland?* 2d ed. Cambridge, 1996.

Stokes, G. *Three Eras of Political Change in Europe.* New York, 1997.

Stone Sweet, A. "Constitutional Dialogues in the European Community." European University Institute Working Paper 95/38, Robert Schuman Centre, San Domenico di Fiesole, Florence, 1995.

Stone Sweet, A., and J.A. Caporaso "From Free Trade to Supranational Polity: The European Court and Integration." In *European Integration and Supranational Governance*, ed. W. Sandholtz and A. Stone Sweet, Oxford, 1998, 92–133.

Strassoldo, R. ed. *Boundaries and Regions.* Trieste, 1973.

Sugar, P., ed. *Nationalism in Eastern Europe in the Twentieth Century.* Seattle, 1995.

Szucs, J. "The Three Historical Regions of Europe: An Outline." *Acta Historica Hungariae* 29 (1983): 131–184.

_____. *Die drei historischen Regionen Europas.* Frankfurt/M., 1990.

Teich, M., and R. Porter, eds. *The National Question in Europe.* Cambridge, 1993.

The TEU—The Meaning of Amsterdam, Representation of the European Commission. London, July 1997.

Teune, H. "Information, Control, and Territorial Political Systems." *Studies in Comparative International Development* 14 (1979): 77–89.

_____. "Development, Modernization, Democracy, and Conflicts." In *Of Fears and Foes: Security and Insecurity in an Evolving Global Political Economy,* ed. Jose Ciprut,. Westport, 2000.

Teune, H., and Z. Mlinar *The Developmental Logic of Social Systems.* Beverly Hills, 1978.

Thaysen, U. *The Bundesrat, the Länder, and German Federalism.* German Issues No.13, ed. American Institute for Contemporary German Studies (Washington, D.C., 1994).

Therborn, G. *European Modernity and Beyond: The Trajectory of European Societies 1945–2000.* London, 1996.

Tilly, C. "Reflections on the History of European State Making." In *The Formation of National States in Western Europe,* ed C. Tilly. Princeton, 1975, 3–84.

_____.ed. *The Formation of National States in Western Europe.* Princeton, 1975.

Tiryakian, E., and R. Ragowski, eds. *New Nationalism in the Developed West.* Boston, 1985.

Tranholm-Mikkelsen, J. "Neo-functionalism: Obstinate or Obsolete? A Reappraisal in the Light of the New Dynamics of the EC." *Review of International Studies* 20, no. 1 (1991).

Urwin, D. *The Community of Europe: A History of European Integration since 1945.* London, 1991.

Vatter, H., and J. Walker. *The Inevitability of Government Growth.* New York, 1990.

Verdery, K. "Nationalism and National Sentiment in the Post-socialist Romania," *Slavic Review* 52, no. 2 (1993): 179–204.

Verney, D. *The Analysis of Political Systems.* London, 1959.

Vincent, A. *Theories of the State.* Oxford, 1987.

Vujacic, V. "Institutional Origins of Contemporary Serbian Nationalism." *East European Constitutional Review* 5, no. 4 (1996): 51–61.

Wallace, W. *The Transformation of Western Europe.* London, 1990.

_____. *Regional Integration: The West European Experience.* Washington, 1994.

_____."Regionalism in Europe: Model or Exception?" In *Regionalism in World Politics. Regional Organization and International Order,* ed. L. Fawcett and A. Hurrell. Oxford, 1995, 201–27.

Wallace, W., and H. Wallace. *Policy Making in the European Union.* Oxford, 1996.

Walt, S.M. "Alliance Formation and the Balance of of World Power." *International Security* 9, no. 4 (1985): 3–43.

Waltz, K. *Theory of International Politics.* Reading, 1979.

_____. "The Emerging Structure of International Politics." *International Security* 18 (1993): 44–79.

Watts, R. L. "Executive Federalism: The Comparative Context." In *Federalism and Political Community: Essays in Honour of Donald Smiley,* ed. D.P. Shugarman and R. Whitaker. Peterborough, 1989.

_____. *Comparing Federal Systems in the 1990s.* Kingston, 1996.

Webber, M. *CIS Integration Trends. Russia and the Former Soviet South.* London, 1997.

Weber, Max. *Wirtschaft und Gesellschaft.* Tübingen, 1964.

Weidenfeld, W., and J. Janning, eds. Europe '96: Reforming the European Union. Gütersloh, 1994.

_____. *Europe in a Global Change.* Gütersloh, 1997.

_____. *Europa öffnen.* Gütersloh 1997.

_____. *Amsterdam in der Analyse.* Gütersloh, 1998.

Weiler, J.H.H. "The Transformation of Europe." *Yale Law Journal* 100, no. 8 (1991): 2403–2483.

_____. *The Constitution of Europe: Do the New Clothes Have an Emperor?* Cambridge, 1999.

Wendt, A. "Anarchy is What States Make of It: the Social Construction of Power Politics." *International Organization* 46, no. 2 (1992).

_____. "Collective Identity Formation and the International State." *American Political Science Review* 88, no. 2 (1994).

_____. "Constructing International Politics." *International Security* 20, no. 1 (1995).

Wessels, W. "Staat und (westeuropaische) Integration: Die Fusionthese." *Politische Vierteljahreschrift, Sonderheft Die Integration Europas,* 1992, 36–61.

_____. *Die europäischen Staaten und ihre Union—Staatsbilder in der Diskussion.* Munich, 1994.

Wheare, K.C. *Federal Government.* London, 1946.

Whitman, R.G. "The International Identity of the European Union: Instruments of Identity." In *Rethinking the European Union:*

Institutions, Interests and Identities, ed. A. Landau and R.G. Whitman. London, 1997, 54–71.

William, A., ed. *Southern Europe Transformed*. London, 1984.

Winkler, H.A., and H. Kaelble, eds. *Nationalismus, Nationalitäten, Supranationalität*. Stuttgart, 1993.

Winn, N. "Who Gets What, When, and How? The Contested Conceptual and Disciplinary Nature of Governance and Policy-Making in the European Union." *Politics* 18, no. 2 (1998): 119–132.

Wollmann, H., H. Wiesental, and F. Bönker, eds. *Transformation sozialistischer Gesellschaften. Am Ende des Anfangs*. Leviathan, Sonderheft 15 (1995).

World Bank, *World Development Report, 1998/99* (Washington D.C., 1998.

Yeltsin, B. *The View from the Kremlin*. London, 1994.

Young, O.R. "International Regimes: Toward a New Theory of Institutions." *World Politics* 39, no. 1 (1986).

Zacher, M.W., and R.A. Matthew "Liberal International Theory: Common Threads, Divergent Strands". Paper Presented at the American Political Science Association, September 1992.

Zagorsky, A., ed. *The Commonwealth of Independent States: Developments and Prospects*. Moscow, 1992.

About the Authors

Francis Campbell, staff member at the Foreign and Commonwealth Office, London/U.K.

James A. Caporaso, professor of Political Science at the University of Washington/U.S.A.

Lenard J. Cohen, professor of Political Science at the Simon Fraser University/Canada.

Andreas Heinemann-Grüder, senior researcher at the Bonn International Center for Conversion and adjunct professor at Humboldt University Berlin/Germany.

Michael Kreile, professor of Political Science at the Humboldt University Berlin/Germany.

Gretchen M. MacMillan, professor of Political Science at the University of Calgary/Canada.

Jim Seroka, professor of Political Science at the Auburn University, Alabama/U.S.A.

Willfried Spohn, professor of Sociology at the European University Florence/Italy.

Henry Teune, professor of Political Science at the University of Pennsylvania, Philadelphia.

Douglas V. Verney, adjunct professor of Political Science at the University of Pennsylvania, Philadelphia.

Mark Webber, professor of Political Science at the University of Loughborough/UK.

INDEX

U

Ukraine, 167, 171f., 175, 179f., 185, 188
United Arab Republic, 173
United Kingdom, 18, 21, 25, 35f., 54, 74, 196ff., 201f., 204f., 216, 230, 240
United States, federalism in the, 18f., 21-33, 35f., 39ff., 66ff., 78, 90, 216, 220
Uzbekistan, 172, 180f.

W

Wallace, William, 231
Waltz, Kenneth, 40
Warsaw Pact, 41
Weber, Max, 196
Wendt, Alexander, 178
Westentorp, Carlos, 131
Western European Union (WEU), 41, 235
Westminster form, 29
Westphalian system, Westphalian state, 4, 8, 40, 83-86, 97
Wilson, Woodrow, 40
World Trade Organization, 188

Y

Yeltsin, Boris, 152, 154, 170f., 181f., 187, 200f.
Yugoslavia, 103ff., 113, 117ff., 148f., 152, 173, 220

POLICY CONCERTATION AND SOCIAL PARTNERSHIP IN WESTERN EUROPE

Lessons for the Twenty-first Century

Edited by **Stefan Berger** and **Hugh Compston**

Policy concertation – the determination of public policy by means of agreements struck between governments, employers and trade unions – continues to thrive in Western Europe despite the impact of liberalizing trends that were expected to lead to its demise. This volume brings together a team of 23 experts with the aim to undertake paired historical and political studies of policy concertation in ten West European countries, which were then subjected to systematic comparative analysis. It shows that overall the incidence of broad policy concertation in Western Europe can be explained by the changing configurations of just three variables.

Stefan Berger is Professor of History at the University of Glamorgan. **Hugh Compston** is Lecturer in European Politics in the School of European Studies, Cardiff University.

Winter 2001/02
ca. 400 pages, 40 tables, bibliog., index
ISBN 1-57181-702-6 Hardback
ISBN 1-57181-494-9 Paperback

UNIVERSITIES REMEMBERING EUROPE

Nations, Culture and Higher Education

Edited by **Francis Crawley,** Free University of Brussels,
Paul Smeyers, Catholic University of Leuven and
Paul Standish, University of Dundee

Higher education plays a vital role in the sharing of the identity and culture of Europe and therefore receives considerable attention from scholars and policy makers. This volume is different in that it brings a philosophical perspective to the debate on higher education in Europe. As a work of applied philosophy, it reflects on changes in European identity with the development of the European Union after the fall of the Berlin Wall and considers the reciprocal relationship between these changes and higher education. By uncovering the unavoidable philosophical problems embedded in policies, the book sets out both to provide a clearer understanding of the current situation of higher education in Europe and to contribute to its development. It attempts to redefine the democratic basis of higher education in the light of social and political change in the evolving European society.

Contents: The Idea of the European Dimension - The Challenge of Multiculturalism - The Response to the Economic Demands - Situating the Individual and Society in European Higher Education - Higher Education in a European Context: Some Recommendations and Conclusions.

2000. 256 pages, bibliog., index
ISBN 1-57181-957-6 Hardback

SEXUAL POLITICS AND THE EUROPEAN UNION

The New Feminist Challenge

Edited by **R. Amy Elman,** Political Science
Department, Kalamazoo College, Michigan

*"... informative and thought-provoking ... useful as an outline of
EU history and institutions ... accessible, informative and useful
... the case studies would be worthwhile reading on women's
studies courses."* **—H-Net Reviews**

*"...provides a rare overview of the development of sexual politics
at the levels of the European union and national government."*
—Journal of Women's History

*"...provides an analytic foundation for assessing the policies and
politics of European integration from a feminist perspective...
helps [to] understand that policy affects gender as a hierarchy of
power, and these power differentials in turn can shape policies...
[an] innovative volume."* **—Women & Politics**

1996. 188 pages, bibliog., index
ISBN 1-57181-062-5 Hardback
ISBN 1-57181-046-3 Paperback

EUROPE'S NEW RACISM

Causes, Manifestations, and Solutions

Published in association with
and edited by **The Evens Foundation**

Europe has seen a tremendous rise in popularity of new rightist political parties in the last two decades or so, claiming cultural supremacy of the so-called native Europeans over foreign immigrants. In this volume, European scholars from Russian to Britain have come together to examine the media and social and legal policies in an effort to determine the causes of this resurgence of rightist and anti-democratic ideologies. They furthermore suggest actions that might help combat racism more effectively

The Evens Foundation is a recent, non-profit organization whose aims are to promote peaceful co-existence, intercultural education, and the integration of Europe. The foundation is based in Antwerp, Belgium.

Spring 2002. *ca.* 304 pages, bibliog., index
ISBN 1-57181-332-2 Hardback
ISBN 1-57181-333-0 Paperback
Culture and Politics/Politics and Culture, Vol. 1